Growing

Up

Greenpoint

Also by Tommy Carbone:

The Lobster Lake Bandits:

Mystery at Moosehead

"Carbone is a natural storyteller in his novel about northern, Maine. His descriptions and dialogue make the characters come alive. I loved the whole book and recommend it highly."

-- The Book Corner
Maine's Journal Tribune

Find Tommy's books at:
www.tommycarbone.com

Growing Up Greenpoint

A Kid's Life in 1970s Brooklyn

TOMMY CARBONE

BURNT JACKET PUBLISHING, LLC

Copyright ©2018 by Tommy Carbone

Cover photo, interior illustrations, and photos all from the collection of Tommy Carbone.
Cover design by Tommy Carbone.

All rights reserved. In accordance with the U.S. Copyright Act of 1976, the scanning, uploading, and electronic sharing of any part of this book without the permission of the publisher constitute unlawful piracy and theft of the author's intellectual property. Use of material from this book, other than short passages for review purposes or used within quotations, requires prior written permission be obtained by contacting the publisher at permissions@tommycarbone.com. Thank you for your support of the author's rights.

Burnt Jacket Publishing, LLC
Maine
20230718ISPBK

Library of Congress Control Number: 2020905854

ISBN 978-1-7347358-5-7
Also available in:
    eBook
    Large Print
    Hardcover

www.tommycarbone.com

For Mom and Dad who made growing up

in Greenpoint fun, were able to make it

there, and gave me the guidance I needed,

allowing me to make it anywhere.

For Gina and Marisa,

so you might know better

where some of our traditions came from,

and why I may have spelled,

"N.O." at times, in one way or another.

Books from Tommy Carbone

The Lobster Lake Bandits

Mystery at Moosehead

The Elephant Mountain Gang

Mystery at Maine's Moosehead Lake

I Am Penobscot

A Novel

Woods and Lakes of Maine - Annotated Edition:

A Trip from Moosehead Lake to New Brunswick in a Birch-Bark Canoe

Hubbard's Guide to Moosehead Lake and Northern Maine

Annotated Edition

Exploring the Maine Woods

The Hardy Family Expedition to the Machias Lakes

David Stone Libbey – He was Penobscot

The Penobscot Man – Life and Death on a Maine River

Katahdin, Pamola, & Whiskey Jack – Stories & Legends from The Maine Woods

Memories

Where in Brooklyn?	1
My Greenpoint	14
The Blackout of 1977	32
We're "Out" of Electric	45
Uncle Ray and the King	61
The Blizzard of 1978	73
Winthro Park	90
Roller Skating at the Movie Theater	109
Block Parties	120
The Candy Man	141
Pinball Players	153
The Greek's	159
Mets or Yankees?	166
Whiff, Slap, Punch	176
The Pope is Coming!	196
We Lost Mom - in Rome	212
Pickles for Nickels	225
Fortune Cookies	236
Greenpoint Fries	249
Swims with the Fishes	262
Pasta and Sauerkraut	275
Goodbye to Greenpoint	290
City Terms	299
Discussion Questions for Book Groups	302

The stories in this book are written as remembered by the author. The characters mentioned in these stories were my friends or cousins; or friends of friends; or cousins of friends. Back then no one was excluded from our street games. When someone asked if they could play, we'd say, "It's a free country."

The names of the characters, in most cases, have been modified. First, my childhood was over forty years ago and I apologize, I cannot remember the names of all the kids I hung out with in Greenpoint. Secondly, some of the characters are in the kid protection program and I am resolute to protecting their reputations. Lastly, where necessary, a few of the characters are composites of multiple personalities to further protect identities and improve the reader experience.

"If dreams and memories sometimes get confused, well, that's the way it should be."

Kevin Arnold
The Wonder Years
Season 3, Episode 19

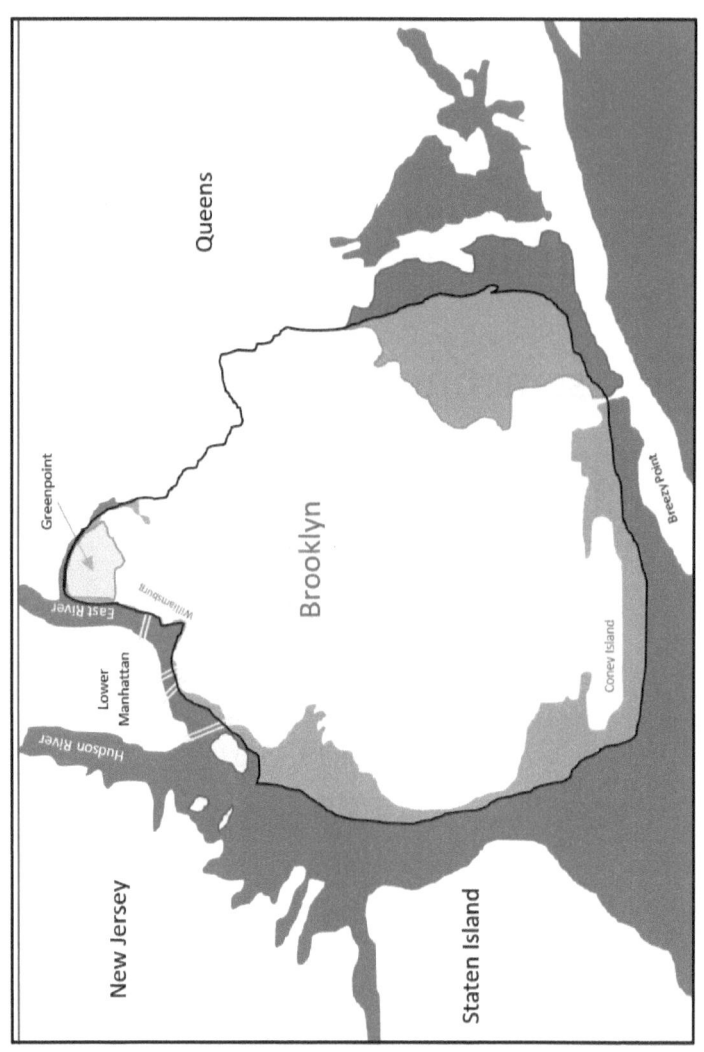

Growing up Greenpoint

xi

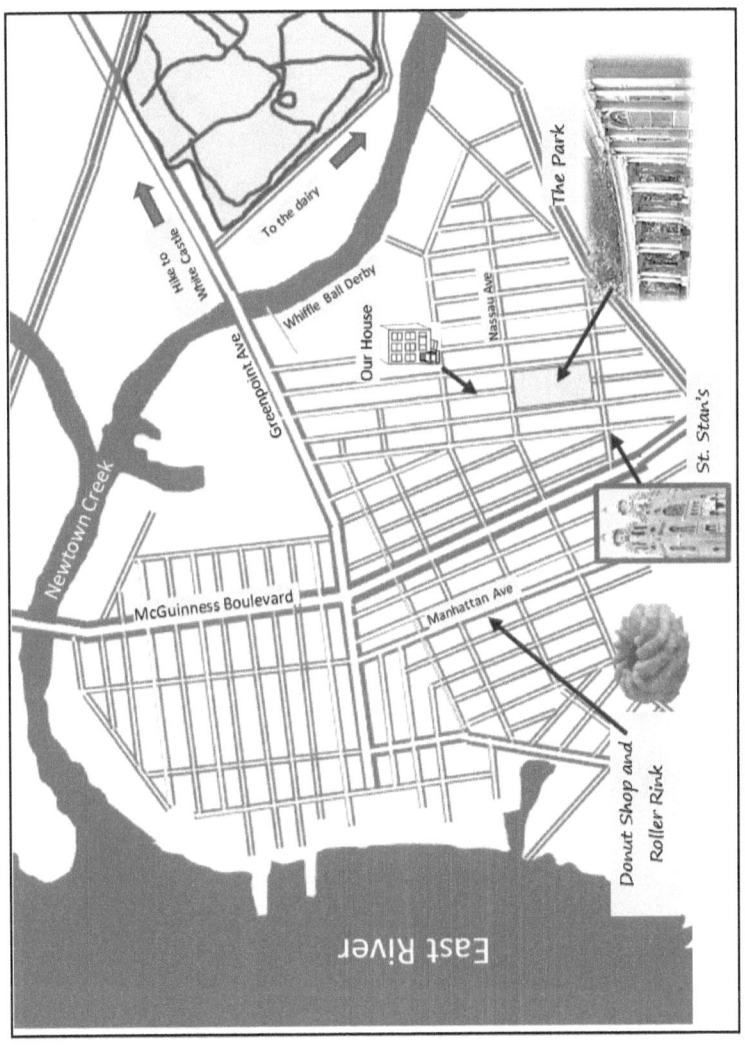

Where in Brooklyn?

"**Watch this,**" said Joe Cusimano, the senior plant operator I was working with on a July Saturday afternoon.

"Watch what?" I asked.

Joe pointed down to the cement walkway that lined the river. Mickey, the most senior plant operator, by years of service and by age, was about to perform the routine clearing of the water intake screens.

I thought to myself, "So what! I've had to clean those filthy trash collecting screens plenty of times." The 'screens' were large metal grates, the size of a car, angled slightly into the Hudson allowing river water in, while keeping debris from entering the plant's cooling water system. And trust me, you may not see the river debris as you drive over it on the GW Bridge, but there's plenty of 'stuff' floating down the Hudson River. Looking back, I can't believe I used to water-ski on that part of the river. Aside from the obstacle course to ski around, I always felt grimier after being in that water than before I had jumped in.

Working at the power plant, I was rewarded with a much closer view of the type of stuff that was floating in the river when it got caught up in the screens. Usually the new operators were assigned to the screen job. I discovered that Mickey was the only senior operator who preferred doing it himself, and nobody was going to argue with being relieved of hard labor on a hot summer day. I was about to learn why Mickey actually looked forward to this particular dirty job.

At the time, I was working at the Indian Point 3 nuclear power generating station north of New York City. While I had worked at coal, oil, and gas power generating facilities before, this was my first nuclear facility. This plant was far cleaner than the fossil fuel plants, where after working a shift, blowing my nose resulted in turning the tissue black. Here the generator floor shined. The cleanliness, however, was accompanied with a far greater sense of danger. Each morning when I passed through the metal detector, put my lunch through the x-ray machine, and was eyed by the guard who sat behind bullet proof glass before he'd hand me my ID badge, I was reminded that this plant was a high security installation. This was made even more apparent as the guards walked around carrying rifles. It was a job I left after several months, but not before learning a great deal from Mickey; a little was about the plant, a lot was about remembering the past.

I watched as Mickey used the grate rake to throw weeds, bottles, wood, a tire, and other undesirable trash into a bin the length of a city bus. Even though cleanup of the river had improved over the years, the Hudson, as with any large moving body of water, had plenty of large debris that would get caught in the grates, requiring them to be cleared twice per shift. Just a few days earlier, it took four of us to deal with a tree stump that managed to come ashore at that exact location and block the grates.

Looking down from the rusty iron bar exterior walkway, I noticed Mickey was carefully picking through the river trash and placing something in a canvas bag. He certainly was taking his time collecting garbage. The day was clear and warm, drawing my attention out into the river and away from the disgusting work Mickey was doing. He wasn't even wearing gloves. Boaters raced by pulling skiers or just enjoying the sunshine on this beautiful summer weekend.

Once he completed his task, Mickey hobbled back up the metal staircase to the generator floor. Whistling and carrying his sack over his shoulder, he resembled Darby O'Gill with a captured leprechaun. When he walked past Joe and I, I would have sworn something in that bag was moving. Mickey entered the corner room that was used as a combination kitchen, lunchroom, and night shift poker room. Joe motioned for me to follow.

We walked into the small grimy kitchen behind Mickey. The room had a two-burner electric stove, an old orange refrigerator, and three microwaves, not one of them in working order. We were responsible to keep a power plant running that could generate one billion watts of electricity from a nuclear reaction, but we couldn't get a microwave to function. The fact that they were never ever cleaned may have had something to do with it.

Mickey dumped his sack on the table and out spilled six oily crabs. They were coated in the greasiest dark mud I had ever seen. Three still had enough limbs to scramble across the table. Mickey threw his crustacean catch into the sink. He washed his hands and the crabs at the same time with the green bar of pumice soap that could easily remove paint from a car. He threw all the crabs, handicapped included, into a big stew pot on the stove and added some water.

Mickey took the caps off the salt and pepper jars and dumped a liberal amount of each into his palm and then dropped it in the pot. He turned the burner to high and reached for the pot cover.

I turned to Joe. "He's gonna eat those?"

"I sure am! What's the problem with that?" Mickey jumped back at me as he swung around to look me in the eyes, his hearing no longer a problem.

"I didn't think it was safe to eat from that river," I said in a low voice.

"I've been eating from this river since I was a teenager, long before you were born. It's fine. You shouldn't let people sway you from eating good food," he snapped, an Irish brogue slipping into his New York accent.

I thought back to my early education during the 70s at St. Stanislaus. We were taught the river was polluted from industrial waste of the 1960s. My mind was conflicted. Could Mickey be right? Were these crabs really 'good' food? I concluded that he was either right, or lucky, if he had been eating Hudson River crustaceans and fish for well over 40 years.

As he waited for his crabs to cook, Mickey went on about how people whined too much about the river not being safe. He told Joe and I stories of catching striped bass and bluefish from his boat. He even talked about working the overnight shift back in the early 70s and fishing for his dinner from a pier just up the road.

Steam seeped out from under the lid of the pot. A smell,

which didn't make me hungry, filled the small hot room. The kitchen had no windows and the aroma of oil, mud, and seafood had nowhere to go. Right about then I really needed some air. I cursed the nonfunctioning air conditioner that was installed through the kitchen wall to the hallway. That may have been unfair, since it was the outlet it was plugged into that didn't work. Again, we could generate electricity to power Times Square forty miles to the south, but management wouldn't schedule labor to fix an outlet for the air conditioner.

When he had determined the crabs had cooked enough, Mickey placed his one pot lunch on the table. Taking out his greasy lineman pliers, he pulled out a crab and cracked into it right on the surface of the table. Noticing that Joe and I were not leaving, Mickey said, "You two gonna just stand there or ya gonna man up and try one?"

Joe made some excuse that he had to go check a pump. Knowing I had this one chance to get on Mickey's good side, I sat down at the table. I observed within days of starting the job, that Mickey would go out of his way to help someone learn about the power plant. He knew everything about the plant. If a system was acting up he could tell anyone, with enough brains to ask him, what valve needed to be replaced without even waiting for engineering to check the blueprint. Well, he'd help the person if he liked them. If he didn't, he enjoyed watching them crawl around in hot, dangerous places, with potential nuclear dust, trying to find the problem. I didn't want to be that person.

Mickey placed a crab on the table in front of me. He probably thought I was wimpy when I pulled some paper towels off the roll for a plate. I didn't care. The table hadn't been washed since the Indian Point site was an amusement park back in the 1920s and I didn't want to be sicker than I needed to be.

The human crustacean in the chair across the table watched me with his one good eye as I picked at the crab. I looked in the cabinet draw, hoping to find some utensils, or if I was really lucky a nut cracker for the shell. Mickey, with his usual lack of patience, grabbed my crab and cracked it open with his pliers.

"Thanks, Mickey."

He asked, "You've got a city accent, kid. What part?" By that year in my young life, I was living in a town on the other side of the Bear Mountain Bridge. Nowhere near the city as far as I was concerned. I tried to explain to him about where.

"Nah, I mean where ya really from? Where were you born? What part of Brooklyn?"

"How'd ja know I was born in Brooklyn?"

"Come on, kid. You telling me you don't think I can tell my five boroughs apart?"

Right away I knew what Mickey meant. My dad's sister from Queens has the nasally Flushing voice, think Fran Drescher as the Nanny. My Uncle John is Fordham Road Bronx. My cousins that moved out to "The Island," the stepsister borough, early in their lives, had no accent, at least not one I could tell anymore.

Impressed with Mickey's ability to distinguish city accents, I said, "I was born and raised in Greenpoint."

"No kiddin. My mom was from Greenpoint. India Street. That neighborhood was always a nice part of the city."

From then on Mickey helped me out whenever I had a

question about a system in the plant. I'm not sure if it was because I was from Greenpoint or because I ate the crab. Since I was later sick to my stomach, which I blamed on the crab, I'm thanking my Brooklyn roots because after that day I declined all his river culinary experiments and he never seemed offended.

"Were you living down there during the blackout of '77?" asked Mickey, fishing another crab from the pot.

"Sure was. That's something I'll never forget. The whole neighborhood, the entire city, came to a stop."

"Did you know that what started the blackout happened right up the road from here?"

While I recalled the blackout happening when I was a kid, I never had a reason to contemplate the reason behind the darkness. I did, however, remember the days we spent in the sweltering July heat and being annoyed there was no milk for my Cap'n Crunch.

Mickey's questions about the blackout stirred up old memories of how I worried we would run out of food, or the looters were going to burn down our house, or our car was going to be stripped bare. Only the last of which actually happened, and that was not until a couple of years after the blackout. What caused the blackout never entered my mind, at least that I can recall.

"No. I didn't know that," I said, now curious to learn what Mickey knew.

Eating his crab lunch and drinking a bargain-brand cola from the agent orange fridge, Mickey told me that he was working a double shift that July night in 1977.

"IP2 was in shutdown for repairs. So, it was only our side running," started Mickey.

As part of my new hire orientation, I had learned that Indian Point (IP) was made up of three separate nuclear reactors, numbered creatively 1, 2, and 3. The older style reactor, number 1, had been out of service since 1974.

He cracked open another crab and continued, "We were shorthanded that night. It 'twas a hot summer night. I think high 90s, hot as hell here on the generator floor. A lot of guys called out sick. Probably they were sitting by their pools or watching TV with the a/c blasting, while they left me here to cover for their lazy rear ends."

He pulled at the meat inside one of the crab legs using needle nose pliers as he continued to complain about his coworkers. He sure was enjoying his seafood lunch, the smell of which was making me nauseous.

"Shoot, they were mostly sick of the heat wave, weren't we all. With the hot temps, we knew demand was going to be high into the night. After my dinner, I did my rounds and walked the exterior. I noticed lightning across the river - up towards Bear Mountain State Park." He flicked his head out towards the river and gave a point with the tip of the pliers in a direction that was symbolic, given we had no windows to the outside from the kitchen.

Mickey made a federal case out of sucking the crabmeat from the legs and went on, "It was real humid that night. Storms were reported up and down the river, dangerous conditions in our business. The senior officer told us to stay in the building unless otherwise directed. He was worried about the lightning.

This made those of us on the shift even more miserable. At least outside there was a slight river breeze. It was even worse when he made us close the bay doors at the end of the deck. Those guys in the cooled control room had it easy, while sending me all over this darn plant to check different gauges."

He cracked another crab, and pulling a flathead screwdriver from his tool belt, he wedged out the meat. Finished with that crab, he pulled two more from the pot. He offered one to me. I motioned I was all set. I was taking my time with the first one, not interested in eating a river crab that could contain more PCBs than a high voltage transformer.

After he yanked out the meat, he picked up a small unlabeled glass bottle, that could have been on that table since Edison invented the light bulb, and dumped an orangey sauce on the crab. Still he used no plate. It was then that I understood who was responsible for the grimy table. I guess if he was eating that many crabs from this polluted river, a dirty table was the least of his concerns.

"I was down in the PAB (*primary auxiliary building*) taking readings just before 9 p.m. Indicators started going off like crazy. I got on the phone with the control room. From the sound of the ringing, every alarm was going off up there too. The SO (*senior operator*) told me we were tripped offline and we were going into shutdown." He broke open his fifth crab and pushed one my way. Seeing mud still caked between the crab's legs, I waved him off, hoping he wouldn't notice. The smell was making me want to run out the door, but I was glued to my seat wanting to hear the rest of his story.

He smacked the side of the hot sauce bottle and drained the

last of it onto the top of his crab. Tearing apart the crab, he more stated than asked, "Some sweet crabs today, huh?"

I just nodded my head, not wanting to offend him. Sweet? Then why the heck was he drowning them in hot sauce? I wondered if the sauce would kill the aftertaste of the crab that was lingering in my mouth. The flat soda I was sipping was doing nothing to cleanse my pallet.

Mickey went on with his memory. "We found out later that night the cause of the initial problem. Lightning had hit the line leading to the substation. The power from the plant here had no place to go. We had no choice but to take her down. This was no drill. We were scrambling. We were too busy to have a clue as to what was happening south of us down in the city. I only found out in the paper the next day."

A few weeks later, I was working the night shift when Mickey volunteered to go pick up the steaks for the overtime dinners. He paged me to come and help him. Before heading over to the restaurant for the takeout, he parked the truck in the substation lot and told me to come along. I thought he had to check on something. Standing next to the chain-link fence, he pointed to the power line that had been hit by the lightning, as if it were one of the top ten New York City area tourist attractions.

"That there's the line that was melted. Breakers tripped out. It caused a big mess. Amazing what millions of volts in a bolt of light can do." He was so animated as he recounted the damage, I almost gave him a five-dollar tip for the tour.

GREENPOINT AVE.

My recollection of that night was quite a bit different than Mickey's. I was not yet ten years old in July 1977, when the entire city lost power for more than twenty-four hours. It's a childhood memory that has stayed with me until this day. We never lost power in New York City. The skyline had never gone dark before; at least not up to that point in my life.

The night the electric went out, I was on my bed watching an old nine-inch black-and-white TV when it flashed off. Along with the TV, my lamp went out and the air conditioner in my parents' window stopped vibrating. Our flat had two sections. All the bedrooms were connected to one another. These were separated from the living room, dining room, and kitchen, by a cheap veneer hollow door. In the darkness, I heard Mom and Dad shouting on the other side of the door in the living room. I jumped out of bed to go and see what was happening. As I was grabbing for the doorknob, the door hit me in the face. Mom was on her way in to check on me and my brother and sister, who were both already asleep.

"The batteries in the flashlight are missing!" yelled Dad.

"I'm getting them. I gave them to Tommy to use for his race cars."

"Are you kidding me!" screamed my dad.

"Check the freezer, there are some in the bag recharging," she shouted back.

Later in life, after I became an electrical engineer, I was never able to convince my mother that keeping batteries in the freezer does nothing to charge them, and in reality, reduces the useful life. Where she heard such a thing, I do not know. It's right up there with, "Don't sit so close to the TV, you'll damage your eyes."

"These batteries in the freezer are all dead!" Dad began yelling from the kitchen where he was using his lighter to illuminate his battery search, testing each one in a flashlight. Mom had found the race cars, removed the batteries, and gave them to my dad. We had run those dead as well.

By now, my two younger siblings were awake from all the yelling. Hearing the commotion, Nana came up from her apartment on the ground floor with an extra flashlight that she handed to my dad. It wasn't much brighter than a match. We were all bumping into one another and feeling our way around in the dark. My little sister, Jeanette, was crying.

Mom lit an odd array of candles she found in the junk draw of the hutch. The flames bounced off the cigarette stained dining room walls. I made shadow puppets, thinking that would entertain Jeanette. Tormented by the flickering shapes, she just cried louder. The one dull flashlight and the candles would be the only light we would have in our apartment that night and into the next.

Dad took the flashlight on his way to the basement to see if it was the main fuse. I stood holding the apartment door open a crack. Dad was going down the stairs when Pop-Pop stuck his head into the hall and said, "Don't bother. The entire block is out. It's not just us. Look outside."

Dad went out the front door to see if he could find out what was going on. I ran back into the apartment to look out the window that faced out on North Henry.

As sirens started to blare, my mom, sister, brother, and I

pressed our faces to the dusty screen. Everything was dark. Not a streetlight was on. Every apartment window on the opposite side of the street contained multiple faceless heads staring back into the night. We had no idea how long the lights would be out or how the city would be impacted by the darkness. The blackout of '77 became one of my vivid memories of growing up in Greenpoint, Brooklyn. It was an odd feeling knowing all the lights, in the city that never slept, had faded to black.

My Greenpoint

The 1970s have been called New York City's dark ages. I was a kid then, and other than the blackout, it didn't seem too dark to me at the time. The decade was sandwiched between the post-war boom of the 1950s and 60s, and the later revitalization era of many urban centers during the late 1980s and into the 1990s. I grew up mostly unaware of the city's despair during the 70s; I suspect most of us kids did. We were just living life in the urban jungle and didn't know anything different. Looking back, the Greenpoint of my youth certainly had an impact on my personality, my outlook on life, and how I view the city – both good and bad - until this very day.

The extent of my childhood neighborhood was a rectangular piece of Greenpoint that started at my front stoop on North Henry Street, went south to St. Stanislaus Kostka School, then northwest past my maternal grandmother's apartment on Nassau Avenue and returned east along "The Avenue" back to our block. When we said "The Avenue," we knew we meant either Nassau or Manhattan Avenue, depending on the context.

"Go up The Avenue and get a loaf of rye bread," meant Busy Bee on Nassau.

"I've got to get up The Avenue and get the kids some glue," meant going to Newberry's Five and Dime up on Manhattan.

When I was a bit older, the rectangle extended past what

was originally my paternal grandmother's apartment at 720 Manhattan Avenue, a number I will never forget as she played it every week. If by chance Nana couldn't get to the corner store, or just didn't have the dollar to play it, she'd yell out the front window to my dad on his trip to the corner, "Play 720. Straight and box!"

Nana and Pop-Pop lived on the second floor at 720 until they moved to the ground floor of the house my parents owned on North Henry. Even with her new address, Nana would still play the house number from The Avenue.

Only on rare occasions do I recall venturing too far outside this rectangle. In fact, as I was writing, I couldn't recall the name of the street one block to the east without the use of the internet. I may have only walked Monitor Street alone, or with friends, three or four times in all the years I lived there. There were a few times Dad had to park our car there and we had to walk around the block to get home. I remember vividly one of those walks when I was young, it felt as if we had left our car in another city. It was a strange and distant land. The houses all looked so different; although they were all pretty much the same as on our street. Two and three-story row houses, sided or bricked, plain or ornate, some with aluminum awnings over the stoop. The street felt longer than our street; although it was the same length. The people on that block looked different; although it was certainly the same demographic of Polish, Italian, Irish, and mostly other European descent as on our block. That didn't matter. I rarely went around that corner, and so it could have been Queens as far as I was concerned.

Most all the homes on the side streets had a closed in space along the sidewalk we referred to as the 'aria,' or something that sounded like that, if not spelled that way. I can find no reference to such a term. Mom says it was spelled a-r-i-a. It seems to me a-r-e-a would align more with a dictionary term, but Mom lived in Greenpoint longer than I did, and she has an entire Brooklyn street vocabulary not documented anywhere, so who am I to argue.

I suspect her naming for this tiny front yard space came about from her saying so often, "Stay in the front area," over and over to us. I spent enough time in that fenced in pen before I could roam the streets, that I can still see in vivid color, a 360-degree panorama from that part of my Greenpoint.

"Can I go out and play, Mom?"
"Stay in the aria"
"Where's Dad, Mom?"
"Down in the aria"
"Can I have a snack, Mom?"
"Take the trash down to the aria first."
"Can we leave yet?"
"Go wait in the aria."

Our aria was a small space, enclosed with a wrought iron fence and a heavy gate that we had to lift to get it to close correctly; certainly, from it being slammed all the time. Dad, or Nana, or Pop-Pop (or all three together) were always yelling, "Don't slam the aria gate!"

In our aria, we had a rickety wood bench that someone must have made from leftover lumber. On a warm summer evening Nana would sit there, talking to people as they passed by, or with my dad who stood on the stoop smoking. It was my job each summer to paint that bench, always a forest green; other than the bicentennial year when I painted it red, white, and blue. I still remember how unstable it felt, swaying back and forth, as I sat on it lacing up my roller skates.

If the adults were in the aria talking about something and didn't want me to listen, they would say, "Tommy, go inside and play." It's strange to remember being told to 'go inside to play.' We always wanted to be out, that's where the action was. We were street kids.

Inside, all my toys were stored in a corner of my parents' bedroom. So, there I sat, counting my matchbox cars and sorting baseball cards, and I could hear everything they were saying down below in the aria anyway. I may have been out of sight, out of mind, but I was not out of earshot. I heard a lot of family and neighborhood gossip that way.

An 'aria' is, by definition, a vocal performance, usually as part of an opera. The term derives from the Greek and Latin 'aer,' or air. Maybe the term aria was endeared to this space when the men of the past generations stood in front of their houses in the evening to get some air, to smoke, and maybe even sing a verse now and then.

Aria may have evolved from the term 'areaway' which is defined as a sunken space used to gain access to a basement. The aria in front of our house was not sunken, but there was a cellar door to get to the basement. Our cellar door was originally a two-section slanted hatch of three-inch-wide boards pieced together. My friends and I would scale over the rail along the top of the stoop and slide down it. Eventually, the half inch thin pine boards started to rot so badly something had to be done. Mom stopped letting us go out even to play in the aria until Dad replaced it. She was worried we were going to fall through the boards onto the concrete steps below and break our necks. The way we jumped on that door, how we never fell through is amazing to me.

Dad broke down and replaced the door out of his concern for security rather than our safety. A good pull on the handle and the inside latch could have been broken by a twelve-year-old. And when we were twelve, we discovered that with a little jimmying the latch would also come loose without breaking the door. On a hot summer day, we discovered cases of Miller High Life, in nips sizes, stored for the upcoming block party on the steps leading to the basement. The yellow beer wasn't that good and given that it was warm, well it tasted just like it looked. We drank a few anyway. Dad blamed one of my uncles for drinking the beers ahead of the block party.

Once through the exterior door, the door at the bottom of the steps leading to the inside of the basement was secured with a simple hook and eye latch on the inside. My little sister could have kicked it in. She never needed to, because she, or anyone else, could just slide a hand in and flip the latch up. It was obviously a very safe neighborhood since these two doors were sorely lacking in the security department.

Dad replaced the rotting wood door with one made of heavy steel that he secured to the ground with what must have been three truckloads of cement. I was given the job of painting the door a high gloss battleship gray. My friends and I discovered that by using Pop-Pop's car wax we could slide down that new door really fast. Since it wasn't wood, it had the other advantage of not giving us splinters in the most painful of places. A chunk of pressure treated pine wedged up in the skin behind my knee cap is something I've never forgotten.

Once that door was waxed and buffed our aria became the place to slide. Kids would line up out the aria gate and onto the sidewalk waiting for a turn. There was a lot of pushing to get up the stoop, climb over the handrail, and slide down the cellar door. This, for some reason, was infinitely more fun than walking up the street to the park and using a real slide. I should have charged a nickel a turn. It was all great until Billy's little brother fell over the stoop rail and smashed his head on the steel door. Billy was the guy I always wanted on my offensive line when we played football; even touch was a full contact, no pad, sport on the asphalt street. While Billy was strong on the field, he was weak in other areas. Instead of watching his brother, he was distracted eating a Drake's Coffee Cake between his turn sliding down the door.

The Nana investigation revealed we had greased the cellar door with an entire bottle of *Turtle Wax*. Pop-Pop was not happy about it at all. I don't know if he took Nana's view of safety, but since we used up his car wax he made it a mission to keep us off that cellar door from then on.

Nana and Pop-Pop (100% Nana) were in charge of watching us when Mom and Dad went off to work in the city, and in this context since we were technically, in "The City," it meant Manhattan. Most things Nana would let slide, but an injury in the aria had to be reported to Mom as soon as the GG pulled into the Nassau Avenue station.

After that when I asked, "Mom, can I go out and play?"

She'd yell, **"Stay OUT of the aria!"**

Once I was out of our aria, all sorts of things could happen. And they did.

Ritchie's house up the block had a true areaway by definition. He had a concrete stairway that led down to an area under their front stoop that was blocked by a full size, medieval looking, iron gate door. Ritchie had this humongous skeleton key that could unlock that outer door. At the back part of this large closet sized area, there was a door made of armor car steel that led to their basement. It had at least five different deadbolt locks on it. They obviously must have lived in the higher crime part of the block or their dad stored way more valuable liquor down in their basement than Miller High Life. When we were little, we used Ritchie's areaway as a kid lockup during pirate games. But by the time we hit twelve, the locked gate became a kissing booth for seventh and eighth graders.

Ritchie's areaway turned out to be the perfect place for our nighttime kiss and don't tell games, or depending on whom you kissed, kiss and tell games. Ritchie was in high school, and at least two years older than the rest of us. He was always pushing the limits with one thing or another and we were willing to go along for the ride. Whatever the game was that Ritchie made up, it meant pairing a girl and boy to make a visit to the areaway. The pairings were done in a not so random order. Ritchie paired up couples that he wanted together, or couples that were already an item, which at our age meant we walked up and down the block to the candy store together.

Everyone would "ooo" and "ahh" as the pair was selected, as if it was some big surprise. Ritchie would follow the couple down the three steps to the iron gate and with a large bang he would slam the door and lock the lock. We would be locked in the dark, for seven minutes in heaven, or hell, depending on your fear of girls (or a girl's dad). Being stuck between two heavy locked doors would probably freak me out now, but back then I was more worried if I was going to turn my head the wrong way and bang the girl's nose.

To make it interesting, and keep things as dark as possible, Ritchie would turn off the stoop light. This made it pitch black, since near his house the street lights were blocked by trees. A few minutes after Ritchie turned out the light, his grandma would come out to the entry hall and turn the light on again.

"Ritchie, why do you keep turning this light off? I'm sure your friends don't want to sit on the stoop in the dark." I'm pretty sure she knew something was going on and she was determined to find out.

Technically, Ritchie's grandma was the reason we were using the dungeon. Earlier in the summer she had confiscated the wine bottle we were using for spin the bottle down in his basement rec room. She took away the bottle, because we drank the few sips of wine that she had left. I don't think she was aware about the kissing games, but how were we supposed to play with wine still in the bottle?

During one of our summer kissing games, Ritchie called out, "Tommy and Erin." Naturally, we faked a protest. Everyone played along pushing us down behind the gate and Ritchie locked us in.

In the dark, close to my ear, Erin whispered, "Tommy, you're not going to tell anyone we did anything down here –

right?"

I wondered how I should play the situation. The older guys were always bragging about bases, so I knew I had to at least kiss Erin. Those striking out were subject to a lot of teasing.

"Of course not," I told her.

With not much to do with seven long minutes, I asked Erin, "What if I just tell the guys we kissed if they ask?"

"Okay," she agreed, knowing it was important for both our reputations. She couldn't be seen as a prude after all.

"So how about we make it real?" I proposed.

A bright light aimed at our closed eyes blinded us with Ritchie saying, "Time's Up!"

Paulie and Lori were paired up next. Ritchie escorted them down into the space between the iron gate and the basement door. We all sat on the stoop laughing uncomfortably, but we were really wondering if they were kissing. Or were they sweating it out, making up some story, and killing time. Erin and I sat close holding hands.

Ritchie was watching his digital watch waiting for the alarm to play, "The Yellow Rose of Texas." Seven minutes never seemed so long. Before the alarm sounded, Lori's scream broke the silence.

Then we heard Ritchie's grandma yell, "Ritchieeeeee!"

His grandma had gone down through the basement and opened the inner door on Lori and Paulie. Lori freaked out, even though they were just kissing (we were told). Paulie pulled on the iron gate but it was locked. He yelled out for Ritchie, but it was too late. We had all scrambled, Ritchie included, along with the skeleton key. That pretty much put a damper on the kissing games for a couple of weeks. Ritchie's dad took away the key and told him we were not allowed to hang out around their areaway. We pretty much eventually found ways to get banned from all areaways and arias on the block.

It seems then, that <u>aria</u> is a fine term for an open-air space in front of apartment buildings, and <u>areaway</u> a term for those arias that have a sunken entrance to the basement. Thinking about the term 'aria,' it also occurs to me that many Brooklyn words and sayings were unique to our lives in the city. The terms just appeared and then stuck, at least for a generation or two. Sometimes, outside the city, we were foreigners speaking a different language.

When we would visit Jersey, people there had trouble understanding us. When we talked about stoopball, they thought it was something we did to pick up a baseball. I once asked a Jersey kid if he wanted to play slap. His mother dragged him away, as if I was going to abuse him. If we were looking for lunch and we asked, "Where can we get a good hero around here?" They'd look at us weird and tell us they didn't know anyone like that.

And heaven help us if we stopped at a Jersey diner on our way back from the lake, and I asked the waitress for an egg cream. Mom would just whisper, "You'll have to wait until we get back to the city for one of those."

If a Jersey lady asked my mom where she bought her purse, Mom would answer, "The Avenue."

The lady would respond with, "Fifth Avenue?" totally impressed because she may have never even been to the city.

Mom would answer, "What? No (drawing out the "o" in

No), Manhattan Avenue." That was the only avenue we ever needed.

Since we didn't spend much time out of the city, heck we rarely left Greenpoint, the slang language barrier wasn't all that much of a problem. All my friends had the same accent and used the same words. Until I was ten, I rarely even left the aria by myself.

*

My brother Chris riding his bike.
"Stay in the aria!"

*

Within the aria there was a concrete space where we kept the trash cans. The concrete slab space was also perfect for burning leaves with a magnifying glass. At the front of the aria was a tiny dirt garden that butted up against the iron fence

An aria fence, complete with the killing spears.

separating our aria from the sidewalk. The neighboring arias were separated with the same iron fencing. This fencing was very dangerous to climb over. It must have been designed in the Middle Ages as a form of birth control for attacking armies. The fence gave the illusion of being easy to climb because it was divided with perfect footholds. The trouble came as you had to bring your leg over to get across. On the top of these fences were what could only be described as spears. The spears would be aimed directly at the male anatomy. A slip of the sneaker and that's all it would have taken to instantaneously perform a sidewalk surgery. The shortcut was made even more dangerous if the climber was wearing shorts.

When I was scaling the aria fences to visit my friends, my nana was constantly yelling, "Tommy, stop climbing over the aria fence. Walk around!" I am pleased to say, I never had a fatal accident scaling over those spears, the minor scar from a close call on my thigh excluded.

The front fence in our aria was lined with poor excuses for hedges and Dad's prized red maple tree, that only seemed to finally take root and grow the year he decided to move us upstate. And if you're from the city you realize upstate is almost within walking distance of Times Square. A city person's upstate, is not Plattsburgh, Syracuse, or Buffalo.

It didn't, but it probably should have amazed me, that this dirt patch, in our modest aria, in the middle of a concrete jungle, was home to frogs and turtles. I spent hours watching the wildlife. Some of the turtles that wandered through were quite large, maybe pets that had been let go to fend for themselves. Sometimes we would capture these orphans and put them in boxes. We'd feed them leaves, old bread, and give them water in bottle caps. I think they enjoyed the free handouts since they would show up every time we were playing in the aria. At the end of the day we'd let them go, knowing they'd be back. I started marking the turtle shells with drops of paint to confirm it was the same set that was showing up each day. My non-scientific experiment proved that sometimes it was, sometimes it wasn't. The highlight one summer was when a mother turtle came walking out of the hedges with a brood of four young ones. Our aria became the hangout that day as if we had just opened a wildlife park. If that family of turtles could make it there, in an aria in Brooklyn, they could make it anywhere. How they found their way to an aria in Greenpoint is shocking since so many people I've met don't even know where Greenpoint is!

When I tell people I'm from Greenpoint, I am no longer surprised that few have heard of it. Even New Yorkers, meaning those from the city and not Poughkeepsie, I've met around the country have been unaware that Greenpoint is part of Brooklyn. I guess I'm just as guilty because I'd surely fail a multiple-choice test to pick out all sixty-one neighborhoods of the Bronx correctly, or all the sections of any of the five boroughs for that matter.

For me, Greenpoint was special, even if it never was a famous section of the city, unlike at least one neighborhood in Queens that has had plenty of advertising. Paul Simon sung about a Queen Rosie from Corona, a borough section on the way to Flushing Meadows Park. There is a King of Corona, but he sells Italian ices on 108th Street, to none other than Carrie and Doug Heffernan. Doug, as I am sure you know, was the King of Queens. Maybe the creators of that TV show were not Paul Simon fans, or Leah Remini's character Carrie may have more aptly been named Rosie. There are plenty of songs about Brooklyn and TV shows set in Brooklyn, but no really famous ones that I am aware of specifically about Greenpoint.

People have asked me if Greenpoint is close to Flatbush, or Bay Ridge, or even Long Island (good grief). Some will say, "I thought Brooklyn, was just, well, Brooklyn." There could never be 'just Brooklyn,' there's just too much that is different between each of the EIGHTY-SIX neighborhoods of the borough.

More recently I have resorted to telling people I was just generically from Brooklyn, leaving out the Greenpoint part. I'm not happy about that, so the next time I'm asked, I might just give the person a copy of this book.

When people hear I'm from Brooklyn, it certainly conjures

up certain mental images. Some think that Brooklyn always was, as it is now. I guess the 'now' is considered trendy, some call it 'hipster.' I'm not sure. Some ask how dangerous it was growing up in the 70s. For some reason they're impressed I survived a mugging – hasn't everyone? A few are familiar with the breakup of boroughs into neighborhoods and when they ask as Mickey had asked, "What part of Brooklyn?" I know immediately they know something about New York City geography, even if they're not totally sure where Greenpoint is.

Greenpoint, the northern most neighborhood of Brooklyn, was for the most part a safe section, even in the 1970s, my own muggings aside. The neighborhood was predominantly Polish. The Polish influence was evidenced, particularly in our section of the neighborhood, where store signs had mostly consonants and very few vowels. I had no way of sounding out a store name – and we were half Polish.

The side streets were mainly residential. The avenue streets were an eclectic group of shops, most of which lined Nassau and Manhattan Avenues. As in many New York neighborhoods, on any given intersection, there was a good chance you could find pharmacies diagonally across from one another. One might be a Polish-American Apteka (Pharmacy); the other just Pharmacy. The other two corners were often delis or bars. Every few blocks there was a pizza place with a takeout window to grab a slice as you walked by – always ready, the ultimate New York fast food. On the way to the Meserole movie theater, I could grab a cheese slice and a Coke at Baldo's window and a pepperoni Sicilian slice at Pizza Prince – a full meal on the go and no time wasted.

The Five and Dime on Manhattan Avenue was a favorite for buying puzzles, matchbox cars, and just about anything else I ever needed. Between Newberry's, the candy store, and the Army Navy store, I never had any trouble Christmas shopping for my parents, brother, sister, or grandparents. If we couldn't get "it" on one of the "The Avenues," we probably didn't need it.

There were no chain donut or coffee shops back then. We had bakeries. The Italian bakery, the Polish bakery, and the Donut Shop. Coffee came two ways – regular and decaf. Fuhgeddaboudit if you think the server would have known back then what to do if you asked for "a venti double mocha chino, skim, no whip."

By the time I was eleven, I was pretty much roaming my rectangle of Greenpoint, at least during daylight hours in the summer, on my own. There were always pickup games of one type or another going on to keep us busy. The kids on the block went to one of several private schools, associated with one of the local church parishes, or one of the PSs – 31, 34, 110, or 126. Since kids were constantly roaming around, different kids would show up to play, sometimes an entire team would come over for a block to block challenge of slap or punch – ball games, not fights. In this way we extended our group of friends beyond our block. If I needed a change of scenery for the day, all I had to do was walk a few blocks and an entire different crew of friends would be hanging out.

Our block of North Henry Street was sandwiched between the park on the south side and some industrial factories on the north, both of which were fun and scary at the same time. The park was nice to have, but seedy at times. The industrial complex, made up of one and two-story brick buildings, included lots where tractor trailers were parked. Since we had been banned from the arias by grandmothers, we would sometimes troll around in those lots to find an open trailer to hang out in and play cards or just sit and make up lies about girls. The lots were an area I would never have roamed around alone, but in thinking about it, roaming with other eleven and twelve-year-olds, even if we were wearing tough looking jean jackets, was probably not any safer.

Growing up in the neighborhood, I always felt we had a lot of family close by. In a way they were, but in reality, three out of four of my mom's brothers had moved away and nine out of eleven of my dad's brothers and sisters had left Greenpoint by the mid-70s. My aunts and uncles had moved to Queens, Jersey, The Island, upstate, and one moved to the exotic location of California. What kept them feeling close was that both sets of my grandparents remained in Greenpoint, within ten blocks of our house. That meant there were always visiting relatives around, and a feeling of extended family close by.

Greenpoint had everything I needed growing up. I took piano lessons from a lady across the street, we had two movie theaters, and a park to play in. I frequented the pizza places, became a pinball wizard, drank milkshakes on the corner, gorged myself at the candy stores, and discovered different 'street' foods to try. I played multiple types of ball games in the streets and learned to dodge grumpy old men protecting their cars. For the most part, my friends and I had plenty to do to stay out of trouble, even if we may have been the ones causing it sometimes.

During the hot summers, I would spend some weeks at my grandparents' cabin in northern New Jersey near a lake. Why I was not at the lake on that hot 95-degree July 1977 night when all the lights went out, I can't recall. I'll chalk that up to good luck because had I been in Jersey, I would have missed out on a very memorable Brooklyn experience.

The Blackout of 1977

The following week, Mickey had scavenged for his lunch again. I was sitting across from him, eating a sausage and pepper hero, watching him pry the last bits of meat from the underside of a crab using his screwdriver. He looked up and asked, "So what was it like down in Greenpoint during the Blackout, kid? How'd your family get along without power? Was there any looting near your block?"

Having worked inside power plants for nearly half a century, Mickey was interested in knowing how important he was to delivering the juice that powered people's lives. I had to think about how to answer him. I hadn't really given that night much thought in the last ten, or so, years. I took a sip of my soda and told Mickey what I could remember.

GREENPOINT AVE.

When the lights went out in Greenpoint on Wednesday night, July 13, 1977, we were not used to the silence. It was eerie. No television, no hum from the forever flickering fluorescent light over the kitchen sink, and no radio blasting the Mets or Yankee game from a neighbor's aria.

The dead quiet only lasted a few minutes until people stammered out of their homes, flashlights flashing, their night interrupted. At the front window, we listened for Dad.

My mother, sister, brother, and I gazed out on our blackened street. Our four heads squeezed next to each other in the window. How different it looked. The street lights shed no light. There was no color. Everything was a dingy gray. The cars, trees, and even the houses all became shadows, one dimensional. The only colors visible on the entire street came from red dots of cigarettes, slowly rising to the mouths of the blackened silhouettes. Between puffs the yells began – stoop to stoop, aria to aria.

"What the heck is happening?"

"Joe – any idea what's going on?"

"Are you guys out of electric too?" (As if electric was sold in a carton, like milk.)

"The whole block is out."

"The park lights are out too!"

"Must be a transformer."

"All of Greenpoint is out!"

"No! It's all of Brooklyn!" shouted a voice from above us, somewhere on a roof.

"It's the entire city. Look over at Manhattan, it's completely blacked out," added a shadow on a roof across the street.

"Maybe it's the entire State."

Not to be outdone, some wise guy (possibly literally) yelled, "It's the whole country. It's the damn communists!" (This was 1977 after all.)

My mother pulled me away from the window. It was bad enough the cold war had us doing weekly drills, hiding under our small wooden classroom desks to protect us from nuclear radiation fallout, she didn't want me to hear about it on my own street too. Besides we had no school desks in our apartment to hide under if a warhead was headed our way at that very moment.

A single siren approached and then faded away down Nassau Avenue. My dad came back up to our apartment and turned on the battery-operated radio. No sound or static came out. Those batteries were dead too. It took him another fifteen minutes, through trial and error, to find a set of four from the freezer bag that had enough power to bring the radio to life.

Contemplating his pile of dead batteries, he said to Mom, "The rest of these batteries are only good as a weapon." He grabbed two old tube socks, taking his time to find a pair without holes, and pushing one inside the other he loaded up. Nothing like hitting an intruder upside the head with a sock full of frozen D's. As I watched him load the socks, I felt it wasn't the first time he charged up a pair for a battle.

Thirty minutes later the radio station announced that parts of the city had erupted into chaos. A reporter was reading reports of looters breaking into stores and stealing TVs, radios, food, furniture, and even washers and dryers.

I asked, wondering what was going to happen to us, "Dad, are the looters going to come here?"

"No. They're robbing stores. We don't have anything they would want," he replied. I noticed he was still grasping the battery socks.

Since Greenpoint had always been a relatively safe neighborhood of Brooklyn, my parents weren't overly worried. Given we didn't really have any commercial stores in our immediate vicinity, Dad was probably right, but listening to the radio reports, I was still a little scared. This feeling was heightened by the reality that our apartment was dark, except for the flickering of a few candles and the end of Dad's Kent cigarette.

The first sign of inconvenience was not so much the lack of light, but how hot it was getting in the apartment. Our one meager window air conditioner was out of service. While the old unit never kept the bedrooms any cooler than a sticky 75, it was now noticeable that it was better than nothing. Not even a slight breeze was coming through the other four windows Mom had opened – in the hopes of getting some air. Keeping his cool, Dad just sat at the dining room table, listening to the radio, smoking, and adjusting his weapon sock.

Pop-Pop, who lived on the ground floor of our apartment building, took a different approach to the darkness. He sat by his front window with his old pistol at the ready; although, that may have just been his typical evening pastime, since Pop's car had been burglarized a couple of times on our block. After he retired he became a traveling salesman of sorts, earning extra income selling construction clothing out of the back of his station wagon. He was going to be sure no looter was going to steal his stock of heavy gloves, thick socks, and long underwear – all things people need during a heat wave and blackout. Maybe our neighborhood wasn't as safe as I thought.

After listening to the radio reports and hearing the sirens, Dad wanted to get a view from the roof. It was already way past my bedtime, but I'd never been on our roof. I couldn't let this opportunity pass me by.

"Dad, can I go too?"

"No, Tommy, you have to get to bed," interjected Mom.

"It's too hot to go to bed. I want to go with Dad."

My brother and sister had already fallen back to sleep, oblivious that we were living in a sauna in the midst of a city-wide crisis.

"It will be alright, Mary Lou. We won't be long," said Dad.

I followed Dad into the hall, excited to be part of the exploration. I wondered if we might see the looters and what we'd do if we did. Pop-Pop sitting in his chair, the door from his apartment wide open, to encourage intruders I think, heard us in the hall.

"Where are you going, Tom?" Pop-Pop yelled to my dad.

"Up to the roof," Dad yelled back.

"Wait a minute," Pop-Pop said.

I looked at Dad and thought, Pop-Pop was certainly too large, and up in years, to have any interest in attempting the climb with us – or was he expecting to tag along?

Standing at the bottom of the stairs, he said to my dad, "Here, take this. Just in case." He was waving the pistol in his hand.

"No, Dad. We'll be fine," replied Dad, who was clutching the loaded D battery tube sock in his right hand. "And be careful with that thing, will ya! Keep it pointed down."

I don't know if Pop-Pop's gun was loaded or even if it had all the pieces. On his basement workbench, I would often find guns in various states of completeness. He had small pistols and a few old guns that Dad said were from the war, what war I have no idea. Maybe he was a collector, who knows, we never talked about it. I never noticed any ammo. When I was caught, one rainy summer day, trying to find parts to make at least one gun that had a working trigger, Dad made Pop-Pop 'hide' his collection elsewhere.

To reach the roof, we climbed the flight of stairs to the third-floor landing. The young, just past hippie age couple, who rented the apartment above ours, came to their door. They asked my dad, as the landlord, and someone in a position they thought should know, when the lights would be back on. He told them he had no idea. I was mesmerized by the hundreds of candles I could see burning inside their apartment as they stood in the open doorway, hugging each other much too tightly given the temperature. The barefoot woman was holding a glass of wine next to her hips, accentuating her cutoff denim short-shorts, jean threads hanging down her thigh. The smoky air that was wafting into the hallway smelled like the *incense* the teenagers used up at the park.

The man, a *Welcome Back Kotter* look-alike, closed the apartment door, bored of Dad's explanation of the situation. I could hear the woman laughing and giggling on the other side. It must have been the wine – why else would she be so happy during a blackout. Dad told me a few years later, when we were discussing that night, that the smell wasn't incense at all.

Dad and I continued walking to the end of the third-floor hallway where an iron ladder rose to a hatch in the ceiling. I recall the ladder had no pitch to it; it went straight up making it scary to climb. The hatch included a locking mechanism on the inside to prevent someone from coming into the house from the attached roofs. My dad had a habit of always checking that lock, at least once a week. When I asked him about it, he told me that thieves could come down through unlocked hatches, entering the houses from the roof. I don't know if we ever had a problem, but he was sure to keep it locked. He was always more worried about someone coming through the roof, than the much easier wooden cellar door in the aria before it was replaced.

Watching Dad climb up the ladder, I wondered if at that very moment, looters might be waiting to jump down the instant he unlatched the lock. Maybe I should have stayed back in the apartment.

Dad undid the lock and pushed open the hatch. I felt a gush of musty smelling hot air, mixed with the smell of "incense" rise past me to escape the building. Dad came back down. He wanted me to climb up in front of him, just in case I fell. I looked up through the small opening into the black night sky. Climbing the rungs of the steel ladder, I realized I was going to be the first one to stick my head through the opening. The climb was longer than I expected, and when I reached the last rung, Dad helped push me up from the ladder to the roof.

I stood motionless in the hot darkness for a couple of seconds, until Dad pulled himself up. The roof, a flat rectangle, was punctuated by several exhaust pipes and the chimney stack. Even though it was already late at night, the gooey tar was soft under my sneakers. I walked to the front and looked down into the aria. The wooden bench looked so small. I ran across the roof to look down into the yard.

Dad yelled, "Go slow. There are some soft spots on this roof. You might fall through!"

I thought, "What! Fall through?" I tested each step after that to be sure the roof was stable.

Looking over the edge, I spied the residents sitting on their fire escapes behind the apartment buildings. They were talking to one another and trying to keep cool. For blocks on end, I could see beams from flashlights bobbing across the rooftops; the curious residents of Greenpoint were out searching for answers. Everyone had the same interest in checking out the nothingness. However, it was far from nothingness in my eyes.

From the roof, I could see the Manhattan skyline across the East River, all dark, the buildings just silhouettes. A few red emergency beacons flashed on the tops of the tallest buildings. I remember how the Twin Towers pierced the downtown sky, they were two branchless trees pointing up in the middle of a dark forest. The Empire State Building marked midtown. In the muted darkness, the rest of the skyline appeared short and stumpy from my rooftop view.

Thinking about it now, how cool it would have been to go up to the roof on a night when the city had power. What a site that would have been. We never did that. We did go up once during the extreme heat of the day later that summer. A few weeks after the blackout, Dad said, "When we were up on the roof I noticed the tar needed some repairs. How about this weekend you help me out?" Of course, he couldn't wait for cooler weather in September.

When that Saturday came around, I was excited to be going back up on the roof. That all changed as soon as I stepped out on the tar. I could feel the searing heat through the soles of my worn-out Pumas; I was a boy on a hot tar roof. On that sunny day, I didn't even notice the city skyline. I was down that ladder to my humid air-conditioned bedroom, before he could hand me a squeegee. I left Dad to the sticky business of spreading tar in the August sun alone. It was not a cool place to be during a summer afternoon. But that night of the blackout, in the dark, with all the unknowns, and all the neighbors I didn't know shining their flashlights, it was the coolest place to be – just as long as Dad had a tight grip on that tube sock.

"Dad, do elevators work in a blackout?"

"Not usually, unless they have emergency power. Why?"

"Do you think anyone is stuck in the elevators in the Twin Towers?"

He looked across at the city. "There wouldn't be many people at this time of night."

That response didn't really answer my question.

"Can we go up to the top of the towers? Billy's dad took him. Billy said the elevator ride to the top was really fast."

Dad was a bit distracted looking around over the edge of the building.

"Dad?"

"Sure. When we go into the city for your eye appointment, we'll go downtown." Later that fall, we went as a family up to the observation deck. When he pointed out our neighborhood, Greenpoint looked so far away, and so flat.

From our position at the edge of the roof, we could now hear the sirens coming from all directions. Police, fire, ambulances, all with their different pitches carried through the air. The reds and blues of their lights, a patriotic New York City aurora borealis, lit up the darkness in the distance.

Then, we noticed the fires. A few miles away, flames were shooting into the dark sky south of us. Dad said, in a tone that I'm sure was significant, "That's Bushwick." From above our dark, calm street, we were witnessing the section of our city that was experiencing the most chaos.

Dad helped me down the ladder. Back in the apartment, we sat at the dining room table and Mom dished out ice cream by candle light. It was already soft, not surprising since our freezer barely worked to keep food frozen (or batteries charged) when there was power.

The voice on the radio was still frantic. "And in Bushwick there are fires and the looting is out of control. The police are helpless against the sheer number of people in the streets. Shopkeepers have taken to defending their property as best they can. These sure are dark times for the city."

Dad turned off the radio. In the silence the sirens seemed to be all that much closer. We had no idea that the blackout would last for more than twenty-four hours in the heat of that New York City summer.

Mostly, what I recall more than the darkness, was the heat. Our apartment would get stifling hot during the heat of a normal summer night. Dad would only turn on the air conditioner, when we had one that worked, during major heat waves. That July was one of those summers when the a/c was essential equipment for all New Yorkers, and this contributed to the even higher than normal electric demand. Even when city residents were told to conserve electricity, most were counting on their neighbor to do so, so they wouldn't have to. Everyone trusted the city and ConEd to have plenty of juice, all the time. They wouldn't have any problems – right?

We were all wrong. The high demand exasperated the problem of the blackout caused by the electrical storm. This was made worse when the utility operators who were advised to cut the load, didn't do so in time.

Since there was no electric, Dad took the air conditioner out of the window in an attempt to lure in a breeze. One more window open didn't matter. There was no breeze and the air temperature was not cooling off.

Our apartment, similar to those of just about all others in Brooklyn, had windows only on opposite ends of the rectangle. My parents' bedroom had two windows that looked out over the street. These same windows normally let in bright light from the streetlight directly across from our house. That lamp would illuminate our bedrooms during the summer as if North Henry Street was in the middle of Nome, Alaska at midnight in July – always bright. This was the first night, since we had moved to this house, that the light was not streaming in the windows, leaving an illuminated runway across the carpet I would use to land my model airplanes.

My sister's bedroom was directly off my parents' room. To get to her room, she would pass through the room, or hallway, I shared with my brother, then through my parents' room. She had her own window looking out onto the street and a door she could blockade to keep my brother and I out of her room. A door, that on summer nights, she left open to steal some of our cooled air-conditioned air, and on winter nights to heist the little heat that would come from the single radiator next to my parents' bed. The small radiator in her room never gave off any heat.

My brother and I shared a bedroom directly in the middle of the flat. No windows. No privacy. Mom, Dad, and my sister would pass through our room on their way to the living room and back. Our room was essentially a hallway with the one closet all of us had to share. The demarcation line between the rooms was the different shag carpets. I had a blue shag and my parents had a mauve color, both of which were supposedly kept looking new with the use of a carpet rake. One of my Saturday morning chores, before I was allowed to go out and play in the aria, was to 'rake the carpets.' I can't say I've seen too many carpet rakes lately. This wasn't a fine-tooth comb for pet hair, this rake was a garden-type rake, big separated teeth, only hard plastic and not metal. When I was five, raking the rug was a fun chore to keep me busy. By the time I was eight, raking a worn-down shag carpet made about as much sense to me as sweeping a lake. When we moved, it was the one thing we didn't pack. It stood there, alone in my empty closet, the only thing left in the apartment.

The other three windows, on the opposite end of our apartment, looked out over our backyard. Windows from those on the next block, looked back at us. To the left and to the right, it was row after row of two and three-story houses encircling the uniform manicured yards with rose bushes, hedges, and tomato plants. Spaces that were so coveted in the city, yet rarely occupied.

At night my room became just a bed and a dresser as my half of the trundle bed would roll out from under my sleeping brother and lift up by a spring. The force of that spring was so strong that if I timed it right, I could pull the bed out, jump on top, and be catapulted into the air as the bed exploded to full height with a cannon-like bang. Once the bed was up, there wasn't even a space between the edge of the mattress and our dresser.

Being the oldest in this bedroom layout, I have no idea how I ended up with siblings. How so many children are conceived in city flats is either a testament to the sound sleepers kids in Brooklyn became with all the background noise, or there is a whole segment of the city dwelling population that have no need for vocal expression during love making.

As the black night wore on, I fell asleep once exhaustion won out over the heat. The next morning, with the sun up and baking the pavement, I woke to an even hotter apartment. I pulled myself out of my sweat drenched bed, annoyed that our air conditioner was broken again. In my sleep-like state, I had forgotten why.

We're "Out" of Electric

I walked out into the living room and turned on the TV, my normal routine, to give the tubes time to warm up while I poured a bowl of cereal. When the large console didn't start humming and buzzing, as if it were going to explode or take off, I became concerned.

"Mom, the TV's not working!" I said.

"We're still out of electric," she replied. (Again, as if the carton was empty.)

"When will it be back on?"

"The City has no idea," she said, as if "The City" was the name of a person sitting behind some giant control board somewhere flipping switches to fill the cartons.

I poured a bowl of Cap'n Crunch and walked over to the fridge to get the milk. I opened the door. It was dark inside. There was no milk carton. The smell from inside the fridge was awful. I crinkled my nose and slammed the door shut.

"Mom, where's the milk?"

"Tommy, there's no milk or anything else. We have no electric. Everything has gone bad. Do not eat anything from inside that fridge!" Based on the smell, I don't think she had anything to worry about.

"I can't eat my cereal without milk!" I yelled. This blackout was getting very inconvenient. What was happening here? What was The City doing? I had no T.V., no milk, and no air-conditioning. This blackout was becoming a big deal.

"Where's Dad?" I asked.

"He's out in the aria."

I changed into my Two Guys discount store jeans and ran down the stairs and through the open front doors. Pop-Pop was sitting on the bench listening to his small transistor radio with his earpiece in. Nana was sitting on the stoop, smoking a Pall Mall, and drinking her instant coffee. Dad was standing at the aria gate, smoking a Kent, and talking to a neighbor. The old-timers on the block were going about their business as best as they could. Mr. Raviolo led the broom brigade sweeping down the sidewalks. Mr. Mazewski was carrying buckets of water from his aria to wash his Chevelle. Billy's grandma was sitting at her front window. Kids were riding their bikes and big wheels up and down the sidewalk, while the moms and grandmothers sat in the arias keeping watch. It was pretty much just another summer day on the block.

Yet something was different. There were a surprising number of dads out on the street for seven in the morning on a Thursday. Most of them were home and just hanging around. Paulie's dad was painting his aria fence, and Ritchie's dad was trimming the tree we always climbed on. Others were enjoying their day off, sitting on their stoops and reading a day-old paper.

"Didn't any of them have to go to work?" I thought.

I was starting to realize the impact electric power had on our daily lives. The subways weren't running and there wasn't much most of the people could do once at work if they could get there. Nobody was going anywhere. No cars were going up the block. Our day playing in the street was going to be that much more fun!

Ritchie's dad drove off to top off his gas tank. He came

back and grumbled, "There's only one station running with a generator to pump gas and they're almost out. All the others are out of electric." Again, with the 'out of electric.'

Standing on the stoop, I asked Dad, "Where does electric come from?"

Dad took a puff of his cigarette and said, "Like our water, they make it upstate." Nana glanced at him with a proud look, wondering how he knew so much. I thought, "They make our water upstate? Huh?"

"How do they make the electric up there?" I asked Dad.

"They have big generator plants," he said.

"What's a generator?" I dug in, now really interested.

Dad crushed out his cigarette on the stoop.

"It's a big machine that turns really fast to make the electric."

"How do they get that machine to turn? Don't they need electric?"

I could see he was starting to think of something he had to go do.

"Nah. They use steam," he replied and he walked over to make sure the steel cellar door was locked.

The brakes on a city bus squealed up on Nassau Avenue, the characteristic air pressure sound carrying down the block, "pssssst." The bus paused for a second. There was no one waiting to get on. It drove away. The heat induced silence was returned to the neighborhood.

"Tom, you should go over to the ice distributor and get blocks of ice," Pop-Pop said.

In my family, we always went to the distributors to buy

stuff, even ice. Distributors, like "The City," took care of everything we needed. We shopped at the milk distributor, the beer distributor, the meat distributor, and the bread distributor. The miles and miles of side industrial roads in Long Island City and Queens were packed with these places that distributed stuff. Why go to a grocery store? We'd drive around for hours on a Saturday to cut out the middleman. Until the blackout, we usually only went to the enterprising man that was taking the water from upstate and turning it into ice to distribute, if there was going to be a block party, a Baptism party, or a First Communion.

Dad looked around. Nobody else was moving their cars.

"I don't want to lose my spot, Dad."

Our VW bus was parked two doors up from our house. If Dad was to move his car now, he'd set off a chain of events with half the men on the block jockeying to move their cars closer to their front doors. My friends and I would get a good laugh out of the spot jockeys as they moved their cars around the street. It was a live action "Frogger" game, parallel parking style.

Pop-Pop's station wagon was parked directly in front of our house. He was the triple crown champion of the spot jockeys. If he happened to come home and someone was parked in what he considered "his spot," he might sleep in his car at the fire hydrant until that spot opened up. He could drive faster than the Bandit (from Smokey and the Bandit), making his imitation wood-sided station wagon maneuver quicker than a Trans Am when he was in hot pursuit of his prize parking spot. There was no way he was going to move his car today and lose his prime spot.

"The radio is saying they're selling out of ice at the stores. What about my fish in the freezer? I'll have to feed it to the cats," Pop-Pop countered, knowing this would get my dad's attention.

~ ~ ✦ ~ ~

Pop-Pop's fishing grounds were on the eastern shores of Long Island. He would bring back coolers full of flounder and a few other types of mutant fish that nobody could ever identify. For these fishing trips, Pop-Pop would leave at two in the morning and return very late in the evening. Being exhausted, he'd dump the fish into his bathtub and cover them with what was left of the ice in his coolers. He'd then go to sleep until the middle of the next day. The smell of the fish would waft up the dumbwaiter shaft that ran through all the bathrooms of each apartment.

The dumbwaiter, certainly not a politically correct term, was the size of an oven door that opened into each apartment's entryway. An electric mechanism would bring the trolley between floors. It was explained to me that in the old days they used it to transport trash to the basement or coal to the upper floors.

My dad and Uncle Tony eventually disconnected the dumbwaiter mechanism and then sheetrocked over the opening. Before they did that, it wasn't just a dumbwaiter, but a totally dead and inoperable one. We used it as a poor man's intercom. The hollow space would carry a yell very efficiently between our apartment and Nana's below us. Our yelling annoyed the renters on the third floor who really didn't care that we were 'having ziti at five o'clock,' or some silly message we felt the need to yell in a shaft. There was no way my dad or Pop-Pop were going to endorse using the phone for these messages because in those days, for even calls within the **same** building, there was a five-cent charge or something. "Ma Bell was always out to nickel and dime everyone," Nana would say.

From his first-floor bathtub, to our second floor flat, to the incense burning lover's nest on the third floor, the smell of fish, following one of Pop's Montauk expeditions, would permeate the entire house. I'd sneak down while he was sleeping to look at the assortment of fish in his tub. The flounders with two eyes on the same side of their head would freak me out. Compared to the four-inch sunnies and perch I'd catch at the lake, his fish were whales. The smell from his tub was only overcome with something far worse when he began to clean the fish the next day.

Sitting at his dining room table, Pop-Pop would scale and gut the fish to prepare and freeze his filets. Neighborhood cats would come by the dozens and line up in the yard below the window. It did not help that he would keep his window open and throw fish carcasses out to the felines. This would only serve to draw more cats to the yard and flies into the apartment. I'm not sure who would become more upset at him, Dad, or Nana.

~ ~ ≠ ~ ~

Smoking his cigarette in the aria that morning, Dad must have considered the ramifications of the defrosting fish, and the number of cats that would appear, if Pop-Pop didn't get a supply of ice. Dad, reluctantly, agreed to lose his spot and drive to the ice distributor, but not before Pop-Pop had one more request.

"See about getting these filled up so I can top my tank off. You remember the gas lines in '73."

Dad sighed and took the gas cans, wondering out loud, "I bet I'm gonna have to drive all the way upstate before I find a station with pumps working."

An hour after Dad left, a truck came down our block selling ice, ice cream, and popsicles. Since the ice distributor also had no power, it was in his best interest to allow the residents to keep their parking spots and instead distribute the ice - block to block.

Mom dragged us out to stand in line at the truck to buy some ice. The blocks the distributor was selling were not in bags, and the huge chunks began to melt as soon as Mom placed them in our outstretched arms. Chris dropped his block; he was not yet four, and the ice busted into a hundred pieces when it hit the sidewalk. Kids all crowded around, grabbing pieces and putting them down each other's shirts to cool off.

With the blocks of ice that survived, Mom moved what food had lasted the night in the freezer, down to coolers in the basement. Pop-Pop packed his fish into his own coffin-size coolers, which had a permanent smell of rotting fish guts, and relaxed now that his catch was safe for another day.

Dad came back two hours later, double parked, and honked the horn. When he opened the sliding door of our red rusted VW bus, a stream of water poured out. He had twenty blocks of ice stacked on the floor. As we had already purchased ice from the truck, he was a bit upset to say the least. We didn't even have an empty cooler for the ice he had bought.

"Why did you buy ice if you knew I went to get ice?" he asked Mom.

"What if they didn't have any left when you got there?" Mom replied.

He had no argument for her good point. Once the neighbors saw he had a bunch of ice, he sold out in a few minutes. He made a pretty good profit on it but had lost his parking spot.

Dad never did get Pop-Pop's gas cans filled. He ended up buying the ice first because he passed by the ice distributor first, and he didn't want them to run out. When he found a gas station that was pumping gas, the line was around the block. If he had waited for gas, the ice would have been water.

Pop-Pop said to him, "Well, obviously you should have gotten the gas first." The heat was taking its toll and everyone was a little edgy.

After we ate every popsicle that was bought from the iceman, the kids were grating on the adults to find us something to do. To stop our whining, Paulie's dad, who had a special sprinkler cap, opened up a fire hydrant so we could cool off.

~ ~ ◆ ~ ~

Paulie's dad was always good for causing some excitement on the block. If it was anywhere near the Fourth of July, New Year's Eve, or just for the heck of it, Paulie's dad would have a trunk full of firecrackers, roman candles, or jumping jacks. Paulie got caught more than once swiping a few packs before the official holiday.

Paulie's grandparents lived on the second floor of their building. Knowing Paulie took after his dad, his grandma was always watching out the window. If we caused any trouble she'd yell out, "Paulie, come home now!" When it came to fireworks, she was extremely diligent. She was always worried a smoke bomb was going to roll under a car and North Henry would blow up. To fool her, Paulie would smuggle fireworks out of the basement in shoe boxes, telling her it was his baseball card collection. We'd light them off, mats at a time, in trash cans up at the park.

The cops came driving into the park on one of the nights Paulie and I had dumped a mat of firecrackers into a can. When we saw their blue lights flashing, Paulie threw a dozen roman candles into the can and we took off. We hid out behind a car on Russell Street and watched the balls of fire shooting into the air in all directions.

Behind Paulie's back, all the guys on the block used to drool over his high school age sister. There was an afternoon, just before school let out for summer, when Paulie caught Joey M. eyeing his sister as she walked home in her Catholic girl's school skirt. The always protective Paulie jumped on Joey and pummeled him. That was the single time Grandma Polumbo sat at the window watching, never saying a word. After that, Paulie earned the reputation of being a protective hot head. Joey never again looked at Paulie's sister, or any other girl for that matter, if Paulie was around.

Paulie's dad also had a friend that came around who sold things distributor style. The guy would park his Plymouth Gran Fury, with dark tinted windows, right in front of the hydrant. My friends and I would run over to check out his fancy CB setup, while the men would gather around as he'd pop the trunk.

Under a blanket, he had all his merchandise still in the original boxes. The latest model toaster ovens, boom boxes, curling irons, VCR's, and one-hundred-piece ratchet sets.

My dad, always wanting to be sure stuff wasn't stolen, would ask, "So where'd you get this stuff?"

"Ah C'mon. Ya know. Down by the docks. Just off the boat. They sell at a discount. Don't worrybout'it," the "distributor" would tell him.

The year the laser disc came out the guy was selling players for something like twenty-five bucks a pop and throwing in a copy of *Jaws*. I watched as Dad held one of those boxes in his hands as I stood next to him, barely able to contain my excitement. It was all great until Paulie's dad ruined it. He said to my dad, "Carbone, what type of TV do you have? Can you even connect that thing to the beast you have?"

Dad said, "Well I guess we'd have to buy a new TV then." He thought about that and put the box back in the guy's trunk.

The distributor said to Dad, "You need a new TV? What size you want? I know a guy." Dad didn't go for it.

~ ~ ✦ ~ ~

On the day of the blackout, we didn't need a TV, we just wanted to cool off. Paulie's dad was just doing his community service when he opened the hydrant. We ran through the freezing cold water, yelling and screaming. It wasn't long before someone called the fire department. When the truck turned the corner and blasted its siren, thirty kids in wet Keds were scaling aria fences and hiding behind azalea bushes. Later that afternoon, Paulie's dad opened up the hydrant again. Within ten minutes, the firemen showed up and shut it down.

They did let us kids climb around the truck, blare the siren, and flash the lights before giving the adults a lecture about conserving water during the emergency.

With the hydrant off, we took refuge from the hot pavement and hung out in the basement (or does that mean we hung in?) as it was the coolest place in the house. Our basement was a long cement bunker the length of the entire house. Dad had installed the counter from his old candy store and configured it as a bar. At Christmas time, Mom would hide the presents behind the bar under a blanket. She should have pre-wrapped the gifts, because she wasn't hiding them from anyone back there. My sister and I would rummage through the presents, guessing which gifts were for us. During the summer blackout, we sat at the bar and played with my plastic Coke bottle soda dispenser that had shot glass size cups. We probably drank a case of warm soda that day.

There were a handful of times, other than the blackout, when we made use of our basement and yard to play with friends. Before we were old enough to roam the streets, we would meet in the yards, scale the fences, and try to keep busy. Being confined to the yard usually meant playing with GI Joes or trying to pull apart Stretch Armstrong. It took four of us an entire afternoon to get that done. When it was too hot in the yard, we stuck to the basement.

It seemed that everyone's basement had some type of train set to play with. Mine was an HO scale with tiny houses on a four-foot by eight-foot piece of plywood. The locomotive had some type of liquid I'd drip into the smokestack and the train would puff white smoke as it went around the track. My activity of choice was to see how fast I could get that locomotive going without causing a derailment.

Billy's older brother configured his Lionel scale trains throughout their entire basement. The train tracks ran around the rooms, up near the ceiling, through cabinets, and into plaster tunnels. He had multiple locomotives, and his transformer table was a giant control panel with switches, levers, lights, and knobs. We were not supposed to play with it, but of course we did.

With no electric, our trains sat idle. My sister and her friend drew a hopscotch course on the floor. Paulie, Billy, and I played a modified game of slap against the wall. Paulie brought over a case of the POP POP fireworks and he threw them at the girls, tormenting them as they hopped along the numbered squares.

Later that afternoon with dusk settling in, we had a BBQ in the backyard. Charcoal was placed in a tiny table top hibachi and was doused with lighter fluid that provided extra seasoning for the burgers. Pop-Pop fried up the flounder from his coolers in a pan over the coals. He gave it away to anyone that wanted any. People seemed to be making the best of a second night without electric. The decibel level from the backyards that evening was the loudest I can remember. Ice does wonders for beer.

The neighbors that had pools were all the more popular. Billy was jumping from his deck into the cool water of his pool. He yelled, "Tommy, come on over!" Mom wouldn't let me go since the filters had all been off for almost twenty-four hours. She said all the other kids would be sick in the morning.

"But, Mom, everyone else is going in!"

"If they were jumping off the Brooklyn Bridge, would you do that too?" I didn't answer, but if they came back up from the water and swam to shore, why not. I had no idea how high the bridge was, so her analogy didn't really make sense to me.

As daylight faded on Thursday night, Mayor Beam had a crisis on his hands never before seen in the history of the city. Con Edison was working madly at repairing the damaged lines and transformers that had overloaded. Even with many repairs completed, only a limited number of sections of the city had their power restored by dusk. If "The City" didn't get the power back on soon, our city could be in for another long night of looting and arson.

And if having no power and looting were not bad enough, New Yorkers were worried about the 'Son of Sam' serial killer roaming the streets. The end of July would mark the year anniversary of the first shooting. It was a dark time, in more ways than one.

With the noise of partying coming from the backyards, it was actually easier to fall asleep that second night, even with the high temperatures. I was out cold before the lights came back on around 10:30 p.m.

We all overslept Friday morning. Dad had put the a/c back in the window as soon as the power came back on. The cooler temperature in the apartment kept our exhausted bodies comfy. We finally woke up when Pop-Pop started banging on the radiator pipes. Dad and Mom had to rush to make it to work. Everything was back to normal in our apartment.

~ ~ ✦ ~ ~

Along with the dumbwaiter shaft, the radiator pipe was our other crude apartment-to-apartment communication system to stick it to Ma Bell and the phone company. Since Pop-Pop was retired, and was always an early riser, he would listen for our footsteps and the yelling we did in the morning. He'd make sure my parents were up for work, so they could wake up us kids for school. If he didn't hear anything happening above him, he would ring the phone. Nobody, and I mean nobody, was allowed to pick up that call at 6 a.m. If we inadvertently grabbed the receiver off the hook all heck would break lose because we'd have to pay the phone company the five cents for the call. The ringing phone was for alarm purposes only. If there ever was an emergency, and someone needed to reach us, they sure as heck better not pick between 6:00 and 6:30 in the morning, because there was no way anyone was going to answer the phone.

Over time, we all would sleep through the phone ringing, especially since we only had one phone and it was at the other end of the apartment from the bedrooms. During the summer the phone-alarm was useless since we slept in the half of the flat with the air conditioner running, so we never heard the ringing on the opposite side of the bedroom door. Dad and Mom would just roll over and fall back to sleep, forcing Pop-Pop to come up with plan "B." This amounted to using his fishing knife or the butt of his .38 to hit the radiator pipe that ran from his front room right past Dad's side of the bed. Pop-Pop would bang that pipe until Dad banged back.

That morning alarm system worked fine until Dad propped a long piece of copper pipe next to his bed. It was his snooze pipe. Pop-Pop would bang to wake us up. Dad would reach for the pipe and without even opening his eyes, he'd bang back signifying we were up. Five minutes later, Pop-Pop not hearing any footsteps would let loose on that radiator pipe something fierce. The pipe banging early in the morning was not so good for the hippies on the third floor who didn't seem to have to leave their apartment until midday.

One summer evening, our entire family was out in the aria and the third-floor dwellers returned home from their lovers-walk in the park. The man remarked about our dumbwaiter shaft yelling and pipe banging, "Do you guys know they sell intercom systems nowadays?"

Nana replied back, "What? You want "The City" tapping into our private conversations? No way are we getting one of those."

~ ~ ✦ ~ ~

As a kid, I never really understood the full impact on the city for being in the dark for twenty-four hours. The blackout affected the Bushwick section of Brooklyn, just a few miles away, in profound ways. The area was in trouble before the blackout, now stores that were barely surviving in that neighborhood would not reopen.

Dad and his brother drove through the streets the following weekend. I wasn't allowed to go with them. I did notice that Dad took the tube sock in the VW bus with him and Uncle Gus. They came back and reported, with all the burned buildings, it looked like a war zone.

There were some changes made at our house after being in the dark. A week following the blackout, Dad bought a fresh supply of batteries. Luckily, we never needed them for the flashlights because I used them for my race cars. Mom stocked up on powdered milk, who knows why, we never used it. Dad went to some distributor and bought cases of canned goods. Over time, Mom would need a vegetable for dinner and she'd grab a can of corn, or peas, or beans. After a few months, we were back to square one, no fresh batteries and no stored food. We just hoped "The City" would not run out of electric again, and the Soviets would keep their finger off the button.

GREENPOINT AVE.

Mickey dumped the crab water down the drain and without even rinsing the pot, he placed it back on the shelf. He used a greasy towel to wipe down the table, smearing the crab juice and hot sauce into a thin film across the Melmac surface.

He then said, "Wow, kid, that's a good story. I only read about what was happening down in the city. We had power around here that was being transmitted on the lines from up north. Sounds like your family came through the blackout pretty good. I always wondered how widespread the looting got. We had plenty of food delivered to the plant, which was a good thing, since I worked three shifts in a row, sleeping in the locker room between making my rounds."

"I guess you're right. All in all, it wasn't so bad. Others had it much worse," I said.

"Some good came out of it as well. The power company developed some additional emergency procedures, gave better instructions to the load operators, and put in some automatic systems," said Mickey as he headed back to work.

Uncle Ray and the King

Once I had tried the river crab, Mickey took it upon himself to give me a culinary education in locally sourced food. The problem was, I could never be sure from where he sourced his selections. Each day he arrived at the plant with a cooler sized for a giant. He always came prepared with enough food in case he had an opportunity to work a double shift or even a triple. Even though the plant provided meals when working overtime, Mickey required between meal snacks. So, I wasn't too surprised to see him carrying two coolers up to the kitchen on a sunny Saturday morning.

While Mickey was on his coffee break, he tracked me down and said, "Tommy, swing by the kitchen at lunch. I've got somethin' for ya." I went about my morning dreading just what Mickey might have in those coolers. I contemplated leaving sick for the day figuring I'd be sick after eating what he was serving anyway.

When noon rolled around, I made sure to first get a steak and cheese hero from the food truck. The diamond pattern stainless steel throughout the inside of the diner on wheels was covered in grease, earning it the nickname, "grease wagon." The guys that worked it knew all of us by name and our daily orders.

I quickly ate my hero and fries before venturing over to the lunchroom. I wanted to be sure my stomach was packed and lined in preparation for the Mickey surprise special. When I walked into the kitchen, Mickey was eating what looked to be a normal tuna hero. I breathed a sigh of relief and sat down beside him at the rusted chrome sided Formica table.

"Check this out," he said as he flipped open the top of his blue cooler. Inside, sitting on a bed of partially melted ice, were clams on the half shell. I wondered what the security guards thought as Mickey passed through inspection this morning. They had an odd fetish of inspecting the details of everyone's lunch box.

"Uh-huh," I managed to say, peering into the cooler at the not so appealing bivalves.

"Try one. Went clamming with the wife yesterday out on The Island. She shucked them early this morning for me."

He pulled one out, squeezed on a little lemon, added a drop of hot sauce, which he added to everything he ate, and sucked it down without even chewing. Recalling I had some bad experiences with raw clams in my past, I wasn't about to tempt fate now and try a clam that was sitting in a pool of semi-warm water, having been shucked six hours earlier, and stored in Mickey's bait cooler all morning. And when he said, they went clamming out on "The Island," I doubt they were out at Cupsogue Beach in the West Hamptons. Knowing Mickey, he might have found a flat off Staten Island.

I dug deep trying to find a way to let Mickey down easy. "I'm pretty full Mick, I've already eaten from the truck." I held out the grease-stained Styrofoam box for inspection before making a show of throwing it into the trash can. Mickey looked disappointed. I had to figure a way out of this one, and fast. I decided to fess up and tell him about my experiences with raw clams.

GREENPOINT AVE.

The summer of '77 continued to be a hot one. Temperatures consistently hit, or were close to, 100 degrees in the asphalt jungle. To try and beat the heat, the weekend after the blackout we went out to Breezy Point. We felt very lucky to have relatives with a place near the ocean, even if that day we didn't get to go in the water. We spent the day on the hot sand because the jellyfish took over the surf. After walking a mile back to the house, we just sprayed each other with the hose. The heat had beaten us again.

A couple of my uncles showed up with buckets of clams they clammed themselves in some local waters. My Great Aunt Dot placed a large platter filled with ice on the deck table and they shucked the different shapes and sizes of clams with dull kitchen knives. My cousins and I kept bugging them to tell us why all the clams were different. To satisfy our curiosity, they called them steamers, longnecks, littlenecks, and cherrystones, and what we thought was the funniest of all, piss clams.

My cousin held a clam by what I now know is the clam's foot. She asked one of our uncles who was known for tormenting children, "What's this thing?"

He replied, "That's where they pee from." She dropped it like a rock.

As they shucked, we stole the top shell of each clam and lined them up on the deck railing. This was a bad idea, as every seagull from Rockaway Point to Roxbury showed up and circled the house, squawking and annoying my aunt.

The adults dug in and ate the clams, either plain or with a drop of hot sauce. I swallowed a dozen of these slimy creatures, covered in ketchup. Later that afternoon, I was violently ill throwing up over the side of the deck. My uncle said I must have done too much playing in the surf down by the beach. There was no connection that MAYBE it was those clams; especially since we never even went in the water that day. Maybe my problem wasn't the clams, but I never ate a raw clam again. Since then I've stuck to steamed bivalves or clam chowder, which back then came one way – Manhattan style. I didn't even know that New England clam chowder was a thing until I was in college.

While Breezy Point was our place for weekend day trips, for longer excursions from the city, we went to the lake. For most of August, my sister, brother, and I were exiled from the city to my grandparents' bungalow in the hills of New Jersey. Why my grandparents called their country place a bungalow, I have no idea. It was a single story, log-sided, structure with two bedrooms, a kitchen, a living room, and a closed-in porch, where everyone hung out. It was, by all other qualifications, a cottage or a camp, with a limited capacity cesspool and water that was only seasonally supplied through above ground pipes with unknown origin (at least to me).

We had a huge shady yard to play in, no old men yelling at us for hitting their cars with a whiffle ball, and cool mountain air at night - no air conditioner needed. We had our own swing set, we built a really poor excuse for a tree house, and we had a clean lake to swim in, even if it did smell a bit fishy on warm days. When I was young, I was happy to spend time in what we called, "the country."

Grandma's country bungalow, winter 1979.

*

When I was I bit older, I was stupidly upset being sent to the lake because I couldn't walk to the corner and play pinball or get a slice of pizza with my friends. Luckily, I had a good, or bad uncle, depending on how you looked at it, close by who made up for it.

Next to my grandparent's bungalow, my Uncle Ray built a year-round home. Uncle Ray was a former Navy Seaman and still a bachelor at the time. He was the uncle my cousins and I thought was so cool, particularly since he let us get away with pretty much anything. Every kid should have been so lucky to have an uncle, like Uncle Ray, in their family.

Uncle Ray was a huge Elvis fan, and in 1977, he wore his sideburns just as Elvis did. He had stacks of the King's 8-tracks that I listened to when he was at work. I memorized almost all the lyrics while thumbing through his collection of Playboy magazines that he kept next to his recliner.

By the time I was twelve, he wasn't spoiling me with ice cream or having a game of catch. Oh no, instead, Uncle Ray left dirty magazines around and took me to bars during the day. While he sat at the bar, I played pinball, always beating everyone in the place. The Jersey guys had no idea how to play against a kid from Brooklyn. Every one of them was afraid to tilt. My machine shaking in that bar in Jersey, was as controversial as Elvis swinging his hips on the Ed Sullivan show. The bartender told Uncle Ray, "Tell your nephew to stop shaking the machine, he's gonna break it."

"But, Uncle Ray, how can I play pinball without shaking the machine?"

He looked at me and said, "Don't worry about it, Tommy. You're gonna beat them either way." He was right. Not one of the men in that bar even came close to my score. It could have been because I was drinking a Coke and they were buzzed already; or more likely, they didn't have nearly as much practice as I did since I played pinball for hours a day after school. You can take the kid out of Greenpoint, but you can't take Greenpoint out of the kid.

Uncle Ray was always on the go, and I was always bugging him to bring me along. One summer Saturday afternoon, as he was getting into his car, I ran over to him and asked, "Where ya going, Uncle Ray?"

He thought about how to answer that question and then said, "To see the bunnies."

"Can I come?" It really didn't matter if he was going to the dump. Going to see the bunnies didn't even register. I wanted to ride in his fancy car, with the moon roof open, blasting *Jailhouse Rock* down the country road.

He smiled and said, "Sure. Why the heck not."

He looked over towards Grandma, who was sitting at the picnic table and yelled, "I'm taking Tommy for a ride with me."

Uncle Ray knew every curve on those back roads, and he'd go over the hills at just the right speed to give me a sensation of weightlessness. After his version of a rollercoaster ride, he pulled into a very high class looking building with a sign that said, "Playboy Club Resort." I wish I could remember what was going through my head when I walked through the front doors with Uncle Ray. I'm pretty sure I had a grin from ear to ear. Inside, the bunnies were strutting around in their high heels, fishnets, cottontails, and rabbit ears. He showed me around as if he owned the place. It was great, until a manager said kids were not allowed, which should have been obvious. Uncle Ray read the manager the riot act, threw down his Playboy membership key and said he'd never be back. That was Uncle Ray. I'm pretty sure he went back. He loved bunnies.

At the time, Uncle Ray was a large tattooed steelworker employed by the Continental Can Company. To see him singing *Love Me Tender* always made me stop and wonder if he was as tough as he appeared. Sitting around the camp picnic table drinking his evening Budweiser, he told us stories about his union conventions held in Vegas. The highlight from one of his trips was seeing Elvis perform.

When he came home from his job on August 16, 1977, he sat down at the picnic table. The radio was tuned to the broadcast giving details of the King's passing. The cans of Bud were piling up fast. He said, "Here's to Elvis," as he opened another can.

My uncle was definitely shook up about the news. Every

night for a week he played his Elvis 8-tracks. Whenever he took me for a drive in his black Oldsmobile Regency, with the red velvet-feel interior, he blasted The King. By the end of the summer, the song order on every Elvis tape my uncle owned was burned into my memory.

Sixteen summers after Uncle Ray gave the King a sendoff from that Jersey picnic table, I stayed at what was then the Sheraton Hotel in South Portland, Maine. At the bar that evening, the bartender asked me, "What floor are you staying on?" He then proceeded to tell me that Elvis was due to stay on that same floor, on August 17, 1977 for a concert he was to give that night in Portland. Elvis never made it.

The bartender told me he was working as a busboy at the hotel back then. He recalled that the windows of Elvis's room had been covered with aluminum foil in anticipation of the King's arrival. He asked me, "Do you remember where you were the day Elvis died?" I sure did. At a picnic table under the shade of a New Jersey pine with my Uncle Ray. It's funny the exact moments we remember.

Back in Greenpoint at the end of that crazy '77 summer, I played Elvis tapes on my boombox while sitting on the stoop. My friends said that Jersey had turned me into some kind of freak. They were all listening to Lynyrd Skynard, Foreigner, and Rush. It wasn't long before I was converted back, adding the Doors, and Black Sabbath, but I still listened to Elvis when inside. I'd also crank up an old record player my dad had in the basement playing Bobby Darin, Johnny Cash, The Platters, and Chubby Checker.

By the end of that summer, things started to look brighter

for the city. The NYPD nabbed the '44 Caliber Killer' and the Yankees began an upward trend to turn around their season, under the management of George Steinbrenner - or was it Billy Martin? Who could really tell who was managing the ball club that year! As a nine-year-old, I didn't care and didn't pay much attention to the antics of the owner and manager. I just wanted to see Reggie hit home runs, watch Thurmon Munson catch, see Randolph and Rivers run, and hear Phil Rizzuto screaming, "Holy Cow." I wore down my Meatloaf album I played the Rizzuto verse in *Paradise by the Dashboard Light* so much - "Holy cow, I think he's gonna make it!"

Come October, I remember moving the nine-inch black-and-white TV from the dresser in my room to the kitchen table to watch the World Series. First, there was a better signal from near the kitchen window. Second, since I shared the bedroom with my brother, I wasn't allowed to have the TV blaring and yelling at manager Billy Martin, like I was Steinbrenner, while Chris was trying to sleep.

The games were probably broadcast on New York's WPIX. I pretty much could have turned the dial on my small TV to that channel and just left it there. It's the channel I remember watching most as a kid. After school, we also watched it for the live video games. This was a big deal since we couldn't afford our own. WPIX would broadcast a space shooting video game during the commercial breaks, giving a caller thirty seconds of air time to shoot and score points. By saying "pix" into the telephone, the operator on the other end would shoot the game controller. Although we never knew there was an operator involved, we just thought the contestant's words were controlling the game. If the player scored the right number of points, and they knew the word of the day, they could win a savings bond.

I was never allowed to call the station since that would have meant a charge from Ma Bell, or so Nana said. Instead, we would play along and say 'pix' when we thought the contestant should say it. Why a major TV station would give up air time for kids, and not use the time for paid advertisement, is hard to imagine now. In addition, they educated the youth financially by providing savings bonds as a reward. It was a simpler time and maybe it kept some of us kids off the streets.

The Yankees getting to the 1977 World Series was something the city needed. It had been a rough year, and an even tougher summer. I remember that October night when I sat in our cramped galley kitchen, on a hard wooden chair, the hum of the fluorescent light over my head, for game six. The Yankees were leading the Dodgers 3 games to 2, and I prayed for the win. My prayer was on top of the prayers the nuns had led us in earlier that day. Sister Theresa was an avid Yankee fan and would get into the baseball season right along with us.

The game was back and forth in the first four innings. As it was a school night, I hoped the game wouldn't go to extra innings. My mother had a strict policy of 11 p.m. bedtime, no matter what game was on, especially when she had to get up for work in the morning.

When Reggie hit his second home run in the 5th inning, I recall jumping up and down. Dad came in from the living room to see what the commotion was about. The TV had such bad reception it appeared it was snowing in the Bronx. I didn't care.

To me, that game was the only thing happening in the world at the time. We were in New York, and the Yankees were winning. When Reggie came out of the dugout after his third home run in the bottom of the eighth, I had tears in my eyes. It was 10:30 and Mom wanted me to go to bed – before the game was over! Was she kidding me? Luckily, Dad was able to explain to her what the last inning, of the last game of the season, meant in baseball, so I could stay up watching.

When the Yankees won, the street erupted like it was New Year's Eve. Paulie's dad was blasting off bottle rockets and firecrackers. Other neighbors were banging on pots and pans. We weren't allowed to do that anymore, since all my mom's pots were dented and had rounded bottoms from the beatings. I went out on the fire escape to yell across to Billy. We were reliving the highlights of the game.

"Did you see that play when…."

"Or how about that third home run. Holy Cow!"

Finally, Mr. Raviolo had enough and yelled across the yards for us to go to bed. He must have been a diehard Mets fan. The next day at school, everyone, including Sister Theresa, was on cloud nine. It was the 21st time the Yankees had won the World Series, but the FIRST time since I was born, so it was a BIG deal for us kids in the city. Forty years later, I watched the game in color thanks to the internet. It's as great a game now, as it was then!

Things continued on an upward trend towards the end of that year, despite our worry of being invaded by aliens thanks to the movie *Close Encounters of the Third Kind*. Dad broke down and bought us the high-tech Atari game for Christmas (probably from the trunk of "The Distributor"). He had as much fun playing those video games as we did.

We really appreciated having our own video games during that winter when we were forced to spend time indoors for a couple of days due to the extreme weather. When January and February rolled around, old man winter hit the city with a few more punches to once again strain the city's fragile finances. Nothing a ten-year-old kid needed to worry about, especially with all the snow!

Dad playing Atari.
Look at the size of that TV!
It's the same TV that was in my Greenpoint bedroom.

The Blizzard of 1978

Blackouts and snowstorms are all great fun when you're a kid with zero responsibility. As an adult, I tend to deal with emergencies and natural disasters with a very different perspective. Now, when a storm may be on the way, I stock up on food, fill up the gas tanks, make extra ice, and in the winter split extra firewood. I still never have the right batteries for flashlights, but thanks to Dad, at least I know what else to use them for.

The thing about the New York City blackout, or any blackout, is there's no way to forecast such an event. There was no mad rush to stock up on ice, batteries, milk, or bread before "The City" ran out of electric. Once the lights went out, I didn't have the worries my parents had to deal with. They had to think about how to feed us, keep us clean, occupied, and as comfortable as the situation allowed. They had to spend extra money we didn't have at the time, to replace the spoiled food, and they were out of work without pay. And I'm sure, knowing about the crime happening just a few miles away, hearing the sirens, and smelling the smoke from the burning buildings, they were worried about our safety. I, however, watched the entire event through the eyes of a child, as if it was all a great adventure, New York City style.

With the summer of 77s stifling heat and lightning strikes behind us, the arson, looting, and worry of the blackout became a distant memory in the lives of New Yorkers, who just picked up and moved on. In the time it takes to flip a switch, we went from no lights, to the summer being over, and we were back in school. By December we had entered our version of winter hibernation. The calm, however, did not last long.

The winter of 77/78 came howling in, crippling New York City once again. In late January and early February, the city was pounded by back-to-back storms, dropping a combined 31 inches of heavenly powder, at least from a kid's perspective. The second storm came just two weeks after the earlier storm that had yet to be fully cleared due to the financial crisis that plagued the city.

In the early 70s of my childhood, the city had a pretty dismal amount of snow. There were certainly some small accumulations, but for it to be fun, we needed at least five inches. This is especially true in Gotham, where the heat from the underground, and all the car, bus, and truck traffic melts the snow like a Hershey bar on a car dash in August – fast and messy.

Other than a few mentionable storms between 1970 and 1982, the 1978 storms were a gold mine for us city kids. Near the end of January, 13.6 inches fell and then a whopping 17.7 inches fell during the two-day blizzard on February 6th and 7th. That was the biggest snowstorm since the Christmas storm of 1947 when 26.4 inches fell on the city. It took 69 years until that record was broken on January 23, 2016 when 27.5 inches buried the city. But in the winter of 1978, I could have cared less for records, it was snowing and it was snowing hard in the Big Apple. There wasn't a kid in the neighborhood who wasn't ecstatic about it!

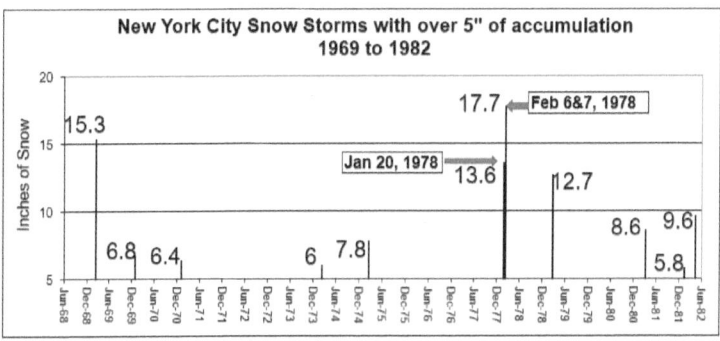

The blizzard roared for more than thirty-three hours. The timing and intensity of the storm caught the northeast coast states by surprise. Most people from New York to Massachusetts started their day as if it was going to be another morning grind. The complications increased due to the limited technology available for forecasting storms at the time.

Monday February 6, 1978 started out pretty typical for my family. It was mayhem. The alarm clock didn't go off. Pop-Pop was banging on the pipes, and Nana was ringing the phone. Dad was yelling, "Nobody pick it up." Two adults were going to be late for work. Three children could not find parts of their school uniforms. We couldn't have cereal because the milk was sour thanks to our mediocre refrigerator. Lady, our high maintenance Dalmatian, couldn't wait as I argued why I had to take her out to the backyard. All in all, the morning was a repeat of every morning in our Greenpoint flat.

WINS news was playing on the radio in the kitchen as Mom yelled that the broken toaster had burned the Eggo waffles again. Dad was calmly smoking a cigarette at the dining room table, trying to wake up. There was some mention on the radio of snow coming up the eastern seaboard. As we had never had a snow day at our school, a forecast of *some* snow did not mean all that much to us. Snow rarely amounted to anything significant and was just a slushy nuisance.

The only preparations Mom made, if there was a forecast of snow, was to pack each of us a pair of the saved Wonder Bread bags into our backpacks. These were our way to have instant boots. Since it was important we didn't get our school shoes wet, and we couldn't afford new boots each year with our constantly growing feet, especially since it never snowed in the city, this was the way Mom dealt with a forecast of 'some' snow. The bags were pulled over our shoes and fastened to our legs with extra-large red rubber bands that pinched off all circulation to our feet.

I would have been scarred for life if a parade of kids hadn't also shown up to school with bread bags on their feet. How a thin plastic bag was to keep our shoes dry I have no idea, because usually it was in pieces by the time we walked one block. I just ended up having polka dot bags flopping around my feet, which became a tripping hazard, when trying to cross a slushy Nassau Avenue with a city bus coming at me. And the bags certainly provided zero traction on ice and snow.

If we by chance did have boots, which in those days were nothing more than a layer of rubber, they were made with metal buckles, not laces, designed to keep them tight. I hated those buckles, they could snap a cold finger off quicker than a rat trap. The other problem with our boots was that they were usually too small. Not only were they painfully tight, they did little to keep our feet warm. To deal with both of these issues when wearing boots, Mom first put bread bags on our feet over our socks. This was supposed to allow our feet to slide into the half-size too small boots. As we protested with our fake screams of pain, she also told us the bags would help keep our feet warm. On that point, she was right.

Once at school, even the nuns were known to mumble a choice word or two (at least those in their vocabulary, such as 'sugar') when trying to pull our boots off that were now fused to our feet from the hot expanded plastic bags. Oh, we couldn't just rip the bags off either. No, we had to be careful to not tear the bags, or there'd be no possible way to reuse them in order to put our boots on to go home in the afternoon. This always caused a big production in the cloak closet with all the students trying to pull each other's boots off. By the time that was done, it was usually time for recess. Heaven help us if they wanted to send us out to the schoolyard and we needed boots. It might take until lunchtime to get everyone dressed and ready to go.

Snow or no snow, that morning we rushed around as usual getting ready. We were so distracted trying to find quarters for the milk cart, and our hats and gloves, if there was any mention on the radio of a big storm coming, or school closures, we missed it.

New York is the city that never sleeps and it rarely gets closed down for snow. Given there had not been a significant storm in almost a decade, nobody was even thinking of closing anything. This ambivalence to snow by New Yorkers is enhanced by the fact that even though traffic might be slowed down by a storm, a good portion of the city's occupants travel to work underground, completely unaffected by the weather. That is, unless it happens to be a historic snowfall and the city is completely unprepared for it. That was the blizzard of 1978.

That morning, the wind was already howling as we left our house and an inch of fluffy snow was blowing around. Mom walked my sister and I the five blocks to St. Stan's, bread bags over our shoes causing us to slip and slide, and we lined up with our classes on the sidewalk. Normally, Mom would then make her way to the Nassau Avenue station to catch the GG, or she'd take a bus over to Long Island City and then take the 7 train into Manhattan.

That day was different. The nuns were standing outside the main entrance talking with a group of parents. Seeing them in their black outfits and habits on a background of freshly fallen white snow is a scene I'll never forget. Mother Superior was explaining to the parents that she had just gotten word that the public school system was to close and she had made the same decision. They did not want to take the chance of having kids stranded at the school during a snowstorm. The sign on the building said it was fine to be used as a nuclear bomb fallout shelter, but they were totally unprepared for a snowstorm. The parents were unsure of what to do with their kids as they had to get to work and had no daycare options. They looked to the nuns for some divine intervention. None was available.

My mom shrugged her shoulders and knowing there was nothing she could do, she just turned us around and we walked back home. This worked out for the better since getting back home at five o'clock during the storm that was developing would have been a nightmare for her.

By late morning, the snow was coming down heavy. We bugged Mom to let us go out and play in it. She took one look outside and told us "N.O.," spelling it out to put additional emphasis on her decision. After saying NO, she'd proceed to tell us what these two letters spelled. "N.O. spells no!"

Sulking, we hunkered down watching the snow from the window thinking we'd wait for Dad to get home from work. My siblings and I were entertained watching the wind blowing the snow sideways. After ten minutes, we were bored and retreated to the living room to watch reruns of *Woody Woodpecker*, *Bugs Bunny*, and *Magilla Gorilla*.

The snow piled up all day long. When it was close to the time Dad should have been coming home, we went back to the window. There was nobody outside on our street and no cars had moved all day. Our street wouldn't even see a plow truck until the next morning. "The City" had too many avenues to keep clear and too few plows to keep up with such a storm.

We watched as a few men on the block came walking home, fighting their way down the sidewalk stepping through snow that was up over their knees. The wind was driving the snow into their faces as they tried to hold on to their hats, while struggling to keep their footing in the drifts.

Finally, we saw Dad. He looked up at the window as he came through the aria gate, expecting us to be sitting there. He waved and smiled as if walking home in a blizzard was great fun. He didn't have snow boots. He didn't have a winter parka. New Yorkers were never prepared for such weather, nor did they let it stop them – well, usually.

Jeanette, Dad, Chris, and me during a much smaller snowstorm in 1977.

Since Mom usually picked up dinner on her way home from work, and she hadn't been out all day, we had canned soup and crackers for dinner. Mom made up for her lack of emergency planning by letting us eat on the couch, which was a big deal since she usually told us "N.O.," when we begged her in the past. She even applied this rule when she was running late and bought us TV dinners to eat out of metal trays with cherry filled desserts.

"But, Ma, it's called a TV dinner!"

"N.O." (spelled out of course).

The night of the storm, we sat on the couch eating our soup. My little sister got her way and we watched *Little House on the Prairie*, an episode I am sure that made our problems of a city blizzard seem uneventful.

The next morning, excited to see how much snow fell, I was up before Pop-Pop started banging on the pipes. I ran to the window and looked out into the street. The snow was still coming down and all the cars were buried under a thick blanket of white. The snow extended from our stoop, out across the aria, across the sidewalk, over the cars, through the street, over the other cars, across the other sidewalk, and all the way to the tops of the stoops across the street. Only a couple of car antennas were sticking up out of the snow. There weren't even any footprints. Mom dragged herself out of bed and came and stood next to me at the window.

"Is there school today, Mom?"

"I sure hope Mother Superior doesn't expect us to get there today, dear."

In the kitchen, Dad was listening to the radio. The news announced that all city schools were closed.

"Holy cow!" I screamed in my best Phil Rizzuto impression. We had two snow days in a row! I never had "off" from school before, unless it was summer, or a Catholic feast day. We never even had a snow day at my school before yesterday. New York City just did not close down.

"Mom, can we go out and play?"

"N.O." was spelled out for me. It was bitter cold and the snow was being blown around by thirty mile an hour gusts. Eating my second bowl of cereal by the front window, I watched the men fight a losing battle trying to keep snow off their cars. Within ten minutes the wind whipped all the snow they had illegally pushed into the center of the street, back over their cars and we could no longer tell they'd even cleaned any off. Pop-Pop did this twice. New Yorkers were never a very patient bunch. After a couple of attempts, they all surrendered to the storm, knowing this time they were beat.

I was watching cartoons, and just before noon I heard Mom say to Dad, "I'm not sure what we will do for lunch and dinner. We don't have much in the house. There's one can of soup left and a few crackers."

"What happened to the emergency food we built up after the blackout?"

"I used it up in the emergency."

"What emergency?"

"The weekly 'we're out of money' emergency," Mom replied.

Hearing this, I started to worry. It was one thing to be snowed in with the day off from school, but to have nothing to eat, that was not something I was willing to accept. This was New York City for crying out loud. There had to be a pizza place or deli open – right?

Dad braved the storm to hunt down and gather food. To keep his feet dry, he put on socks, covered those with a Wonder Bread bag, then pulled on another sock over that. Finally, with Mom's help, he forced his black loafers on. He returned an hour later with enough bread, cold cuts, and Entenmann's cakes from the Busy Bee Food Market to last us an arctic winter.

Late Tuesday afternoon the snow stopped, or at least

slowed. The wind was still howling and whipping the snow off the roofs. We were only allowed to go out as long as we stayed in the aria. It probably would have been safer to play in the center of the street. The men who lost the battle clearing their cars, started to worry about all the snow on their roofs. One of them decided it would be smart to shovel the snow off the roof and drop it three stories down to the aria. Many of the other men followed the leader.

Dad watched and said out loud, "I wonder if Tommy and I should go shovel off the roof? It's probably pretty heavy up there."

Mom was hearing nothing of the sort. "Not with these winds. Neither of you are going up there!"

Mom let us back out to play when Dad went to clear the sidewalk. It took thirty minutes to get bags and boots on our feet. We had to be strategic on where we played to not get pounded with snow that dropped from three stories above. Once the roof cleaners had finished, we had a grand time jumping off the stoop into piles of deep snow that some kids disappeared into, never to be seen again.

Dad, Pop-Pop, and all the men, working like a small army brigade, shoveled a path along the sidewalk from one end of the block to the other. The snow was now piled four to five feet high in the arias. Old ladies were yelling that the men were killing the hedges and prized rose bushes. Within an hour, a foot of the snow was blown back into the path. We were losing the war.

Given we didn't have the proper gear to be out in such weather, it was dangerously cold with the wind chill. After an hour or so of shoveling, with us kids mostly playing, we all went back inside to get warm.

Unlike the blackout a few months earlier when all the families on the block came outside, this time everyone hunkered down inside. Nana watched her game shows and we played our high-tech Pong video game. That night we had hot chocolate and watched *Happy Days* and then *Laverne and Shirley*.

Heading to bed, I asked, "Do you think we'll have school tomorrow, Mom?"

"I sure hope "The City" will have the streets cleared by morning. Goodnight."

Wednesday morning, I woke up and hiked the twenty feet to the kitchen to hunt for Cap'n Crunch. Sitting at the kitchen table scooping up the captain's orange sugar squares, I couldn't believe my ears when the radio report said that the schools would be closed for an unprecedented third day. This was unheard of. The city had been stopped. The crews needed another full day to clean up and move the snow. Holy cow! Three days in a row.

We had the entire day to play in the snow! Mom and Dad had to go to work, so they left Nana in charge. My sister and little brother had to stay inside, but I went out to the aria to climb on the snow. Nana sat at her front window and watched me from the warmth of her cozy apartment in her housecoat and slippers. Within minutes, Billy, Paulie, and I slipped down the street and out of her view.

Every adult that could stay home was working on the cleanup. In general, New Yorkers don't do well with lots of snow. There's just no place to put it. Pop-Pop, and all the men of his generation, would shovel the snow from between their cars into the middle of the street. The plow would come along and it would just plow the snow into the space between the cars one car length further down the street.

Once the plow turned the corner, all the men appeared again, shovel in hand, pushing the snow back into the center of the street. This scene would be repeated several times during the day with each pass of a plow. The poor fellow parked in the last spot on the street seemed to take the brunt of it as eventually the mass of plowed snow would encase his car until it melted in May. Maybe this was how the system was supposed to work and the city made good use of the older men of Brooklyn by not ever ticketing them for their actions.

After running around throwing snowballs and playing snow football, Pop-Pop said I had to help with the cleanup. I thought for a moment that maybe I should have stayed hidden inside, but then decided to make the best of it. Paulie and I started taking the snow that was plowed back between the cars and carting it to the aria. We were making a mountain to save until summer. When we reached the section between the front of Pop-Pop's station wagon and the back bumper of Mr. Raviolo's Chevy Chevelle, the screaming began. Mr. Raviolo came zipping down his front stoop brandishing his shovel and yelling, "Hey, you kids, you leave that snow where it is!"

Paulie and I just looked at one another. First off, we thought we'd be doing him a favor clearing the snow, and second, we were helping the men obey the law by not putting the snow in the center of the street. We stepped aside and a seventy-something Italian man from Sicily proceeded to take back the snow we had already piled in the aria. He took shovel after shovel and piled it into the center of the street. He yelled at us the entire time he shoveled.

"How do you expect The City to take away the snow if you put it in your aria? You're gonna cause a flood! Capito? Ma perché non state a scuola?" (Understand? Why have you not gone to school?)

I sarcastically yelled back, "Perché it's snowing! Non scuola oggi." I had to yell it in Brooklyn-English-Italian as I didn't know too many words in Italian, unless they were curse words I had heard from Dad, or Pop-Pop, which I was not allowed to use. Roughly, I tried to say, "It's snowing, there's no school today."

With no place to put the snow, the plows had pushed it in the spaces reserved for fire hydrants, waiting for available backhoes and dump trucks. Once the plows turned the corner, the men figured the hydrant spaces were fair game. They went about moving all the snow they could to the hydrant spaces, making piles ten feet high.

Paulie took one look at the mountains, and taking charge, yelled, "Let's build a fort!"

All of a sudden, kids that didn't want to shovel a square of sidewalk were moving mountains of snow. Kids multiplied like cockroaches and came from every apartment climbing over the snow piles.

Using this packed snow, a child army went to work. Paulie's dad shouted directions. He had us make two circular forts a story high at each end of the no parking hydrant space (okay, maybe they were three feet high). We connected the two fortresses with a twenty-foot tunnel. We had to fix the tunnel multiple times as the warring teams would try to crush and bury anyone slithering through it. I'm surprised we didn't bury a kid or two alive that day.

We protested and yelled when the firefighters came by to clear the space in front of the hydrant. They were pretty sore at the plow operator for plowing in their hydrants that they then had to shovel out. Our whining was not helping. They busted our tunnel in two, but then they must have felt bad. They proceeded to shovel the snow up on the sidewalk so we could rebuild our tunnel, snaking it around the hydrant. This worked out great, until they left. The owner of the apartment building must have been lurking in the hall, because as soon as the trucks turned the corner, he was out complaining.

He had spent the morning pushing the snow off his sidewalk into the hydrant space. Now it was back along with twenty screaming kids. He yelled in Polish as he proceeded to break apart the tunnel and shovel the snow into the center of the street. Our brigade retreated to the opposite sidewalk. Behind the parked cars, we made more than one hundred snowballs as he continued destroying our tunnel. It's amazing how fast child armies can work. Crazy Four Fingers Frankie from Nassau Avenue ran home and came back with a bucket of water for a snowball dip. Frankie had five fingers, but he threw a baseball, football, and we learned even snowballs, or ice-balls in this case, without the use of his pinky.

On the count of three, we let loose with an air attack on the man. He ran back into his house getting pelted with iceballs from twelve-year-old kids. Everyone in Brooklyn was a little crazy during snowstorms. We rebuilt the tunnel and this time the man didn't come back out to bother us.

On Thursday, schools unfortunately reopened, and we had to sit in our classrooms while we dreamed about being out in the snow. That afternoon, we walked home in the slush and were mortified when we reached our block. All the snow had been removed, not just near the hydrants, but the entire block had been scraped clean. All that was left of our fort was a brown, slushy film. Wisely, the department of transportation waited until all the youth were back in school, until they demolished the forts and carted away the snow. Had we all been home, there would have been two dozen kids locking hands and blocking the plows from entering North Henry Street.

The snow grinches had taken it all. It was as if the big storm never even happened except for the piles we were able to secure in our arias. Mr. Raviolo stood smoking on his stoop with a big grin on his face, satisfied there would be no flooding.

Within a couple of weeks, even the last hold-outs of small, dirty piles of snow were gone. What was left along the gates was stained yellow thanks to the canines and felines of the streets. Frankie thought he could save the snow by stocking up snowballs in his grandma's meat freezer down in his basement. He totally forgot about them until July when he went looking for a root beer popsicle.

In a case of really bad timing for an unfortunate little kid, Frankie found them again when little Joey Junior was walking by licking an ice cream. Frankie came running with the frozen balls, excited to throw them at something. Joey Junior dropped his cone and ran home after being beaned in the back by a five-month-old ice ball thrown by Four Fingers. After being yelled at by Paulie's grandma, which was totally acceptable in those days in a version of community policing, Frankie brought out a milk crate of the ice balls along with a wooden baseball bat. We used these for batting practice down at the lots. Shattering an ice ball pitch in the middle of summer is all fun and games until someone gets a shard of ice in the eye. Paulie only had to wear the eye patch for three weeks and luckily, had no permanent damage. I wouldn't be surprised if Frankie now owns an ice distributor.

The snow being removed from the streets really bothered us kids. Even though we had backyards that were full of pristine, footprint free snow, it just was never as much fun as playing in the streets dodging plows, firemen, and old men. On the street, we always had a dozen kids at any given time of the day running wild. No matter who had to go home, someone else was coming back out.

With the snow gone from the streets, we decided to play tackle snow-football in the park. In the middle of the winter, with two feet of snow on the ground, the park was pretty safe. I suspect that during the cold months, the riffraff found other places to hang out, but that was not always the case.

Winthro Park

Growing up I never knew the park at the end of our street by its official name. I knew it by its original name, Withrop Park, but we never sounded out the "p" at the end, so it was just Withro Park. The name didn't really matter to us. We referred to it the way we did "The City" or "The Avenue." It was just "The Park." Sometimes, due to the strong smells, typically urine or wet rotting oak leaves, Nana referred to it as, "Stinky Park." Forty years after swinging on the swings, sliding down the slides, climbing the fences, and running through the fields of dust, I looked into the controversy of the park's name.

The land for the park was acquired by the city in 1889. It was originally named Winthrop Park after Winthrop Jones, a borough assemblyman. Jones not only acquired the $132,000 for the purchase of the land, he also was the son of the parks commissioner. Jones died before the park was officially opened in 1891.

In 1941, the park was renamed for Monsignor Edward J. McGolrick, the pastor of nearby St. Cecilia's Roman Catholic Church. The Monsignor, who had recently passed away, was loved by the community, or at least enough of the residents and one parks commissioner, to make the name change. Since Winthrop Jones had no children or known family in the Greenpoint area, there was no opposition to the renaming. And so it goes with time.

The renaming presented a dilemma. Would the residents refer to the park by its full new name, Monsignor McGolrick Park, which is a full seven syllables? Or would the old name stick?

"Let's get the guys together for a ballgame."

"Where?"

Do you think a kid would answer with, "Monsignor McGolrick Park."

Or would the kid say, "Winthro" or just, "The Park," each two simple syllables. No doubt the older generations going out for a stroll might also shorten the name in the same way.

Thirty-five years after the renaming, everyone I knew always referred to the park using one of the shorter options, because that's what stuck. If you're from anywhere around the city, you just don't have time to waste on extra syllables.

While the park was mere feet from our houses, we only used it if we were kicked off the street, or we needed more space for a full two-team baseball or football game. The park had a few large fields that were worn down to hard bare dirt, making every baseball or football game a mud or dust bowl depending on the season. It wasn't that the fields were worn down from play. I rarely saw people playing on them, other than a few of us kids. It's just they were never maintained. Growing grass, at least not the kind for kids to play on, wasn't a top priority for anyone in the near bankrupt city government. It didn't matter to us anyway, we preferred to play on the cement to prove how tough we were.

The park's playground area had a metal monkey bar set that I am surprised didn't kill a kid or two every summer. The metal bars were thin, slippery, and five feet off the ground at the center. The whole twisted metal sculpture was set over cement with rocks and sharp pebbles protruding through the surface. The park's designer was either the scarecrow from the *Wizard of Oz* (no brain), or someone who hated kids. Nana would bring a bottle of rubbing alcohol and a box of band aids whenever we went. By the time we were headed home, we were covered in blood stained gauze.

The monkey bars were not the only park attraction warranting first aid. The large slide was a behemoth of a metal structure. It had to be a story high (well, maybe not) and had a ladder that must have been repurposed from a defunct ladder truck. The narrow steps went vertically straight up with a slight backwards tilt. Kids would hang off the side of the handrails, making it even more difficult for someone to climb up the ladder – of course, totally on purpose.

The slide surface itself was a polished metal. Over the years, it was take-off smooth thanks to thousands of kids sliding down it. The ladder wasn't nearly as much of a challenge as the dismount off the slide. At the bottom there was no sand or mulch to cushion a landing. The slide was set over the same hard cement with embedded rocks and sharp pebbles protruding through the surface that was under the monkey bars. The end of the slide was bent in a slight upward u-shape, Olympic ski jump style. The dismount of choice was to slide down as fast as you could, ride the curve so it would launch you in the air, and land standing on your feet. You can imagine how that worked out, especially for little kids with short legs. The bottom of the slide area looked as if the children of Greenpoint just took an enemy beachhead. Kids would be bloody, screaming, and lying all over the pavement. If they didn't move out of the way quickly, they would get a second pounding from the next kid who would dismount and land on top of them, most certainly on purpose, to avoid hitting the pavement themselves.

The park's most popular attraction, for the eight to twelve-year-old crowd, was a cement circular slide. To get to the top we had to go inside the bowels of the cavity and climb the ladder to the top. The pee smell in this dark, damp, concrete bunker was overwhelming, especially on a hot, humid summer day. For some reason the older urchins who used the park at night for their incense burning, also used the inside cement floor of the slide to pee in private, when any tree would have done.

Stepping inside the bunker to climb the ladder, there was always a half inch film of wet goop that would stick to the bottom of our shoes; the same shoes that went up the ladder that we climbed with our hands to get to the top. It was gross; I knew it even then, but it didn't matter. That cement stinky-park slide would keep us occupied for hours in a game of torture.

We put up with the smell mainly because we enjoyed the danger. Kids would push you up the metal ladder to get you to the top. If you made it up to the top, kids that had claimed the top as a hangout, would be waiting to push you down the slide. Getting pushed down, however, was preferred to getting pushed over the edge to the concrete below. It was a rough playground.

Grandmas, who took their grandchildren to the park to play nice with other youths, had no way to see what was happening up at the top of the slide due to the high sides. The killer slide circled down, probably not a long run, but long enough for it to be a gauntlet as hoodlums sat on the sides and hit and kicked you at every turn. This was mainly done to kids who didn't live on your block as a way to take ownership of the slide for the afternoon. If your block showed up with enough kids to have a majority of hitters and kickers, eventually the others would leave. It was never consciously decided that this was the strategy, it just happened. Competition was fierce and block blood was thicker than neighborhood blood.

The killer cement slide was immortalized in the background of a classic picture of George Burns, Art Carney, and Lee Strasberg. Withrop park was used as an on location set for the film, "Going in Style" that was released in 1977. These days movies seem to be made all over NYC, every day of the week. Back then this was a big deal for our little neighborhood. My dad was a huge Art Carney fan. He told me Carney was the man who played Ed Norton, on *The Honeymooners*. The reruns of that show were watched religiously in our house. By the time of the park filming, Carney was older, and I didn't recognize him at all. I did recognize George Burns from TV specials I watched with Grandma. I didn't see the work of the great Lee Strasberg until later in life when I was old enough to see him as the character Hyman Roth in the *Godfather Part II*.

We all tried to get as close as possible to catch a glimpse of the movie stars. We stood around the perimeter of the park and waited for hours. Sometimes the crew would move us to a new spot so we wouldn't be in the background of a shot. We thought it was great when the three stars walked onto the 'set' from a trailer and gave us a wave. The three of them sat on a bench as a scene played out with the infamous Winthop Park slide in the background.

A studio original of the black-and-white photo of these three icons, sitting on that park bench, with the Winthrop graffiti covered cement slide in the background, hangs on my wall. Seeing them sitting there brings back bittersweet memories of that park, the sounds, the not so pleasant smells, and that killer cement slide.

The slide proved to be seriously dangerous for my younger brother, Chris. I was maybe twelve at the time of the incident, and Chris was six. I have no idea why I was allowed to take him to the park, but I don't recall any other family members being with us the afternoon the slide claimed him as a victim. Chris was climbing the rusted-metal, half-inch round slick and greasy pipe ladder in front of me. The ladder also had no tilt. In fact, like the metal slide, it also tilted backwards, so as I climbed up, I had the feeling I was going to fall off. Maybe this was part of the intended fun of these slides back then. In keeping with the theme of the monkey bars and the metal slide, the concrete slide was another nightmare attraction the park's designer employed. There's a good probability that if there were any Winthrop family around during the park renaming, they may not have been opposed for good reason; this place was a kid killing field.

The day Chris became the slide's latest victim, he was maybe three or four rungs up when his hands slipped. The fall was only slowed by his front teeth latching onto the rungs of the ladder. When he came crashing down, I tried to stop his fall and we both hit the sticky pavement. When I lifted my head, I saw blood pouring from his mouth and covering his t-shirt. His two front teeth were hanging by threads. I recall everything going silent. His mouth was open. He must have been crying, screaming, yelling. I could hear nothing. Kids' faces were peering down from the opening above. One, two, five, eight or more faces looking down at us laying in the pee pit. Their mouths were moving, screaming. I heard nothing.

I grabbed Chris by the arm. He was too big to carry. Running and dragging him, my hearing came back, and his screams were piercing. We ran from the cement playground area, across the first path, to the Nassau Avenue entrance. We stood at the curb, waiting for the traffic to clear, so we could cross. All the people on the street were moving in slow motion, while the cars and buses were speeding by at warp speed. Blood was gushing from his gums. He was choking up blood. An old lady screamed.

Two men came over and looked at Chris. They said something about going to the hospital. I pulled away. We had to get home. They stopped traffic to cross us over the avenue. I pulled on Chris's arm and we ran. The half a block to our house never felt so long. I don't recall anything after that except my own stomach hurting. I suspect Nana was home? Or maybe Mom? His teeth turned out fine. Luckily, it was his baby teeth that had been knocked loose, although I suspect that dentist bill was an unexpected expense. That was the last time I recall going to play on the killer playground at the park.

The park became a dangerous place of another kind as the

decade wore on and turned into the 80s. We were warned by parents and teachers, "**Do not** cut through the park. Keep to the streets."

There were older kids from our block that hung out in the park, high school age, although they likely hadn't been to school in ages. Within that crowd, there were those beyond their high school years who made the Sweathogs look youthful. I figured since I knew some of them, the warning to not cut through the park didn't really apply to me.

This older gang of guys and a few girls looked cool in their jean jackets; the backs were painted with murals of Zepplin's *House of the Holy* and Floyd's *Dark Side of the Moon* album covers. They listened to The Doors, idolized Jim Morrison, and smoked cigarettes and weed on the park benches at the far side of the park. They carried knives and would melt away at the first sign of a cop car driving along the roads outside the park. Paulie, Ritchie, and I would linger around to listen to their music, until they chased us away. I didn't realize at the time, that there were other gangs that would come to the park from other neighborhoods to cause trouble.

At the center of the park there's a brick and limestone shelter pavilion. The structure was built in 1910, designated a New York City Landmark in 1966, and listed on the National Register of Historic Places in 1980, allowing it to be saved from a wrecking ball, even as it fell apart on its own. In the 1970s we could walk through the building. At night and on rainy days, the park gang would stand around in there smoking funny things. Over the years it went from a cool hang out, even if it reeked, to a dangerous place to venture. This was partly due to the human element, but more so from the pieces of the ceiling that would crash to the ground at random times. As the structure was in disrepair, with no funds to fix it, and no authority to knock it down, "The City" surrounded the entire pavilion with a chain-link fence to keep the delinquents from hanging around inside. That didn't protect the rest of the park from those up to no good.

When I was in the eighth grade I would sometimes go home for lunch. I don't know why the school allowed eighth graders to wander off school property in the middle of the day, but they did. I suspect it was because many of us lived within a few blocks of the school and mothers, or grandmothers, were home to cook a lunch of hot pierogi, kielbasa, or lasagna. My friends and I took full advantage to leave the building and go home for a quick break. For me, there wasn't anyone cooking lunch at home; I could have easily brought my baloney and cheese sandwich to school, but that wasn't cool.

Oddly, we could leave the building as individuals for lunch, but we couldn't enter the building unless in our class group. When we would get to school in the morning, each class had a designated location along the Newell Street sidewalk. We would line up military style, double file along the brick wall. A nun would pace up and down the formation, keeping order. My eighth-grade class lined up under the sign bolted to the brick wall, identifying the building as a bomb shelter. The last time I looked, the same faded sign was still there.

At eight o'clock sharp, the bell would ring, the double doors would open, and as a unit, we would march in. Heaven help me if I wasn't there before the outer doors shut. Being late meant I had to go to the main door and ring the bell. The huge heavy reinforced door (obviously to protect against a nuke) was locked and could only be opened from the inside. If I was late, I would have to ring the bell two or three times, before the secretary would push open the door and escort me to the office. Once inside the office, I'd have to wait until morning announcements were over for a pass. This made my late entrance to homeroom even more dramatic, because even though I was a mere thirty seconds late to the front of the building, fifteen minutes had now passed before I could join my class.

By the time I finally arrived at my classroom, the morning and afternoon snack money had already been collected. I believe this was part of the intended punishment for being late. I lost out on having a chocolate milk and bagel for morning snack and a pretzel and juice for the afternoon. This was painful because nobody was going to share any of their snacks with anyone who was late. Each of these items cost a quarter, so I always tried to bring a dollar. That was big money in those days, five bucks a week. Some days I was lucky to scrounge five nickels from the change draw. Sometimes my mom didn't have a dollar to give to me, and I had to bring a snack packed in my metal *Happy Days* lunch box; not cool, even if the Fonz was carrying my apple.

I measured the school day by four critical points; morning snack, lunch, afternoon snack, and the dismissal bell. After morning snack, the minutes would tick by slowly, but never as slow as between 11:30 and 11:55. At five minutes to noon, we lined up watching the clock with the white background, large black numbers, and a red second hand and waited for the lunch bell. No class could exit their classroom before the bell. We'd just wait in a line, the boys punching one another to kill time. When the second hand reached twelve on the synchronized clocks throughout the building, the mechanical bells would ring, dismissing hundreds of hungry kids.

In an orderly fashion, resembling dogs being let off their leashes in a room full of steaks, classroom after classroom would file into the hall. From the top floor of the building, the seventh and eighth graders stampeded down three flights to the lobby. Some unfortunate souls would descend one more large flight to the basement / bomb shelter / purgatory lunch room, where volunteer Moms served hot dogs with sauerkraut for a dollar every Friday (Lent excluded). All other days, the lunches were soggy peanut butter and jelly sandwiches, or warm bacteria-growing egg salad that Moms had packed in brown paper bags; there were no ice packs and nobody died. A lot of the 7th and 8th graders would exit the windowless heavy double doors to Newell Street.

By the time we reached the corner of Driggs Avenue, small groups would form based on who was going in what direction. Everyone we passed knew we were from St. Stan's. The boys all dressed in blue polyester pants, light blue shirts, and dark blue clip-on ties with a small silver cross emblem. As we walked, our group would thin out as friends ducked away into apartment buildings or down side streets. I was supposed to take a left on Humboldt Street and then a right on Nassau Avenue, sticking to the streets. I didn't do that. The shortcut through the park saved me two whole minutes.

My walk home on one particular day, was similar to most other lunch runs. I was walking with Jimmy, Paulie, and Billy, talking about Sunday's Giants game. It's as clear in my memory as it was cold that January day, our breath steaming in front of us, all four of us - lost in our laughter.

As we approached the center of the park, close to the fence enclosed pavilion, near the benches where the North Henry Winthro Gang would normally hang out at night, a group of unknown delinquents surrounded us. There were six or seven of them who we didn't recognize at all.

"Give us your money!"

Combined, we had what amounted to a buck fifty total. Jimmy contributed a dollar since he had been late to school that morning and still had his snack money.

"You need to bring us more money!" said the largest kid wielding a knife, his unwashed hair weighed down over his ears by the grease. "On your way back to school, you come back this way and bring $10 each."

They took our hats, gloves, and coats. I was wearing my matching NY Giants wool hat and gloves, my favorite Christmas presents. Aside from being pissed they took my stuff, I was worried I was going to get in trouble for getting my winter gear stolen.

"We might give these back to you if you bring us the money!" spat the shortest one through his crooked buck teeth.

The four of us hustled through the rest of the deserted park, shivering without our winter coats. At the park exit, I ran out across Nassau Avenue and sprinted down North Henry Street.

Nana was always watching for me at her window to make

sure I arrived home okay. Usually by the time I unlocked the stoop door, she'd be in the hallway to greet me and see if I needed anything. On that afternoon, I scaled the stairs and opened our entry door on the second floor when I heard her ask, "Tommy, is everything all right? Where's your coat and hat?"

"Everything's fine, Nana," I said as I closed the door.

Inside I sat at the dining room table shivering – from both the cold and the experience. Not knowing what to do, I called my mom. She was working miles away, across the East River, high up over the Avenue of the Americas.

"What is it, dear?"

"They took my coat." I cried into the phone.

"Who took your coat?"

"A gang in the park."

Now that should have sparked a lecture as to why I had cut through the park, but it did not.

"Stay there. I'll call your dad and see if he can get home."

"No. No. I need to go back to school."

"You stay home!"

Of course, I didn't listen. I ate a quick baloney and mayo sandwich and stole five dollars from the emergency envelope in the china closet junk draw that we were never to touch (it was for emergency milk, bread, and batteries for blackouts). Why we called the hutch a 'china closet' is a mystery. It wasn't a closet and it held no real china. Mom had a collection of never-used plates, which were probably lethal lead crystal, on display behind the sliding glass doors. The good dishes reserved for Easter and Christmas were packed away in zipped, padded cases, away from our nosy hands, on the shelves behind closed doors in the lower section of the hutch.

I looked in my closet for a coat to wear in the thirty-degree temperature. There was a blue knitted sweater with a matching waist belt my grandmother made for me. Without hesitating, I grabbed an old jacket that was two sizes too small and my faded Jets knit cap and headed out the door. By then, Mom had called to alert Nana to keep me captive in the house.

Nana was waiting, guarding the front door to the street. I could see her tiny shadowy figure in the darkness of the hall at the bottom of the stairs.

"Tommy, your Mother said to wait for your dad to get here." Nana, being all of ninety-five pounds, knew she had no way of making me do what I didn't want to do. It's a good thing Pop-Pop wasn't at home, he would have decked me.

"I'll be fine, Nana. Really." And I jumped down the front stoop.

Part of me had to go back to not be bullied. The other part of me went back because I expected the others to go back, and I wasn't going to be the only one who stayed home. Sister Mary might not call me a sissy, but the guys would. Sister Mary, on the other hand, might just head off to the park with Mother Superior, brandishing rulers and hand brooms, to kick some butt themselves. They were very tough.

I knew I could not walk through the park, even as I touched the five-dollar bill in my right pocket. But if those guys were to corner me along the street, I might be able to get away by giving them the family emergency money.

I walked along Nassau Avenue staying close to the line of cars, hoping for cover. I doubted those guys would come out of the park, but they might have been watching me that very second from somewhere on a park path behind the trees.

I half ran the short block to Russell Street and then crossed over at the Jiffy candy store. I never crossed at the end of the block. It was always safer to cross in the middle. In the middle, I had only to watch out for cars going straight. At the corner, stops were optional and cars would turn unpredictably, and sometimes come down the wrong way. Crossing at the corner, even if there was a crosswalk, was a dangerous proposition.

I ran past Humboldt, past Diamond, and hooked a left on Newell Street. I made it in plenty of time for the class line-up on the black asphalt playground bordered by the school, an apartment building, and an eight-foot chain-link fence. I wanted to pull the gate closed behind me as I ran in.

Once in line, I looked around for Jimmy, Paulie, and Billy. As we were required to line up alphabetically, we were always in the same position. They were missing; the requisite spacing for their body types left by the other students. This was a problem. Did they stay home? Did they get pinched by the gang on the way back? Where were they? I had a choice to make. Do I tell my teacher? Or keep my mouth shut? My brain froze when I spotted the huge black blur headed my way.

For a large nun, Mother Superior could really move. She was even impressive on the basketball court. She joined our gym class one day and my jaw dropped as she took a lay-up shot in her habit and block heels. She made it easily. We all broke out in applause.

She approached my class line, "Thomas Carbone, please come with me!" I fell out of line as the rest of the uniformed student body watched and wondered what I had done. Mother Superior was always levelheaded, but then again, I never had a reason to make her angry before. While most all of the nuns were sweet ladies, it was a known fact that they had no problem disciplining kids who were out of line, and they had the full support of all parents. I had my share of rulers or hand brooms brought down across my knuckles for making a wise crack or two, but that was nothing to the wrath Billy had experienced during seventh grade.

~ ~ ✦ ~ ~

The smack heard around Greenpoint, happened back around Thanksgiving of that year. Sister Theresa was giving a lesson, walking up and down the aisles between the desks. She was asking serious questions about the pilgrims.

"What was the name of the ship the pilgrims sailed on?" Sister Theresa asked. A hand went up. "Yes, Miss Lynnkowski?"

"The Mayflower?"

"Is that a question or an answer?"

"An answer. The Mayflower."

"That is correct. And who can tell me why the pilgrims sailed to this new land?"

No one was volunteering an answer. Sister Theresa, in her silent black shoes, came up the aisle behind Billy. Uncharacteristically, he had miscalculated where she was at that moment. She, however, was in stealth mode, knowing Billy might be gearing up for one of his wisecracks. On this day, his wise crack was more off color than usual.

Billy whispered to us, "To get away from the nuns."

Sister Theresa was much bigger than Billy, who was a large boy for his age, surprised him when she was right behind him as he made his remark. I saw him shiver when she bent down, close to his ear.

"Please apologize for that remark, Mr. Balzuski!"

"It could be true."

Billy was on a roll, too bad his roll was out of line. So, not only was he incorrectly answering the question, he was insulting and disobeying Sister Theresa.

Sister brought her hand back, not even taking time to get the ruler. She swung at Billy's head. Billy ducked. She had wound up like Reggie Jackson stepping back to take a swing, and like Reggie often did, she whiffed. The momentum of her long arm was on the return swing as Billy's head was coming back up, a big smile on his face, until the sound of the crack.

Sister Theresa's World Series size gold ring hit Billy square on his jaw. Billy's head snapped back. He was stunned. Sister Theresa was shocked as well, as I don't think she expected Billy's head to come up. He was sent to the nurse and did not return the rest of the day. He never made another wise crack, at least out loud, all the way through the end of eighth grade. He told us that Mother Superior had come to see him while he was getting checked by the nurse, but he said nothing of what she said or did, other than, "Don't mess with her."

As I followed Mother Superior's black dress into the building, I felt a chill in her shadow. Inside her simple office, a small space with a large gray steel desk, a phone, a file cabinet, and a large crucifix, she had me sit in a metal chair along the back wall. She said nothing. Her chair creaked as it shifted on its wheels. She opened a black notebook with a gold cross on the cover and made a few notes.

A few minutes later, the secretary led in two men in beige shirts and brown ties that arced over their bellies. They were introduced as detectives. What kind of higher power had the ability to get the NYPD to have spare manpower in 1982 for this type of crime?

I don't recall much of what happened or what they asked after that. My dad arrived and talked to the detectives for a few minutes and I was sent back to my afternoon classes, which I thought was great since I had paid for my pretzel with extra salt.

It turned out that Mom had called Dad, and Nana had also called Dad once I ran by her. I'm sure she cursed Ma Bell the entire time for charging her for a call in such an emergency. Dad had called the school. Mother Superior had called the police.

As to how the official investigation turned out, I never found out, but there were two 'investigations' that proved effective.

When the Winthrop gang found out I had been robbed, they asked for descriptions and decided to take care of things. They were likely more upset about some other gang trying to take over "their" park, than my mugging, if you can call it that, but it was fine with me nonetheless.

The Winthrop gang staked out the park. Evidently the intruders came back one afternoon looking for more victims. Some of the Winthrop gang were hiding in the cement bunker of the pavilion. Chain-link fence around the pavilion didn't matter to these guys who somehow managed to have keys to all the park buildings and pad locks. Other members of the gang staked out the park exits to block all ways of escaping.

Once the intruders had made their way to the center of the park and took seats on the benches waiting for school kids, the Winthrop gang slowly surrounded them. It was no match the way I heard it.

Dad and an off-duty friend did their own 'investigation.' One night when I was watching a re-run of *Sanford and Son*, he came home and placed my stolen gloves and Giants hat on the living room coffee table. When I pressed him to tell me how he found them, he just said, "Those guys won't be around this neighborhood anymore."

I found out later from him that the perps had walked over from East Williamsburg. His police connections had an idea who they were and where to find them. It wasn't hard to spot them since they were wearing the stuff they stole from us. I never wore those gloves and hat again. I don't think Dad intended that I wear them; he was just sending me a message. The issue had been taken care of – Greenpoint style.

Roller Skating at the Movie Theater

Fridays were always pastry day. I'd stop on my way to the power plant and pick up a box to bring to the crew. The adorable nonna-like lady behind the counter would smile as I pointed out my order. She'd carefully pack the sfogliatelle, biscotti, pizzelle, cornetti with chocolate, and a dozen mixed cookies and then tie the white box with a piece of cotton string. With a "Buongiorno!" she'd send me on my way.

    Spotting me in the break room grabbing a huge chocolate brioche from the box, Mickey said to me, "You'd better watch whatcha eat, kid. Those sweets are gonna kill ya one day."

    I gave him a head nod, my mouth full of the flakey goodness. What I was thinking was, "Here you are eating a steady diet of river trash food, with who knows what's in it, and you're telling me not to eat this delicious pastry?"

Since childhood, I've had a sweet spot for good pastry. Maybe it was the Italian pastries I had growing up, since no relative ever visited without bringing a bakery box, or maybe it was all the times Dad would take me for a French cruller, but I would come to realize later in life that not every city, state, or country felt the same way about the critical importance of sweet pastry (most of Italy excluded). Nowhere was this fact more apparent than some locations I have visited in Asia, where fried dough was more likely to be filled with jalapeño peppers than covered in a sugar glaze.

Twenty years after Mickey's warning that I was going to die from eating delicious sweets, I was more worried about dying in an earthquake. My flight had been cancelled due to weather and I was stranded in Tokyo. I wandered around near the area of the Shinjuku station, which makes Grand Central resemble a small train depot, trying to find something for dinner. I happened upon a place called MOS Burger. Being in a country known for eating seaweed, I wondered if maybe the final S had just fallen off the sign. It wasn't obvious that MOS stood for mountain, ocean, and sun (I had to look it up).

In the window, I noticed a promotional poster for one of their burgers. What caught my eye was that the bun appeared to be a French cruller, although my mind told me that was impossible. French crullers were always my favorite and here I was on the other side of the planet staring at a poster with what looked to be the twisted airy donut I loved so much. At that moment, in that train station, hungry as I was, there was nothing I wanted more than a true French cruller. As I couldn't read any of the words on the poster, I went inside and ordered two versions of the specialty burger by pointing at the pictures.

I didn't think that the bun was going to be a French cruller donut, but it was. The first 'burger' was a spicy chorizo sausage patty. I didn't eat too much of that one because it included tomato, onions, and lettuce, and these weren't toppings I wanted paired with a sweet donut.

The second 'burger' was a more reasonable combination, even if there was technically no burger. Between the sliced cruller halves, there was a piece of chocolate cake, layers of a berry sauce, and whipped cream. (Good thing Mickey didn't see me then, he might have called in the cardiac unit). I picked it apart, scraped off the sauce and cream, tasted the cake, and ate the cruller. It was certainly a food adventure. Sitting at that counter, eating that donut / burger, and watching the commuters rush to catch their trains, brought back cruller memories I shared with my dad in a donut shop on Manhattan Avenue.

GREENPOINT AVE.

Growing up in Brooklyn in the 70s meant there were always great donuts and pastries to be found, and I'm not talking about those chains you see on every corner today. I'm recalling the places that hand-crafted delicious and unique treats. One of them still exists, in the same storefront as it did so many years ago.

What was simply known back then as the "Donut and Coffee Shop" is now the "Peter Pan Donut and Pastry Shop." I remember there was a counter that snaked back and forth in U shapes along the length of the shop. This allowed the server to fill coffee cups of six to eight customers by pretty much spinning around. The patrons were also able to conduct lively conversations in their own little coffee communities. The topics of the decade were politics and if the Yankees might win a pennant. When I looked several years ago, the counter was still configured in the same setup.

On Saturday mornings, my dad would sometimes take me to the donut shop if he had errands to run, and if he didn't, he'd find some reason to go up the avenue. As he had a thing for coffee and donuts, this was one of his regular hangouts. Dad pretty much knew everyone in the donut shop. Before they moved into our building on North Henry, Nana and Pop-Pop lived directly across the street from the donut shop, and Pop-Pop would come down and join us. I'd sit on a stool at that counter, looking at the display case of donuts and cookies trying to decide what to get, while Dad and Pop-Pop had coffee and talked family business.

It was during one of these father-son-grandson Saturday morning conferences, when I was sitting between Dad and Pop-Pop at the donut shop and I had my first French cruller. Every stool was occupied by Greenpointers complaining about the 84-day strike at the Daily News, Post, and The Times. They were done taking sides, they just wanted their dailies back!

Dad ordered a French cruller. I had never had anything French, so that's what I ordered too. The French cruller, a glazed, twisted, round donut, may not be French at all, but rather German or Dutch. I've since talked to people from France and they are not familiar with the French cruller of this type served at The Donut Shop, or Dunkin Donuts for that matter, being eaten in France. None of that mattered to me at the time, as far as I knew back then, that was my first taste of French cuisine, French or not. I smiled as I caught Dad watching me bite into that donut. On that morning, I became hooked on the airiness of the glazed French cruller donut, which, to this day, I prefer over any other donut.

When I was twelve or thirteen, I'd make trips up the avenue and stop in for a cruller. The waitresses knew me as "Little Tommy." I was seated at the counter eating my cruller one afternoon, when Dad walked in for a coffee. The waitress looked at my dad and said, "Like father, like son." I wasn't sure what she meant; I didn't start drinking coffee with him until I was maybe fourteen.

Some afternoons, I'd make a detour into the donut shop for a snack after a skating session next door. Of course, that was after the Meserole Theater on Manhattan became a skating rink. The Meserole Theater, turned skating rink, provided early training for Greenpoint kids who had to later learn how to merge onto highway traffic in a car. When the theater was converted to a roller rink, all the seats were removed to make room for the rink, which was a circular pit down from the lobby. To access the rink, we had to skate down a highly waxed ramp. The ramp had an incline that was good for picking up speed. At the bottom, the skaters were in constant motion going in circles.

Rolling down the ramp, I could barely see over the wall, it was dark, and strobe lights were flashing, so I mostly used "the force" to merge into the moving traffic. Along the side of the ramp there were bronze handrails, a relic of the theater, that the less skilled skaters would cling to on their way down. I'd come down the ramp at light speed. After more than a few collisions, possibly with unreported concussions, the management posted bouncers at the bottom of the ramp. If we were caught speeding, a monster with scary looking tattoos, wearing tight leather pants, who was somehow agile on skates, would grab us by the shirt and drag us to the side for a timeout. Since he could only grab one kid at a time, we'd wait at the top, for just the right moment, and then speed down in a pack to get past him.

The roller rink in the early 80s was the place to go. The girls made fashion statements with their high hair, short skirts with leggings, or hot pants. The young ladies who were not permitted to wear short skirts, by overprotective dads, would just change when they arrived. They'd pull on a mini-skirt over their pants and then shimmy off their pants right in the skate lace up area. There were no helmets or knee pads, and everyone was dressed to impress.

The music played at the rink was disco. The DJ was surrounded by records and spun vinyl behind a huge mixing panel from inside a glass booth overlooking the rink. A blue ceiling light and the hundred-dial LED control board resembled the bridge of a Star Wars battleship. Billy and I would skate over to his door and bug him with requests for Pink Floyd's *The Wall* or Queen's *Crazy Little Thing Called Love*. He'd ignore us and play songs for dance-skating. He played Donna Summer singing about *Bad Girls* and *Hot Stuff,* The Sugar Hill Gang rapped out *Rappers Delight,* and the Village People had us contorting our bodies into the letters YMCA as we sped around the rink with hands in the air.

Today, the theater turned skating rink is a chain pharmacy. The ramps lead down to the beauty aid section. If you look up you might even see the old disco mirror ball still hanging from the ceiling.

Getting to the rink was always an adventure. It was only a half mile from our apartment, but as a small kid, the trip felt a lot longer. There was traffic to contend with and annoying "Don't Walk" lights that were a pain when I went screaming down the street on skates. Greenpoint could pack an awful lot of slow people, who got in the way, over nine short city blocks. When I was running late, I'd skate right down the center of Norman Avenue.

To go even faster, I'd grab the back of a truck. The smell of exhaust and the noise of the city would fly by as I bumped down the street. The most difficult part was navigating metal manhole covers, because there was no way I could skate over those grates. For the most part, I just had to memorize where they were on each block and let go of the truck before running over one. Forgetting to do that would mean an immediate and sudden stop of the wheels. I'd go from skating to hopping on my skates, trying to stay upright and not get run over by a car.

Back then, we all skated on city streets without pads and helmets. Besides, a helmet would have messed up my hair that was probably sprayed with an ozone killing can of Mom's hairspray.

Getting across McGuinness Boulevard on skates was a challenge. At the intersection with Norman Avenue, McGuinness was a seven-lane boulevard made up of four traffic lanes, a turning lane, and two parking lanes that drivers decided to use as a passing lane if there were no cars parked at the corner. In the center of the boulevard there was a small cement pedestrian island. Since the light rarely gave enough time to get all the way across, the light would strand you on this thin piece of pavement as cars, trucks, and buses went whizzing by in both directions. The center island was always packed with grandmas pushing their foldable shopping carts. They'd never make it across in one change of the light.

I had a lot of hair back in 1980...

On skates it was a bit of a suicide mission. Getting to the corner when the 'walk' sign was beginning to flash, 'DON'T WALK,' I'd skate even faster, only to realize I was not going to make it all the way to the opposite sidewalk. Mid-street I had to somehow figure out how to stop on the cement island, and not push someone's grandma into oncoming traffic. This meant I had to strong arm a pole. Someone's nana would give me a lecture, "Does your mother know you're skating across the boulevard?" I'd reply, "Sure, she's on skates a block ahead of me. I'm trying to catch up." Good thing the light would change and I could take off, or she would have hit me with her purse full of bingo markers – it was all permissible back then. It was way riskier skating home in the dark. Parents never came to pick us up with their car. They'd lose their parking spot! These were our survivor games, we didn't need any TV reality show for it.

At some point the rink instituted a policy of no street skates allowed. It was a dead giveaway we were wearing street skates if we skated up to the ticket booth to pay. They didn't want skates that had wheels with embedded gravel scratching up their nice polished floor. To get around this rule, I'd skate to within a half block of the rink and then change into sneakers. Pretty much everyone was doing the same. This was a necessity since no one I knew could afford two pairs of skates – one for the rink and one for our games of full contact street hockey, without any pads, of course.

Getting to the rink through the city streets, and getting down onto the rink from the ramp, were only two of our challenges. Once down on the rink, we had to get out of the pit and back up to the lobby when we wanted a break. To get up the exit ramp, I'd have to skate fast enough to build up momentum to make it to the top. Skaters without enough speed, or no leg strength, would have to pull themselves up the ramp using the handrails; not a way to impress the girls.

When the DJ played *Endless Love* the exit ramp would get more congested than the L.I.E. at five o'clock. I think the DJ got a kickback from the lady working the snack counter, because her sales of fries skyrocketed every time he played something slow.

One of my main reasons for being at the rink was Alison. She had 80s fluffy brown hair, wore her sweaters tight, and her dance training made her a great skater. The first time I saw her, Billy and I were sitting at a table looking down at the skaters in the pit, while we ate a large order of fries smothered in ketchup. The brunette in the white sweater, school uniform skirt, and black leggings was skating with her friends, smiling and laughing.

"Who's that girl?" I asked Billy.

"Don't know, but that's a St. Cecilia skirt." He was spot on. St. Stan's, St. Cecilia's, and St. Anthony's, all had particular uniforms, so it was easy to tell who went to what school.

"Do you know anyone she is with?" I asked him.

"Nope," he replied and stuck his hands back in the fries. He wasn't much for catching on.

"I'll be back," I said, leaving Billy to his grease sticks.

I skated over to the top of the on ramp and watched as Alison came around with her friends. Timing my descent just right, I slid past the bouncer at a controlled speed and ended up directly between the beautiful skater and her friend.

"Oh, sorry about that. The ramp was really fast," I shouted over *The Best of Times* by Styx.

She smiled, making it easy for me to be bold.

"Wanna skate together?"

She looked at me and said, "Sure."

We skated away from her friends, and soon we were doing twists, twirls, and holding hands. Alison and I would meet at the rink every week to skate together. That rink kept a lot of us kids off the streets. We would skate, flirt, eat oily French fries with way too much ketchup, and play Space Invaders.

My friends and I would try to impress the girls showing off with our skating moves. It was great while it lasted, but the disco-skating trend faded away, and the rink closed down. The building sat empty for a number of years before it became a retail store. Many memories were made where they now sell greeting cards, cosmetics, and those "As Seen on TV" products.

Before it was a roller rink, the location was the Meserole Theater. I saw *Jaws* there in 1976. The second film of the double feature was *Lifeguard*, featuring Sam Elliot. Both films were rated PG. Good thing for me *Jaws* was shown first, because Dad dragged me out of there as soon as half a boob was shown during a kissing scene. Forty years later, thanks to the internet, I watched the full feature of *Lifeguard* to see what the problem was. I didn't miss anything – flesh or acting wise.

Since I was upset about missing the second feature, Dad took me to The Donut Shop next door for a snack. He bought me two French crullers and a hot chocolate. To this day I always get two French crullers, one is never enough, just as long as they are not used as burger buns – ever again!

GREENPOINT AVE.

It was out of old habit that the box of donuts I brought to the plant always had French crullers. I tried for weeks to get Mickey to try a donut.

"Mickey, have you ever even tried a French cruller?"
"Can't say as I have. Never tried French food."
"Why not just give it a taste?"
"Nah. That stuff will kill ya."
"Mickey, remember when I tried that blue crab?"

That did it. Mickey sat down and tried a French cruller for the first time in his life. He took a small bite and then another bigger one. "Blimey. That's pretty good! Way better than a regular old dry cruller."

At that moment, seeing the smile on Mickey's dirty wrinkly old face, I had an idea of how my dad felt the first time he bought me a French cruller. I just wonder if kids in Japan would feel the same way if they ordered a cruller here in the USA and it DIDN'T come with a chorizo patty and tomato slice. Yuck!

Block Parties

Mickey and I were on our way back from a takeout food run for the overtime crew when we hit a detour. The side street we normally drove down was blocked off with a blue wooden police barricade, the white letters exclaiming, "Police Line – Do Not Cross."

I peered down the street to see triangle multi-colored plastic flags hanging across the road along with the occasional string of Christmas lights. The entire street was devoid of vehicles and all the neighbors were out having a grand old time. It was nice to know the tradition of neighbors partying with neighbors was still going strong.

"Why don't they have this party in the park!" Mickey barked.

"Then it wouldn't be a block party, Mickey. What, you never went to a block party?"

Waiting for the red light to change, I could see he was thinking. "It's been a long time," he answered.

Block parties, unlike street festivals, are usually held on a single city block, with the people that live on the block, plus the friends and relatives that drop by for the free food and drinks. For me, it was a nice way to remember the parties we had on North Henry. Mickey just grumbled about his dinner getting cold and having to drive two blocks out of the way.

GREENPOINT AVE.

The barbeques in the yards the second night of the blackout, and the snow days of the '78 blizzard, were the random occurrences when <u>everyone</u> came out of their flats wondering how the city ran out of electric or how the city let so much snow fall. The only pre-planned times when EVERYBODY on the block came out were the block parties of summer.

Our block parties were no small event. **No Parking** signs were posted and the NYPD would deliver the blue wooden horses to signify our street was closed to traffic. In the early morning, men began moving their cars off the street, with a lot of vocal complaining from the older residents. Mr. Raviolo would grump walking to his Chevelle, "Feste, feste, feste, sempre feste." (Parties, parties, parties, always parties.) If he were back in Sicily there would be celebrations weekly for one Italian name day or another. He should have been grateful because we didn't even have a block party once a year, a situation I thought was an outrage.

Watching the men move their cars, I always wondered where they went to park. There never seemed to be any extra spaces for blocks in any direction on regular days. Where did a hundred cars go when the street was closed? And if these vehicles were parked on less accommodating streets near the factories, was there a rise in the thefts of AM radios and hubcaps?

At the exact time noted on the signs for all cars to be moved, a street cleaner appeared followed by a tiny NYPD meter maid car, which was followed by a line of tow trucks. It was city revenue coordination at its finest. A ticket, a towing fee, and an impound fee. What a way to begin a festa.

Once the official cleaning was complete, which really just swooshed the dirt around from what I could tell, Paulie's dad would take the matter into his own hands. He'd open all the hydrants to give the street a full wash down. The men, led by Mr. Raviolo used push brooms to sweep any standing water and residual dirt down the sewers.

Even though we had Withrop Park at the end of our street to play in, block parties were special occasions for us kids. We celebrated having a car-less street to ride our bikes on without the fear of a car door opening up unexpectedly, into the front tire of our bikes. I was fortunate this only happened to me twice. Two occasions during my childhood when it would have been nice to have a helmet.

With the street closed, there were no grandmothers standing along the curb yelling at me and my friends to watch out for the cars. There were no men yelling at us for hitting their hubcaps with a hockey puck and no double-parkers blocking our stickball court. This was OUR street for the day. The kids ruled!

Once the cars were gone and the street was cleaned, the setup began. Strings of flags were dropped from second floor windows down into the arias and a runner ran them across the street, holding the flags as high as possible so as not to decapitate an unsuspecting tike on a trike. It was mayhem with kids of all ages riding two, three, and four-wheel vehicles with complete disregard for any road rules. Once the runner reached the aria of the house across the street, a rope would drop from the second story. The runner would tie the end of the flags to the rope and the apartment dweller would pull up the flags.

To not be left out, some of the third-floor residents did the same. Sometimes a crisscross pattern would develop as a second-floor flag would inadvertently be tied to a third-floor rope in the rush. This was repeated up and down North Henry Street in synchronized fashion that would amaze even Dr. Seuss. The entire block would be decorated for the festivities in under three and a half minutes. It wasn't symmetric, but it was colorful.

While the flags made the block look festive, there was always the risk in how the residents secured the flags. Some would tie the end of the rope to their bed post; others just closed the window down on the last plastic flag at the end of the string. This usually was not a problem except the time that the go-kart races started before Paulie's grandma was done baking the lasagna. The mishap that occurred, requires a bit of background.

The block party go-kart race was the event I always looked forward to. Our go-karts were crude, handmade by ten to twelve-year-old kids. We would spend every day from the time school let out in June until the night before the block party getting our karts ready. These karts had no engine, so if you're imagining loud, gas-powered go-karts, that's not what we built. Neither were our karts soap box derby car designs that normally have a closed, somewhat aerodynamic, front. Our cars were made from wood with a basic center beam, axles of various designs, four wheels, and a seat. Seems simple enough, but we'd spend weeks designing to get it right.

No adults were supposed to help in the construction. I was always suspicious, but a bit envious, of the karts that were somehow welded together with lightweight aluminum and included power steering. Other kids went for fancy over function. It was those cars that usually fell apart before reaching the finish line. For the karts that followed the rules, the center beam was an old, half rotted two by four we pulled from a dumpster down at the lots. Many of the karts were constructed from stolen and broken up pallets and lots of nails that were too small for the job.

It was not unusual for anything on wheels to go missing and be chopped to assemble a kart. If we determined that a part would give us an edge to go faster, it was fair game. For weeks before the block party, grandmas, little kids, and mothers started to complain they were missing wheels. The front wheels for a go-kart would be stripped off a carriage, a grandma's grocery cart, or a sister's tricycle left unattended in an aria, entry hall, or basement. The rear wheels were often stolen from a younger sibling's Big Wheel or Red Flyer wagon. We had first class chop shops in secretive places. Mine was the dark basement boiler room, a place I'd go at no other time, other than to build my kart. I worked day and night in that dingy, scary, hot cinder block room that smelled of unburned oil with asbestos flaking off the pipes. The furnace in that room was the size of a city bus. This was several years before *Nightmare on Elm Street* came out, but I'm pretty sure Freddie was growing up behind that furnace; I heard him laughing every time the darn thing kicked off. Freddie, or not, that's where the work had to be done. It was important that nobody see the design, or know where it was being assembled, for fear of go-kart espionage. We were cold war neurotic.

When I went dumpster diving at the lots up past Norman Avenue, I couldn't find a 2x4 long enough, so I had to piece together a center beam with odd size boards using 12d nails. The seat for my kart was a cut open wooden milk crate found behind the dairy distributor when I went on a milk run with Dad. The words, "THEFT PUNISHABLE BY DEATH," were spray painted on the side. I made the seat more comfortable with the cushion swiped from Pop-Pop's driver's seat (also punishable by death, in the more painful Neapolitan style).

I designed the cheapest mode of steering using a 2x4, that was loosely attached to the main beam, with a long nail that went through and was bent around. My feet on the front axle were used to guide the kart. The rear wheels came from my brother's not-so-old orange and yellow Big Wheel. I was grounded for two weeks because I dismantled his Christmas present. The punishment was worth it though, since those wheels gave the kart a 'monster-kart' look, and a rumble sound. I learned a lot about the center of gravity and drag by building that kart. The lighter the kart the better, since once the pusher let you go the outcome was entirely up to momentum. The only other requirement was the kart had to stay in one piece, at least until passing the finish line.

When I finished building my kart, Dad took me someplace secret to give it a test drive. I made him cover it in sheets, before we carried it from the basement to the van, to keep nosy eyes from seeing the design. He didn't even tell me where we were going. Dad drove all the way out to Flushing Meadows. This was one park, where the word park, was never needed, it was just, "Flushing Meadows." Interestingly, this was yet another of the city's parks that had its name changed, even though no New Yorker was going to add extra syllables to call it *Flushing Meadows Corona Park* when the original name was perfectly fine. Sorry Corona, you already have a Queen (and King) anyway.

With Dad, Chris, and Jeanette in Flushing-Meadows park ~1978. Look at those handle bars on my bike. I even had a custom speed shifter on the bar! I see I'm wearing my Mets cap.

~

After testing the kart on a flat path, Dad thought it would be great fun for me to try it going down a hill. His idea probably had more to do with the fact that he was trying to push me while smoking a cigarette and he was tired of running.

We located a path with a suitable grade and he gave me a push to start me down the hill. About midway down the hill, I realized I was picking up a lot of speed. The Big Wheel plastic tires were rumbling and sent walkers scattering. At eleven years old, I had yet to learn about momentum and acceleration, but being in a live situation, I figured it out pretty quickly. At the bottom of the hill, there was a curve. Dead ahead was a patch of bushes. I had three options. I could allow the kart to pick up speed and try to steer with my feet into the turn, which I figured would have resulted in a high-speed pavement roll-over. In shorts and wearing no helmet or pads that was going to be painful. I could just plow into the bushes hoping they would cushion the crash; assuming there were no rocks, fences, or other obstructions behind them.

My third option was to test the brake, which was mostly for show, an unnecessary accessory for the real race day. The brake mechanism was a thin piece of wood, nailed into the main beam that could be pulled back against the rear tire. I never figured on having to use it, since North Henry was as flat as an open can of Coke that's been in the fridge for a day. The stopping during the real race was done after the finish line Fred Flintstone style, with our heels dug into the asphalt. The flat course meant we needed a good push off and a light car to go the distance from the start to finish. Nobody wanted to be the driver of the car that ran out of steam ten feet from the finish line. That was the ultimate embarrassment. Given our priority was on picking up enough steam to make it across the finish line, we never even considered needing a brake to stop. We mostly used it to generate extra noise during practice runs to intimidate the competition. We'd scrape the bumps on the plastic wheels with the wood producing a 'ch, ch, ch, ch,' sound that drove Mr. Raviolo crazy. On that afternoon in the park, on that hill, I went with my third option. The brake was getting tested with a live crash dummy.

As I pulled back on the piece of wood it scraped against the black plastic tire, making a "sheering" sound. The brake was not designed to hold back an accelerating kart and the lever was too short to grasp enough of the tire surface. It became obvious that nailing a thin piece of wood to the frame with a 12D nail was not a sufficient design to stop a kart going fifteen miles an hour. The wood popped off in my hand. With no time for a plan B, I braced for a rollover collision with the bushes and let out a scream.

Opening my eyes, the milk seat crate was lying directly next to my head, its message, "THEFT PUNISHABLE BY DEATH," staring me in my face. When I picked myself out of the thorn covered hedges, I assessed the kart damage. The 2x4 center beam had cracked, the two front carriage wheels had flown off like frisbees, and one of the rear Big Wheel plastic tires had split open into two pieces.

I kicked the stupid kart and told my dad I was dropping out of the race. He was hearing nothing of it. We carried the pieces of the racer back to the VW bus. Back on North Henry, under the cover of darkness, Dad helped me smuggle it through the aria and back into the basement. It was critical to keep the test run disaster a secret. Go-kart races at a block party were close to being the Belmont Stakes, where bets were taken and big money could be won – at least five bucks by the gambling grandmas and certainly by my nana.

Dad helped me spread the pieces of the kart out on the basement floor. He told me that I should examine the failure points and design a better kart. I spent the next week making trips up the avenue to the hardware store buying long bolts, huge washers, and metal rods with my poker earnings. I learned about the benefits of cotter pins to hold on a tire instead of reusing old push caps.

I skated up to the lumberyard on Clay Street and came back with a brand new six-foot 2x6 for the center beam. Getting across McGuinness, which is now referred to as Brooklyn's "Boulevard of Death," carrying a beam on skates drew complaints from both grandmas and truck drivers. When I reached the center island of the boulevard, the beam was sticking out into traffic on both sides. Ladies yelled I was going to knock them into traffic. Horns blared as I tried not to get pushed to an early death.

Back in the boiler room, I connected the front axle to the new center beam. The higher performance axle was acquired from my grandmother's grocery cart with the rubber wheels still attached. She was always so supportive; it was better anyway for her arm strength to carry the groceries the six blocks from the A&P.

This time the steering was a rope tied to the left and right of the axle that operated as if I was holding the reins of a horse. This left my feet free to operate a robust foot brake I had designed for emergencies. To give the kart a jacked-up look, the rear wheels came from a carriage in the basement; one I figured my mom didn't need any longer, not knowing she had promised it to a lady who was pregnant. The added height also served to give the runner a higher stance than being awkwardly bent over for the push off. My new seat didn't have the menacing message that I considered bad karma. Instead, I used the plastic seat from my brother's, already made useless, Big Wheel that was missing wheels from the first kart design. Being close to the Fourth of July, the last thing I did was paint the kart red, white, and blue. My re-designed kart was crafted to be light, sturdy, and look cool. If it didn't bust apart going over a manhole cover or pothole, I had a chance.

The go-kart race was the highlight of the block party for me and my friends. The girls spent an hour with chalk drawing and decorating the start and finish lines in anticipation of the race. Before the race, the karts were lined up for inspection behind a big bubble letter START line, which was drawn from one side of the street to the other. Men with intentions of placing a bet would walk up and down the line of cars assessing the viability of a win.

Aside from having a fast car, I needed a fast partner to win the race. A significant amount of bartering and jockeying would go on to secure the fastest runners on the block. Our street had several fast runners who could provide a significant advantage in winning and bribes were not uncommon to secure the best partner. The runner would push the kart out of the starting gate and up to the release line. From there, we were in freewheel until crossing the finish line.

At ten minutes to race time, the course was double swept to ensure no rock, bottle top, or grain of sand would otherwise slow down a kart or cause the pusher to fall. Our street never was as clean as just before a go-kart race.

The races were held as elimination rounds with three or four karts speeding down the street at a time. I lined up with the first heat; my kart's front tires touching the chalk line. I knew my car had a chance, but my runner Billy was built more as a defensive lineman, than a sprinter. I just hoped he could get a good start.

When Mr. Mazewski raised his flag, yelling out, "On your mark, get set, GO," he dropped his arm and the flag came down. The runners dug in and started pushing. The problem was that more than his flag dropped. With the lasagna not yet ready, Paulie's grandma came to the window. Caught up in the excitement, she opened her window to cheer on the racers. Paulie's grandpa had not figured on anyone opening their bedroom window when he simply closed the sash on the flags earlier.

Grandma Polumbo's cheer turned to a scream when the string holding up the flags flew out the window. There may have been a collective, "O Dio," as Paulie's grandma tried to grab the rope unsuccessfully. With the runners pushing us, oblivious to what was happening two-stories in the sky above them, the karts sped down the block. A live version of the Whacky Racers was underway. Dr. Seuss would have been proud of such a moment coming to life after such determined decorating.

Half way to the finish line, I saw the flags floating down through the air in slow motion. A mental calculation told me I could make it under the flags before they caught my kart or me around the neck. There was no way I was going to use the brake and risk losing the race.

My mental calculation was wrong, along with the calculations of the entire set of lead cars. None of us made it under the flags. When the line of karts hit the falling string of multi-colored plastic party flags it became a slow-motion demolition derby. The flags caused the karts to get tangled up, spin out, and knock into one another. Of course, nobody was wearing helmets or pads. Adults were yelling in the mayhem. Wheels came off karts, jumped the curb, and rolled into spectators. Mr. Collins, whose first name I'm pretty sure was Tom, had made the mistake of setting up his liquor on a flimsy folding table right at the curb with VIP seating for his relatives. Joey Junior's kart took out a liter of Smirnoff, a bottle of rum, and a fancy gold ice bucket stand that held a cheap bottle of wine.

Paulie's kart dismantled completely on impact with the curb, leaving him sitting on the ground astride a 2x4. Lori and three other girls ran over to see if he was injured. He played the disaster pretty good. The four of them helped him to his feet and waited on him the rest of the day. He came out a winner in my book.

I stood up, pulling flags from around my neck, and realized that my re-designed kart had made it through without a single piece coming loose. It was a very satisfying moment and made the test run out in Flushing Meadows worth all the thorns and scratches.

Luckily, no kids were decapitated and Mr. Collins had plenty of booze to re-supply his guest table. Mr. Mazewski immediately called for the flags to be hoisted up, tied securely, and for the karts to get lined up for the next race. The broken karts that could be repaired would re-race last. They were taken into the pit at the fire hydrant where a team of kid mechanics hammered, nailed, sawed, and taped things back together.

The good news was that Paulie's grandma heard the oven timer and brought down a perfectly cooked lasagna for the competitors to share. The bad news was that Billy decided it would be fine to eat a huge plate of it before pushing me in the re-do race. Billy just didn't have enough left in him to push me off fast enough. Maybe it was the lasagna. Two karts were out in front of me with the lead. Unfortunately for them, they bumped into one another and their wheels locked together. I coasted around them to victory. Billy came running to the finish line, and yelled all out of breath, "We did it! We did it!"

I said, "Billy, didn't you see what happened? We got lucky, man."

After three rounds, it was down to a run-off between the final four karts. With Billy eating a second helping of lasagna, I told him, "Billy, this isn't personal, it's business," and I fired him as runner. I went over to recruit Paulie, who was always the faster runner, even with a fake injury.

He was reluctant at first. "I don't know, Tommy, I told the girls I hurt my leg. How's it gonna look if I push your kart?"

"Paulie, there's four girls, right?" I asked him.

"Yeah, so?" he replied.

"Think about how it's gonna look if you run the race, with this so-called injury, AND we win. Seven minutes in heaven multiplied by four!"

At the start line, Paulie, took hold of my shoulders, his girls cheering on kart 15 (Thurman Munson's number). When the flag dropped, Paulie pushed off and we had the early lead. I have no idea who the final winners were that year. It's not stored in my memory. There were no trophies that I recall. Paulie probably remembers the hugs at the finish line from his cheerleaders. My memory is about the building of the kart, the test runs, the endurance of the competition, and that marvelous lasagna.

In the days after the block party, we couldn't use the karts in the street, so we would run them up and down on the sidewalk. Mr. Raviolo would yell each time we went by his house. "Silenzio, Silenzio!" He eventually got his wish as the karts would only last a week or two going over the cracks and bumps on the sidewalks – thanks to the same gravelly cement that was used at the park playground. We'd move on to other summer interests and store the pieces of the karts in dark corners of our basements until the next block party. Usually, we'd forget about them and just steal, I mean borrow, new parts for our new and better models.

Years later, when we were packing to move, Dad and I found that red, white, and blue kart under the basement stairs. I took it out to the street and gave it to some eight-year-old kids. It was the first time they had seen a go-kart. They didn't know what to do with it. A kid scraping a watermelon flavored imitation Italian ice from a waxed container groaned, "What we spos to do with that? There's no pedals!" What had become of this city!

Our block parties were filled with orchestrated games and activities coordinated by the ladies of the block association. All along the street something was going on to keep the kids occupied and the adults out of the beverages until later in the afternoon. There were whiffle ball games, talent shows, bike races, running races, and jump rope competitions.

The teens that were learning to play drums or guitars would have a battle of the bands. Nana asked me, "Do they call it *hard rock* because it's hard on everyone's ears?" The music committee wisely limited each group to one song. Sometimes there were singing competitions. My sister Jeanette sang, "The Sun Will Come Out Tomorrow." Sitting next to her she had a small tan dog she had found roaming the streets a few weeks earlier. That dog had so many fleas the day my sister brought her home, we could have started a flea circus. Mom made her tie the dog up in the aria until Dad came home with some chemicals. I have a feeling Jeanette had it in her mind, when she first saw the dog, that she needed a prop for her singing debut. She won the competition in her age group, the dog just sitting by her side scratching and taking in the applause. The dog was her "Sandy" although that's not what she named her. After the song, everyone was asking her, "Is your dog's name Sandy?"

"Mindy," she'd answer.

"Mindy? Hahaha, Where's Mork?" Everyone laughed except my sister, who didn't see the irony.

Soon after the talent show, the serious cooking would begin. Barbeques, hibachis, charcoal grills, Coleman stoves, and even the occasional kitchen stove would appear on the sidewalks. Some neighbors borrowed folding tables from the Knights of Columbus; other families would bring out their entire kitchen set to the sidewalk. Hot dogs and hamburgers were cooking at almost every house, along with Polish, Italian, and Irish dishes of kielbasa, sausage, and bangers.

Relatives and friends would arrive from other blocks, neighborhoods, boroughs, and I think even other states. Some ended up never leaving, thinking we partied in the streets all the time with free food and booze. We ended up with a family of eight Italians who took up residence in our basement. They were family friends, but we referred to them as Uncle Jerry, Aunt Emmie, and cousins. After realizing we didn't always drink and dance in the street, they packed up an overloaded station wagon, the SAME model and color as the Griswold's, with a homemade wooden roof rack, and headed across the country to settle in Vegas.

To wash down all the food, coolers were stationed along the aria fences. The thing to do was to make your way from house to house socializing, trying different grilled meats or antipasti while getting to know your neighbors better. Mostly for the adults, they were just getting smashed as they went house to house. The kids roamed the block getting high on sugar from all the cookies, cheesecakes, and pastries. By midafternoon card games for adults sprung up at various tables along the street with five, ten, and twenty-dollar bills being held down with empty Schlitz bottles. By now, even Mr. Raviolo was in a good mood.

The partying was not without oversight. The NYPD officers from the 94th precinct would stop by, mostly to inspect the food choices. They would park their patrol car at the end of the block near the blue barriers. Leaving their lights flashing, they'd stroll down one side of the street and up the other. Our good men in blue would sample the sausage and peppers and homemade cannoli. Pairs of partners would show up throughout the day and evening. Sometimes they would stop and have a game of catch.

The local firehouse would not be left out and would bring along the truck for the kids to jump on. The moms and dads would feed any public servant that happened along, whether they were from the local precinct, the local engine company, or anywhere else they happened to come from. Given the amount of NYPD and NYFD employees that would come around during a block party, I suspect a call went out over their radio, "411. Block Party. Great Italian Sausage and Kielbasa, North Henry Street." If the temperature was hot, the NYFD would put a special sprinkler cap on the fire hydrant and then let her rip. This would also signal the start of the boat races.

Weeks before the party, everyone would start constructing their boats. Even some of the adults took part in this competition. Many of the boats were made from popsicle sticks, forcing us to eat a lot of ice cream bars from the guy that drove the ice cream truck down our block every day. Those that couldn't eat enough ice cream made their boats from paper or cardboard. Speed wasn't the object, finishing was. As the high-pressure water from the hydrant filled the gutters, kids of all ages would place their boat into the torrent. Some boats would sink from being too heavy or flip over if too light. Only those boats that were light, watertight, and counterbalanced to handle the flood of water would stay afloat. The boats would float down the length of the street, headed for the sewer, which was blocked with a screen to keep the crafts from heading out to Newtown Creek. The objective was to get your boat to the end of the street before it was swamped. As the boats went by the grandfathers would cheer, especially if they were winning money. Self-appointed officials would clear the gutter of shipwrecks that were blocking passage of the next race. Without fail, some wise guy would drop in a store-bought plastic boat or rubber duck just for a laugh.

    The plastic flags floating down over the street during the go-kart race were only a minor safety issue when it came to things strung up across the street. The high-class part of the block would run strings of Christmas lights along with the flags. These weren't the tiny LED lights of today. The year being what it was, the strings were hundreds of large five-watt incandescent bulbs, pulling enough wattage to stress the New York electrical grid once again. The adults failed to consider, in the hanging of these lights, that they were directly over our whiffle ball court. Not that we were trying, but hitting the string of lights with even a whiffle ball would cause a rain of glass in the outfield. Mr. Raviolo was at the ready with a broom, yelling and screaming about the shattered bulbs. Adults came running from all stoops moving us to another section of the block to play. By evening, when the extension cord was plugged in, half the bulbs had been smashed. That didn't matter to the adults, who were mostly tipsy by now. They would all "Ooh and Ah," the moment the lights were energized.

To use up even more juice, neighbors hauled out their hi-fi stereos, each blasting different singers. Sinatra, Bobby Vinton, and The Clancy Brothers, belted out Italian, Polish, and Irish songs from the speakers in the arias. As the sun set, a real band would appear or stereos would be turned up, and the party intensified. The younger children would have already passed out from exhaustion, allowing the adults to get serious with their partying. This meant for us pre-teens and teens, we had leeway to get into some trouble, not on purpose, but in the dark, at a city block party trouble seemed to find us. This was doubly true with Ritchie around. Ritchie swiped a six pack of nips from his dad's cooler that he, Paulie, and I finished off in his aria under the shadow of a tree.

After gulping down the Miller High Life, Billy said, "I don't feel anything. Why are these so small?"

I realize now why nips, the small 7oz beers, were a favorite of the block party coolers. As the men (and some ladies) would make their way from house to house, a full-size beer can or bottle would be too much. You would get to the next house and not be able to accept a beer, as you would have one that was still half full. The use of nips meant you could finish a beer in a reasonable conversation time and move on to the next house to have your next one. By the time you drank the equivalent of a six pack, you would have had an opportunity to visit with twelve neighbors. Now why doesn't that sound like a good idea? What could go wrong?

Once Ritchie had smuggled away some of the nips, we

became even more brazen. Walking up and down the street, every house had essentially an open bar on the sidewalk in front of the aria gate. Soda bottles were on the tables right next to the hard alcohol. The street was fairly dark thanks to the earlier breakage of most of the Christmas lights. My older cousin, who I'll call Angie so as not to incriminate her, who couldn't have been more than seventeen, was standing next to an unattended alcohol table. Ritchie, being one with words, flirted and sweet talked her into mixing us drinks. Angie must have already been drunk because she was flirting back with a fourteen-year-old. She secretly made us screwdrivers and rum and Cokes.

I'm not sure how many drinks it took, or if it was the mixing of the two, but I remember Nana chasing me home with a flag pole. Nana knew all the Italian curses and pushed me up our stoop and into the house yelling at me for being a drunk.

"You get upstairs and get to bed now!" she yelled.

I have no idea where my parents were at that point. They may have already been inside or they could have been visiting along the block. As soon as Nana went back outside, I snuck out and jumped over to the neighbor's aria, narrowly escaping an early vasectomy from the iron spears, and made my way down the block again.

The next thing I remember is Dad throwing me in an ice-cold shower and me heaving all over. He never spoke of that night after that. I didn't try another rum and Coke until my senior year of college. The smell made me sick even then and I still can't stand that drink.

The Candy Man

When there wasn't a crisis at the plant, which was rare, Mickey and I would swap stories about the city while eating lunch. The day I bought a knish from the grease wagon, Mickey was sitting in the lunchroom eating one of his homemade crab cakes. Walking out of the plant the night before, the guards laughed as they inspected Mickey's lunch cooler because it was filled to the top with dirty river crabs. I now knew what he had planned on making with his catch. As we ate, we started talking about candy stores.

"Ya know, candy stores were the corner hangout back in the day. We'd all sit around at the soda fountains, some of them even sold knishes like you're eatin there," said Mickey.

"We had places like that in Greenpoint when I lived there."

"Are you sure, kid? There aren't many places like the ones I'm meanin just now."

"No, really. In fact, my dad owned a candy store with a soda fountain counter."

"No kidding. Did he make egg creams?"

"Of course! My dad was famous for the way he made egg creams!" Or so, Mom has told me.

I don't know if I ever had an egg cream Dad made at the candy store, but he made plenty of these delicious fountain drinks for us at home over the years. I would have never guessed that Mickey had a thing for egg creams, seeing that he only drank generic brand diet sodas.

"There's a place not far from the plant that makes a pretty good egg cream. I'll take you over there sometime," Mickey said.

I had forgotten all about Mickey's offer, until the next time we went to pick up the steak dinners. By now, I had been working at the power plant for a couple of months and he trusted me enough to drive. I think he enjoyed having a chauffeur. On the drive to get the takeout he asked me to stop at a dive corner store. I figured he needed some gum or he wanted to play the lottery.

"Come on, kid. You're gonna try Manny's egg cream." I looked at the front of the store. Across the window was a sign that read, **Deli-Grocery-Beer**. It didn't remind me of any candy store or soda fountain I'd ever seen before. I wondered what type of convenience store was making egg creams. I can't say I remember the taste of the egg cream or the quality of the foam too well. I was more worried about the filth in the place and the greasy glass Manny served the drinks in. It certainly didn't leave a great impression.

Making a good egg cream takes a bunch of practice and a lot of pride. I sampled plenty of these drinks around Greenpoint growing up; none as perfectly mixed or with a foamy head as good as the ones Dad would make us.

GREENPOINT AVE.

Roaming the streets of Greenpoint on hot summer days, Billy, Paulie, and I were always trying to find ways to cool off. We drank more than our share of ice cold Cokes, and they had to be very cold. If a candy store didn't keep their soda cooler near freezing, we'd boycott and buy elsewhere. No matter where we were in the neighborhood, when we finished drinking our Cokes, before pitching the bottle, we'd rub it back and forth across a manhole cover to get the glass rim to pop off. We'd stick the rim in our pocket for our nighttime skelsy games under the street lamp on our spray-painted skelsy court in the hydrant space. Skelsy was played by using a thumb and index finger to shoot the bottlecap around the drawn court. Sometimes we played just for fun, but mostly we played for money.

There were times, during our roaming, when we mixed it up and cooled off with a soda fountain malted or an Italian ice. In my opinion though, the most thirst quenching and delicious drink for cooling off was an egg cream in a chilled glass. The first time I ordered an egg cream when I was with my friends, I was surprised to learn they had never heard of this drink.

After seeing *The Empire Strikes Back* at the Chopin Movie Theater, Jimmy, Billy, Paulie, and I were walking down Manhattan Avenue. Billy said he needed a drink, even though he had just downed two large Cokes during the movie. We stopped in the candy store at the corner of Nassau and Manhattan. We went right to the cooler and each of us grabbed a soda. I picked a Yoo-hoo. I was about to pay when I noticed the sign on the wall, **Egg cream's - $1.00**. The place was more of a soda fountain, than a candy store, so I figured the guy must know his way around a seltzer sprayer.

I put the soda back and ordered a chocolate egg cream. The guys were pretty sore at me. They wanted to pay for their drinks and keep moving, as if they had someplace to be.

"An egg cream? Why the heck do you wanna drink eggs. Who do you think you are - Rocky?" asked Paulie.

"It doesn't have eggs in it," I said.

They watched impatiently as the thin man, with a toothpick in his mouth, made the drink. I thought they were going to have a cow when the man set the drink down on the counter in a tall frosted glass.

"What the heck, man? You gotta drink that here?" complained Billy.

The man behind the counter, sensing the less refined nature of the crew, dumped my egg cream into a Styrofoam cup, charged me an extra nickel, and in the process completely ruined the foamy head. I thanked him and we took off down the avenue.

It wasn't as good as Dad's, and maybe the cup had something to do with it, but I enjoyed the refreshing taste all the same. A few days later, Billy got to wondering what this drink was all about.

"So what was that egg cream again?" he asked while we sat on his stoop listening to the Yankee game.

"It's chocolate syrup, milk, and seltzer," I told him.

"So, like a chocolate milk."

"No, not at all."

"Like a Yoo-hoo then?"

"Better."

He thought he'd give it a try, so we walked up the avenue to the candy store. This time I ordered a vanilla and he ordered a chocolate. He said it was alright, but then he bought a Yoo-hoo to wash it down.

~ ~ ✦ ~ ~

Sitting at that soda fountain with Billy brought back candy store memories from my toddler days. Dad's silent home movies show me using the candy display rack in his store to keep myself upright while I 'stole' candy from his inventory. I was literally a kid in a candy store. To get me to eat some fruit, Dad would hand me a way-too-heavy candy apple from the box on the counter. I'd lick at the outer coating, holding the paper stick with two hands trying to keep the apple upright.

Dad's candy store in the late 60s and early 70s was at the corner of Eckford and Nassau. He had an old-fashioned soda fountain where he dished out sundaes and he made malteds with his green Hamilton Beach machine, and he made <u>lots</u> of egg creams.

I'm told that Dad was the king of the Greenpoint egg creams, and ladies would walk blocks for one of his special drinks. The legend might be true. In 2017, I stumbled on a blog post where someone asked the group members what they missed most about the old-time Greenpoint. A lady responded, "I miss the egg creams from the candy store at Eckford and Nassau, back in the late sixties." If that's the case, she would have had egg creams made by Dad. Mom says Dad always made a production when frothing up the syrup, seltzer, and milk, probably with a bit of flirting for the ladies as well.

Beyond all the sweets and drinks, Dad also sold paper goods, light bulbs, mouse traps, school supplies, and sometimes tools. Items were stacked high to the ceiling. He had to use a ladder to get customers what they needed. It was the neighborhood candy and general store. Maybe he was ahead of his time with the convenience store concept.

Back in those days, Dad's fountain counter was a hangout for the men. Dad always had a huge flat cardboard box on the counter full of cherry cheese danish and French crullers that were delivered before sunrise. The men, Pop-Pop included, would sit there on a Saturday morning, refilling their coffee and talking. (Although, now that I think about it, they may have been waiting for the numbers guy.)

Once my sister came along, Dad took a job that didn't require him to be up for work at five in the morning and not get home until after eleven at night six days a week. I don't think he ever was happy about working for someone else. Years later, we'd still stop into the store if we were passing by and needed to get something. It was at that corner, where I had my first, and only, sighting of a New York streaker. I remember it well.

Dad parked our red Volkswagen bus just off the corner of Nassau Avenue and ran into the store for a pack of Kents. It was a summer night, dusk just falling, and all the van windows were open. As Dad was headed back to the van, I heard him yell, "Don't look, Mary Lou!"

But it was too late, she'd already been mooned. A male streaker flashed in front of the van. My mom screamed and covered her eyes. Dad was laughing so hard he couldn't even open the door to get in the van. I watched as a naked butt ran up Eckford Street and disappeared out of view. Mom was not amused and could not figure out why so many people had taken to streaking through the streets in 1974.

There were a lot of streakers back in those days. They used to run across the field at ballparks. Supposedly, Yankee Yogi

Berra said something to the effect, "We couldn't tell if the streaker was male or female. They had a bag over their head." Yogi also said, "I didn't say most of the things I said," so maybe he said that, maybe he didn't. Gotta love Yogi!

Before we drove away, a lady from the neighborhood came out of the store after Dad. "Tommy, why don't you teach the new owner how to make a real Brooklyn egg cream? His are terrible, no foam!"

Dad looked at the woman, one of his longtime customers, and said, "Sorry, Dorothy. I've tried."

~ ~ ◆ ~ ~

Very few candy stores comparable to those of my 1970s memories exist anymore, not as they once did anyway. Most of what were traditional candy stores have given way to chain convenience stores. While convenience stores sell candy, these establishments can never rival an old-fashioned corner candy store. Sure, they stock candy, ice cream, and soda. Yes, they sell chips, cigarettes, lottery tickets, and even Spaldings (sometimes). But these 'conveniences' sell a whole lot more stuff that make them more not a Brooklyn candy store, than a candy store. These stores have gotten so complicated with their all-the-same merchandising that they are just too impersonal to be a candy store. In my youth, candy stores felt welcoming, were part of the neighborhood, and each store was unique in some way. Sometimes we'd walk blocks for a particular penny candy that only a certain store carried, or to get a knish that was always browned just right.

On my walk to school each morning I'd pass by three of these traditional candy stores. On the corner of North Henry

Street, just across from the park, there was a candy store – our candy store. Walking into this store, we were always eyed by the same proprietor, Nick. He always wanted to check if we had money to spend or if we were just there to bust his chops. Nick stood behind the counter, every single day, with little patience waiting for us to make a decision on what chocolate bar we were going to buy. When all we had was a single quarter to spend, it was the most important decision we might make all day. Nick, on the other hand, just wanted to get back to watching his shows on a little TV he kept next to the register.

"Come on, you kids, I ain't got all day!" he'd complain with the typical New York level of patience. Since we knew he did have all day, we tormented him.

We'd counter back, "Sure ya do, Nick, where else ya gotta be?"

He knew we were right and he had to just put up with us killing time to choose a candy. We didn't have anywhere else to be either. Nick dealt with us kids coming in three, four, or five times a day, sometimes in a single hour. We might buy a nickel's worth of candy, or a single penny piece each trip just because it annoyed him. At ten and eleven years old, we were in the store so often, Nick knew our names and who our parents were. We were his regulars, along with the men (and sometimes Nana) that showed up to meet the 'numbers' runner in the evening hours. Playing the numbers was illegal, but very commonplace in those days.

Nick's candy display case was full of our usual favorites - Snickers, Hershey's, Milky Ways, Almond Joys, and Mounds Bars. Each could be had for a quarter. We also bought a lot of

Candy Lipsticks, Chocolate Babies, Whatchamacallits, 100 Grands, Gatorgum, and the classic Reggie Bar, named after Mr. October 1977, Yankee Reggie Jackson! Besides the bars of chocolate, Nick's store had boxes of 'penny candy' on the counter. These <u>unwrapped</u> candies were open for our grubby hands to pull out a piece at a time.

My favorite unwrapped candies were the chocolate-covered raspberry jelly bars. Nick didn't sell these. For these, I'd walk up the avenue to the fancy candy store at the corner of Newell Street. This wasn't a place I went to often, since they sold special chocolates that were expensive. At this store, a pleasant lady placed candy for customers in little white boxes, tied up with a string. I could never afford an entire box of chocolates, so I'd buy a single rectangle jelly bar at a time for a nickel. I haven't tasted a bar since, that comes close to the deep rich chocolate and jelly taste of those candies I picked from that open box, in that small store on the avenue.

The regular candy stores also had big boxes of Swedish fish, the red jelly-like candy with an addicting taste. While these candy fish now come in multiple colors and are sold in little plastic packages, back then they were red, and only red, and were sold loose in an open box. I'd take handfuls and fill a small brown paper bag. Depending on the store, there was sometimes a scoop to use, but more often, we'd just stick our fingers in the box and pull out a handful, secretly stuffing our mouth full before filling the bag. The candy man would either weigh the bag or charge a quarter if we really filled it. I can recall gorging on these as a meal. Since it was fish, imported from Sweden, it must have had some nutritional value.

Between innings of whiffle ball, the North Henry gang of kids would run into our corner candy store for a sugar snack and a soda. If I had some real money in my pocket, I'd have Nick make me a malted. Back then we never called these ice cream drinks "shakes," even if there was no malted mix added.

Another of our favorite ways to cool off on a hot day, was with an ice. Nick sold real Italian ices, the kind usually found at pizza places. These ices were not the rock-hard ice in a waxed cardboard cup scraped out with a wooden spoon. These were the real deal; ice scooped from a freezer-well in the counter, cooled to just the right temperature to keep it soft and not icy. The ices came in one of only three flavors - lemon, chocolate, or cherry. The ice was pushed into small white paper accordion cups. To eat them, no spoon was needed, we just squeezed as we ate and then slurped out the melted goodness that was left.

~ ~ ♦ ~ ~

One hot summer day, between whiffle ball innings, our gang walked up to Nick's to grab some drinks. Everyone headed to the cooler and grabbed sodas. I walked up to the counter and said to Nick, "I'll take a chocolate egg cream."

"A what? You know I don't sell eggs here!"

Only ten years had passed since my dad had given up his store. Nick's candy store was only seven short blocks along the avenue from where Dad used to serve up egg creams. Yet, Nick didn't know what an egg cream was? The other guys started laughing at me as if I had lost my mind asking for creamed eggs. I paid for a Yoo-hoo and went back to our whiffle ball game thinking, "What has happened to this city?"

Later that night, I asked Dad to make egg creams. You

would have thought I had just told the old man that Jerry Vale was on his way over to sing. He ran to Busy Bee for U-Bet syrup and fresh seltzer. He was in heaven. When he returned, he went into production mode. He pulled the bag of batteries out of the freezer to make room to frost his special egg cream glasses.

After he set up the glasses on the kitchen table, he said, "Now, I don't have a real seltzer dispenser with high pressure, so this isn't exactly like the old days." My sister, brother, Mom, and I watched as he put a good amount of chocolate syrup in the frosty glasses. He added a bit of milk. Then he pumped up his seltzer siphon - it was the next best thing to a soda fountain seltzer dispenser.

He held a spoon in the glass and with some type of expert hand-sprayer motion, he choreographed the making of what he called his Greenpoint Classic Eckford Egg Cream. The five of us sat at the dining room table drinking our egg creams as if it was some special occasion.

You can still find places that make egg creams around the city, along with some traditional hold out candy stores, but they may not be around much longer.

Dad saved his fancy metal cup holders and egg cream glasses from the candy store. They were displayed in our 'china closet' as if they were silver. We used them to have fancy egg cream nights.

Dad's Greenpoint Classic Eckford Egg-Cream

- Whole milk, really cold is best. If you can't drink whole milk, don't have an egg cream!
- Chocolate syrup. Fox's U-Bet was the kind my Dad used. He always said it was the authentic syrup for egg creams. That could be because the syrup originated in Brooklyn, same as the egg cream itself. During Passover, it is made with sugar and not corn syrup. Dad always said the sugar version was better. He'd stock up on it from a Jewish deli in Queens. I also really enjoyed vanilla egg creams, made by simply substituting Fox's U-Bet vanilla syrup.
- Seltzer water. You can use pre-made, pre-bottled, store-bought seltzer, but using a soda siphon gives the seltzer more force and fizz to put a foamy head on your egg cream. If it doesn't have a foamy head that sticks to your upper lip when you drink it, it's not an egg cream.
- Tall, chilled glass, best when frosted in a freezer.
- Long spoon.
- Add a good amount of chocolate syrup to the frosty glass. Depends on your taste. Anywhere from a ¼ inch to 2 or 4 tablespoons. I don't know. I never measure, I do it by eye. Experiment.
- Add an inch or so of milk, or ¼ cup. Depends on the size of the glass you're using.
- Using the seltzer dispenser, angle it in against the spoon for the best foam. If you don't have a pressured dispenser, add the seltzer a little at a time while stirring.
- Work up a foam for an airy head by stirring vigorously.
- Enjoy!

Pinball Players

About the time I turned twelve, I started to hang out at the back of the candy store where Nick had pinball and video games. This was always a problem for Nick because one of us might have a quarter to play and eight kids would hang around watching. If everyone wasn't buying something or playing, Nick would chase the stragglers out to the street. He also suspected that some kids could pick the lock and turn the machine to free play. He was right.

After he had kicked the kids out to the street, Nick would then get annoyed that they were standing around outside on the corner. When he'd go out to chase them away, he sometimes would have me watch the counter. I was never employed there for money, but he did cook me a free knish now and then. Standing behind the register, I felt like a big shot taking candy money from kids, even if it was only for a few minutes.

As an unofficial employee, I had more privileges to hang out at the machines, even if I wasn't playing a game. That was rare though, since I was addicted to pinball and played as often as I could. Given all the hours I spent pushing flipper buttons, I never knew pinball was banned in the city from the 1940s until 1976. In 1976, I would have been eight, hardly the age to be hanging out in a corner store playing pinball. But by 1980, well that was a different story, and by then, pinball was once again legal and machines were everywhere.

In the 1940s, New York Mayor Fiorello La Guardia banned pinball in the city. The mayor saw pinball as gambling and he didn't want New York City urchins having their money stolen from them. While the ban was in place, illegal pinball parlors thrived in the back rooms of bars. What the mayor failed to realize was that city kids didn't need pinball to gamble. We gambled in broad daylight on every street corner with cards and dice. I won and lost a lot more quarters that way than I ever did playing pinball.

Even after pinball was back, we played cards on the corner for money on an overturned box, dice against a brick wall, or used walnut shells and a small rock to gamble for money. The whole setup was really a pyramid scheme. The older kids introduced us to the gambling games and took our nickels and dimes. We in turn indoctrinated the younger kids and took their pennies. It was a way to educate the youth, you might say. The gambling supported our pinball habit. Nick would reluctantly trade twenty-five pennies for a quarter so we could play.

Once the official pinball ban was lifted, the popularity of playing took off in New York City. In Nick's store he would have four to six machines lined up along the back wall. He'd rotate the machines every month or so. We played pinball machines with images of Kiss, the Black Knight, Charlie's Angels, and Sharpshooter. I would play pinball all day if I didn't have to stop to eat. It was a good thing the only LaGuardia around at that time was the airport in Queens, or the mayor may have sent me to some program for wayward youth.

Our main goal in life became getting high score bragging rights with our initials up in lights on these machines. If anyone held the high score on a machine for too many days, Nick would hit reset to give others a chance. It was bad for his business if other kids couldn't get their initials on the machine for at least a few hours. If someone was to beat a standing high score, nothing less than a Greenpoint version of Paul Revere's ride would occur. A kid would ride through the streets on his bike screaming, "Joey Picks His Nose just got high score on Galaxy!" This would spark an all-out march to the store to get high scores back. Nick's register would be ringing non-stop as everyone stocked up on Snickers, Raisinets, and Dr. Pepper to watch the showdown begin.

The one problem was that Joey Picks His Nose was pretty good at pinball and playing after him was always a cooties situation. Whether it was true or not, he acquired his nickname because some girl said she saw him pick his nose while playing left field during a ballgame. He would get teased pretty bad about it. We would make Nick give us a wet napkin to wipe the flipper buttons before we would play after Joey. Eventually, we shortened Joey's nickname to Joey P.H.N. because we couldn't be bothered with so many words. Over time everyone forgot why we even called him that, and we tired of saying the P, the H, and the N. His nickname from then on became Phin, efficiently taking the five syllables of Joey PHN down to one. Parks commissioners weren't the only authority permitted to change names!

For some reason, there was a summer Nick didn't change out Captain Fantastic after the usual few weeks. By August we played all day on a quarter, racking up nine or ten free games in a row. Some of the gang would hang out around the corner playing cards and listening to a boom box. When the shooter wanted a break, we'd rotate. We held that machine all day long for a twenty-five-cent investment.

The entire street of kids showed up to get in on the action. Jimmy, Little Joey, Phin, Nicky Nickels (his last name was Nichols but we called him Nickels because he never had a quarter to play, only nickels he traded for quarters; I always wondered how he always had so many nickels), Tracy, Four Fingers Frankie, Johnny Hydrant (he was always running home to pee), and JJ (whose grandma called him John-John, but he'd kick the crap out of anyone else who called him that), all took turns playing. If a player wasn't that good, and they started losing the free games we had racked up, Paulie or I would take over to win them back. When the sun went down and the girls came out, we gave up the machine to the smaller kids, who pretty much lost all the free game credits in less than five minutes.

The next day when we tried to repeat our success, we found that Nick had increased the point score so high, we couldn't pop one free game. We boycotted his store the rest of that day and bought our soda and candy from Jiffy a block away.

Nick came out of the store and asked, "Where'd you guys get your sodas and candy today?" He was pretty down about it. The next afternoon, Nickels came running out of the store yelling, "Nick lowered the point score back down guys!"

Our protest had worked. Even if Nick wasn't making a lot of money on the pinball, he was losing out on a lot more from his candy and soda sales if we weren't playing in his store. If La Guardia had been mayor then, he'd probably ban pinball again on account of it causing an increase in cavities.

When school started up in September, we were bummed that Captain Fantastic was no longer at Nick's. That disappointment turned to excitement when we found it had been moved to the candy store up on Driggs Avenue. The lady was pretty shocked that we were scoring free games the first time we played. We rotated in and out, playing for free until closing time. The owner didn't seem to mind too much because we kept her malted machine humming.

In addition to the candy, ices, and malteds, Nick and the competing candy stores sold knishes and really bad tasting hot dogs. Then, somewhere towards the late 70s, frozen food choices started showing up for sale in candy stores. Plastic wrapped grilled cheeses, hamburgers, and tiny pizzas could be picked from a freezer case and handed over to Nick behind the counter. Nobody, but Billy, ate these candy store convenience-foods after trying any item once.

Knishes were a different story when it came to acceptable candy store food. These delicious thick potato squares came in a box and were refrigerated, never frozen. Nick would slice one open and place it in the toaster oven on his back counter. Once the crusty edges started to brown, he'd place it on a piece of wax paper and smother one side with mustard – our choice of either Gulden's Spicy Brown or French's – and then sprinkle the other with salt and pepper. He'd slap the two halves together and hand us our golden knishes through the service window to the street. We just didn't have time to waste opening a door and taking another ten steps to go inside to place an order. This was doubly true if we were in the middle of a ball game. We'd run to the window, order, and run back to the court. When the knish was ready, Nick would place it at the window. We'd run back around the corner to Nassau Avenue between an inning to grab it.

Along with slices of pizza from the pizza places, those candy store knishes were a staple of my street food diet. That was until the day I discovered a new tasting food available from another neighborhood corner establishment.

My pinball machine.

You can take the kid out of Brooklyn, but you can't take the Brooklyn out of the kid.

The Greek's

A few days before my thirteenth birthday, Mom made a dinner I didn't care for. It probably was fine, I can't recall what she made, I was just being almost thirteen. I suspect I was being obnoxious and pushing my limits.

I sat down at the table and pushed the food around my plate. Mom asked, "Is something wrong, Tommy?"

"I don't like this." It's a good thing Dad wasn't home yet, or I would have been sitting at the table until I ate the dinner.

"Why not?" Mom asked. When I didn't answer, she said, "You don't like it, get your own dinner!"

So that's what I decided to do. I raided my piggy bank, which was an actual pink pig with a round plastic plug on the bottom, slammed the apartment door, and walked up the block. As I stormed down the street, I figured I was going to get a knish, soda, and a Whatchamacallit from Nick's and play some pinball. What I ended up eating, at the place across from the candy store, was a total surprise. Had I been given the choice before I tasted it, I would have certainly eaten whatever it was that Mom had cooked.

The September evening was warm, and the early setting sun was spreading shadows across the sidewalks. I jiggled the change in my pocket as I strolled past the grandmothers sitting in the arias. When I reached the corner, about to go into Nick's,

I noticed a sign flashing in red letters, "Open," on the opposite side of the street.

The sign was hanging in the doorway of a lunch counter my dad always called, "The Greek's." The faded sign over the front forever read "Luncheonette Fountain." I have no idea if the owners were Greek or not. I had never seen anyone going in, or coming out of the place, and I didn't know anyone that had ever eaten there. My friends and I had never even considered it. We ate at the candy stores and the pizza places, not diners, delis, or luncheonettes. At almost thirteen, I figured I was old enough to go out for a real meal, so I made a decision to skip the candy store and try some Greek food.

I stepped inside and noticed there was nobody else there, not even someone behind the counter. No lights were on. Did the name, luncheonette, mean it was only open during lunch? I stood in the doorway and looked at the line of swivel stools that were bolted to the floor. The back wall was covered in stamped stainless steel that reflected the setting sun in a kaleidoscope of rays. The rays bounced off the stainless coffee urns, to the stainless cake platters, to the stainless syrup dispensers and spread out over the faded red counter. I was about to turn and leave when a man, dressed in a white shirt, a white apron, and white pants, came out from the back room and said, "Have a seat. I'll be right with you."

Now what was I going to do? He didn't ask if I wanted something. He told me to sit.

I walked to the counter and shimmied up on a stool that would not stay still. It kept rotating me in a circle. The man with the droopy jowls, thick untrimmed eyebrows, and stubbly beard gave me a look to stop fooling around. I stuck my foot out straight under the counter to brace myself from spinning.

The place smelled like one big burger. I felt warm and I realized there were no windows open and the air conditioning wasn't running. I started to feel a little dizzy; or was that just because of the spinning stool?

The man came over and asked, "Whatcha you wanna order?" in an accent from somewhere other than Brooklyn. Since I didn't know any Greek people, he could have been Greek, I had no idea. He certainly wasn't Italian, Polish, Irish, or Brooklyn – the four nationalities I knew at the time.

I looked up at the two plastic signs that hung over the prep area listing the full menu.

Some of the wall menu from the Sunview. It was the same for years, maybe decades. Hamburger $1.15 Cheeseburger $1.25 Hot Dog $1.00	

I dropped my money on the counter and counted it. The owner watched me with a concerned look on his face.

"Hamburger please."

"You want ta' onions on that?"

Onions? On a burger? The sign said nothing about onions. As I didn't want to appear I didn't know how to order a Greek burger, I must have said, "Okay." Or maybe nodded my head instead of shaking it. I watched with concern as he dropped a humongous handful of sliced onions on his greasy grill. I started to feel a bit queasy.

The room was getting darker and darker as the sun disappeared behind the park trees. The lights he switched on were dim. The fixtures were covered in grease. The onions sizzled with a chunk of butter melting over them. He threw a thin slice of beef on the grill. The onions towered over the patty.

I thought, "How many onions was this guy going to put on my burger?"

I swung on my stool and looked out the window at Nassau Avenue. I considered making a run for it, but the stool wouldn't stay still and it swung me right back around to face the man. He frowned at me. I stuck my leg out again to brace myself.

"You wanna soda?"

I looked at the menu.

I separated the $1.15 for the burger into a pile.

I had maybe another fifty cents in change, mostly pennies.

He looked at my pitiful pile of silver and copper.

"A soda is free with ta' burger today," he said sadly. I think he was happy to just have a customer. From the fountain he filled a small glass with "Coca Cola" written on it in white letters and placed it in front of me.

"Thank you," I said and took a sip. It was flat. And warm.

"You like-a cheese on ta burgr? Just-a ten cents more."

"Okay"

He dropped more butter on the grill and placed the sliced bun on top of the butter.

I thought, "What was he doing? Butter on a burger bun? I never had a cooked bun before. What was I doing here? Onions and a cooked buttered bun? These Greeks sure have some strange food ideas." I considered if I bolted, I might make it home in time to eat whatever it was Mom made that I complained about.

He flipped the onions and the burger, wiping the spatula on his already grease-stained apron. I watched his image flick on the wall of diamond pattern stainless steel as he cooked. The last of the sunlight filtered through the smoke from the burger as it rose to the vent above. When I noticed he could see me in the stainless-steel wall, I stared down at the counter.

He peeled off the packaging from a slice of individually wrapped Kraft cheese singles and gently laid it on the burger. It was the same kind of cheese we used at home. Maybe this wouldn't be so bad. The man, who looked to be as old as my grandfather, placed the burger on one of the toasted buns and piled the onions high over the patty. He plated it on a large white ceramic plate that made the burger look lost and lonely. He placed the other half of the bun on the plate next to it. Using his fat fingers, he picked two thick pickle slices from a container on the counter and with some artistic thought gently placed them on the edge of the plate in slow motion.

I thought, "This was looking pretty good. A free soda, even if it was flat, and free pickles."

He slid the plate with the only meal he had to cook over to my spot. I hunched toward the counter, I was barely able to reach the burger from the black vinyl stool. The man slid a bottle of Heinz and a napkin holder my way.

I stared down at the pile of cooked onions covering my burger. If Mom had cooked me this meal, I probably would have stormed into my room in a tantrum, screaming that she had ruined my burger.

I shook ketchup from the glass bottle onto the stack of onions, hoping to cover up the onion taste. I balanced the top bun over the onions, wondering how I was going to get past having a buttered bun and a burger covered in onions. My right leg that was still wedged under the counter to hold my stool from spinning, was starting to cramp up.

I lifted the burger, ketchup covered onions oozing out the sides, and took my first bite. I remember thinking, "This is pretty good." I savored the next bite. The caramelized onions were not like any onions I had ever tasted. The buttered and toasted bun had me wondering how I ever thought an untoasted Wonder Bread bun was the best thing since sliced bread.

The man was dumping water on his grill, steam rising into the vents as he scraped and cleaned. He turned and asked, or rather stated, "It's okay!"

"Yes, very good," I managed to get out with my mouth full of juicy burger greatness.

He nodded and grinned, saying, "Good."

When I finished the burger, I pulled a paper napkin from the dispenser and wiped my face and fingers. The white paper turned orange from the grease. The man took the plate and had it washed before I even finished my soda. He placed a slip of paper in front of me. I looked over my first official restaurant check.

Burger 1.15

Cheese .10

Total $1.25

I put a $1.25 in change on the slip. I was too young to know about tips or complementing the chef. I slid off the stool and walked out onto Nassau Avenue where a city bus was just pulling away, bellowing exhaust. Across the street, there were shadowy figures in the park. I turned and walked home on the deserted sidewalk. The street lamps were just flickering on.

When I entered our apartment, Mom was sitting in her rocker watching TV. "Do you want me to make you a grilled cheese?" she offered in a truce.

"No. I'm good. I had a burger with onions and cheese," I answered, proud of myself.

"You did! Where?"

"At the Greek's," I said, as if I was a regular, and walked into my room.

The next week, I beat some little kids in poker to win money for more Greek burgers. I went back to the luncheonette the next Saturday afternoon and many Saturdays after that. When my friends went into the candy store for the fifth inning stretch, I went to the Greek's for a burger with fried onions. It never seemed to ruin my dinner and to this day I love a cheeseburger with caramelized onions and Heinz ketchup on a buttered toasted bun. Simple and delicious; Greek or not.

I was eating a burger there, during one of my Saturday afternoon ballgame breaks, and as was typical, I was the only one in the place. After the man finished steaming the grill, he turned on a little black-and-white TV he had in the corner. He turned the dial until he found the Mets game. He turned to me and asked, "You follow ta Mets?"

"Sure, when they're playing." He laughed, getting my joke about the 1981 player strike that lasted most of that summer.

Mets or Yankees?

The day Mickey asked me, "What team do you root for, kid?" I knew he meant baseball. Next to eating blue crab out of the river, Mickey's other favorite pastime at work was listening to baseball games. He told management his earpiece was a hearing aid. It wasn't a total untruth. The rest of us knew the wire ran to a little transistor radio in his pocket to aid him in hearing the ballgame. Mickey didn't just listen to any games, only the Mets.

I had to think about how to answer Mickey. Many New Yorkers have one team – Mets or Yankees – and would never support the other, no way, no how. I never had a problem with that; I enjoyed both the Yankees and the Mets. It might have been different if there had been a subway series while I was growing up, because then I would have been forced to choose. I liked the Yankees because of the drama. I knew more Mets stats because Dzia Dzie ALWAYS listened to and watched the Mets.

My mom was born from two Polish-Americans and we always referred to her dad as Dzia Dzie, which we pronounced ja-gee. Come to find out there is no Polish word spelled that way for grandfather, so it's just another word, like aria, I learned from my mom that she made up, I guess.

The correct spelling would have been Dziadzia, an

Americanized Polish term for grandpa pronounced ja-ja. This is a variation of Dziadek, which is the more traditional word for grandfather in Polish. We used neither of those spellings. We spelled it Dzia Dzie, on every card we ever wrote out. Wrong every time. Whether Dzia Dzie knew we were spelling this wrong, I don't know. He wasn't one to worry about such silly things. Grandma, on the other hand, that's a different story.

Every birthday and anniversary Dzia Dzie would give her a card. He'd sign them, "All my love."

Mom says Grandma complained to him one year, "Anthony, how come you never sign the cards you give me?"

"What are you talking about, Kitty? I've signed them for forty years the same way."

"You've never once signed your name. How will I know who they were from when I'm older?"

"Kitty, who else is giving you cards signed all their love?"

Dzia Dzie had a simple way of looking at things. He even taught me a simple way to add, subtract, multiply and divide while I thought we were just playing rummy. I didn't catch on he was giving me a math lesson with every game until I was much older.

By the time I was watching baseball, the Giants and the Dodgers, the last to play a subway series against the Yankees, had long left New York. Dzia Dzie told me about the excitement in the city during those games and how the subway was packed with men who wore jackets, ties, and fedoras to go see a ballgame. When I was growing up, Dzia Dzie and I always wished for a subway series between the Mets and Yankees, but that didn't happen until 2000, after Dzia Dzie was gone.

I told Mickey, "I grew up watching the Mets with my grandfather. But I also followed the Yankees."

Mickey smiled, showing a missing tooth on the left side of his mouth. Then considering my answer asked, "How can you do that? What if there was a subway series? Who'd ya root for?"

Since I didn't answer, Mickey went into a story recounting the 1986 World Series between the Mets and the Red Sox. It was a series I remembered well. The Mets came as close to losing the series as a team can with two out, two strikes, in both the bottom of the 8th and again in the bottom of the 10th. Then they pulled off a phenomenal win, extending the Red Sox's Curse of the Bambino. Even die-hard Yankee fans loved the Mets that night and were partying in the streets.

GREENPOINT AVE.

Only kids in 1970s New York City were fortunate to have two each of the major league baseball, football, basketball, and hockey teams. The Yankees, Mets, Knicks, Nets, Jets, Giants, Islanders, and Rangers were the teams of my youth.

I will not get into physical location of the stadiums because while some might not play their games within the boundaries of the "city" or even the state, it's really no different than the 49ers not playing in San Francisco or the Cowboys not playing in Dallas. And while the Bills play in New York, they are not the New York Bills, they are the Buffalo Bills. So, by this association, to me at least, all the other major league city teams were our New York City teams. (My apologies to the rest of

New York State and Jersey, but that's just the way the ball is thrown, bounces, dribbles, and the puck flies.)

In my Greenpoint, most kids were either a Yankee fan or a Mets Maniac; a Knicks fanatic or a Nets nut; they idolized the Islanders or ranted about the Rangers. This made for year-round fun, entertainment, and arguments.

Having two major league teams for each major sport was a curse at times. If both teams were playing poorly, we were doubly depressed. We had a love-disappointment relationship with our teams. We never hated our teams, we were just tough on them, as if any of us could do any better. We all had a bit of a Steinbrenner complex.

Unless I was at Dzia Dzie's apartment I rarely watched a regular season game on TV. We had no wide screen TVs or media rooms to kick back in and relax. Heck, we didn't even have a remote control. To switch between two or more games, we had to get our butts up and turn the dial. That is, if you could find the darn tuner dial. The round dial on our set would fall off and roll under the couch so often we started using needle nose pliers to switch channels. At least if those fell from the top of the TV they didn't roll.

Dzia Dzie had a remote for his TV that was the size of a brick, with the numbers one through thirteen on it. The plastic box had a long cable that attached to the TV. He could change the channels by pushing buttons. He loved his remote because for the first time he could switch back and forth between different games without getting up off the couch. I can only imagine what he would have thought of having a seventy-inch television with the ability to watch a split screen of four games at once and using voice commands to control it all.

There was no picture-in-picture on his TV. When Dzia Dzie wanted to keep up with two games at the same time, one played on the TV and the other on a radio. My grandmother hated the sound of a single ballgame blasting from the "boob-tube," as she called it, and it really annoyed her if Dzia Dzie was listening to two games at once. He resorted to watching one game on the TV, usually his Mets, and the earpiece from his handheld radio fed him the other game in his ear.

At our house we didn't have the new invention called cable TV. We had an antenna we called rabbit ears. Our TV would drop out pretty much at the most important part of any game I was watching. I'd jump up to twist and hold the ends of the thin metal tubing. Sometimes, Mom would add tinfoil in odd shapes to get a better signal; that was about as useful as Wonder Bread bags on our feet during a snowstorm. Then there were times when our console set, a beast weighing more than a city bus, which housed a meager 19" cathode ray tube, would flash, crackle, and then go completely black. When this happened, my dad would mumble at that old TV.

He'd slide the beast away from the wall to remove the very flammable piece of peg board rear panel. Eventually, he just left the back off since he tired of removing the screws every couple of weeks. I'd crawl back behind the set with him for a closer look at the electronics. The innards of the TV looked dangerous. The cavity was full of coils, wires, transformers, and lots of tubes. Finding the tube that may have blown became a guessing game. To deal with this dilemma, Dad had a box of spares stored inside the console. Not once did he get lucky and have a tube that would bring the TV back to life. More often the TV would sit dead for days as he went back and forth to the electronics store up The Avenue for different tubes. Since they wouldn't take back used tubes, he just added them to his collection. Finally, after a week, Dad would replace the correct tube and the beast would hum back to life. In the summer, no one was happier about this than Nana, since she could get back to watching *The Price is Right* and *Family Feud*, when she was supposed to be watching us.

For me, having a working TV to watch the game was only really necessary during the playoffs, the World Series, or the Super Bowl. For most all other games, I listened to a radio as we played our own game in the street. On weekends someone would bring out a boom box so we could blast a game as we played baseball with bats and mitts in the park. Full team baseball was rare because we had to have the right number of mitts for fielders since not everyone owned their own. If playing was sometimes a problem, listening to games caused other problems.

Arguments would break out over what game we should listen to (or not) – Yankees or Mets; Jets or Giants? Sometimes two radios would be going during the overlap seasons once football started in the fall and the baseball playoffs winded down through October.

These dual seasons caused a conundrum in the neighborhood. Should we bring out the baseball gloves or the football gear? The basketball or the hockey gear?

Football season opened with us all getting bruises and bloody noses. If there were nerf balls back then, we never had any. Our footballs were hard and pointed. They stung when they hit you in the chest.

In 1979, my mom was working at the Manhattan office of the Uniroyal Tire Company. She brought home a promotional football signed by Steelers Bradshaw, Greene, Harris, Furness, and Greenwood. A younger cousin of mine took it outside to play when I was at school. He dropped it, it rolled into the gutter, and into a puddle it went. All the autographs washed away.

For our North Henry football league, we'd choose teams and play two-hand touch right down the center of the street. Sometimes, we'd get crazy and we'd call, "no out of bounds" rules. We'd have players in the street, between cars, and on the sidewalk. The huddle would go something like this:

"Billy, you go down past that green Ventura, take a square right up on the sidewalk, go down two more cars cut across the street, and hide behind the van. (He wasn't going to get the pass anyway.) Jimmy, you run straight down the center of the street until you get to the Gremlin, then run up on the sidewalk, I'll throw it to you there."

The men on the block would yell and scream if the football ricocheted off their cars. We would all have to scramble, if one of us stumbled to catch a hail-Mary and banged into a car that had an alarm that would start blaring from the slightest bump. North Henry was notorious for car alarms going off at all hours of the day and night. These alarms were a novelty in the 70s and all the men needed to have one to protect their AM/FM radio with six presets in their Impala, Cutlass, or Skylark. Of course, we never ran down the block rocking cars trying to set them off all at once.

When the Yankees were hot in 1977 and 1978, parents had to break down and buy each kid a mitt. We spent a lot of afternoons in the park playing baseball during World Series fever. If we didn't have enough kids or enough time before dinner, we'd have a catch on the block. Having a catch with three, four, or more players could be accommodated with an arrangement that snaked back and forth across the street. Kids would position themselves on sidewalks, on stoops, and on the manhole cover in the center of the street. The ball would zigzag back and forth in a random pattern. It all would be great until somebody was feeling powerful and would attempt a throw they should not have, with parked cars and a street lined with large ground-floor picture windows.

A long talked about throw during the 1978 World Series between the Yankees and the Dodgers wasn't made in the Bronx or LA, but rather in Greenpoint. We were over on Russell Street playing catch with our new gloves and a hardball. Nickels was positioned on the manhole cover in the center of the street and tossed it over to me on the sidewalk. I tossed the ball to Four Fingers Frankie, who was on a stoop. Frankie's throw should have gone to Phin just up from me on the sidewalk. That's not what he decided to do.

Instead, Frankie turned, looked directly across the street, and launched a line drive at Tracy, who was standing on the top step of a stoop. On a good day that would have been a remarkable throw to get accurate. On a split decision rush throw, likely to grandstand for the high school girls sitting on a car hood, it was a disaster in the making. The ball left Frankie's right arm and we all immediately knew there was no way it was going to make it out of the aria, over the sidewalk, over the parked car, clear the street that was 2-plus car widths wide, to allow for double parking, over the other parked car, clear the sidewalk, miss the fence, rise up and into the glove of Tracy on the top step of the stoop. Who did he think he was? Mickey Mantle? Frankie's throw was more Reggie than Mantle. How did Four Fingers think he could throw a ball that far with a bent back pinky finger!

The ball made it across the aria, over the sidewalk, over the parked car, and it cleared the street. Then the ball lost steam. It skimmed off the top of an Oldsmobile, setting off a piercing alarm, and taking a bad hop. If it had stayed straight, it probably would have been delivered right into Tracy's mitt. Whether Frankie had put some English on it, or the cracked vinyl hardtop on the Olds was more to blame, we'll never know, but that ball skipped and curved to the left.

The thin pane in that ground floor window was no match for a hardball, even if thrown by a sixth grader. The ball pierced through the window like a bullet. It was the sound heard around the block. A large crack spread out from the hole to each corner of the window. Nickels, Frankie, Phin, and I all froze. Tracy, however, jumped off that stoop, ran through the gate, and bolted home. I think he thought it was his fault, as if somehow, he should have caught that ball. As he exited that aria, he slammed the iron gate behind him. Whether it was the slam or the timing just coincided, we'll never know, but the rest of the window came sliding down and crashed on the concrete in the aria.

At that moment, a grandmotherly lady appeared in the glassless window frame. A young girl stood next to her. The grandchild was pointing at the missing window and calling for someone. An older man came into view and looked out at us. The girl hadn't been calling Dzia Dzie (ja-gee) so it was foreign to me, but now that I know better, I suspect she was using the term Dziadek. Time stood still for the twenty seconds this all happened. Then the grandma yelled something in Polish. She screamed it in a high pitched, screechy soprano, carrying over the blasting car alarm. For the first time in all of those years, the <u>aria</u> lived up to its name made-up by Mom. We all took off for our home streets.

Word got around, and playing hardball on the street was thus permanently outlawed by an amendment to the block association rules through order of the Brooklyn-Burger-Meister Meister-Brooklyn-Burger. From then on, we grumbled about having to walk the half block to Winthro Park to play with a hardball. Of course, we didn't want to do that, so the gloves were thrown in the closet and we pulled out our hockey sticks and pucks. Having a slap shot contest on a city street, lined with park cars, and flanked with houses with ground floor picture windows was probably not the smartest idea to ever happen in Greenpoint.

Whiff, Slap, Punch

Whiffle ball must have been invented for city kids. Whoever gave us a ball you could take a full swing at on a city street and not break a window in a car or house should be awarded a national holiday. Or, at least, have a park named after them. Although, if we shortened that park name it'd go from Whiffle Ball Park to Whiff Park, which in the 1980s could have described every park in the city. But we didn't need a park; every side street in Greenpoint was prime real estate for a whiffle ball game. We even played inside, using the third-floor gymnasium of the St. Stan's annex. The ball would bounce off the ceiling and the gates covering the windows making playing the outfield more challenging than Fenway's Green Monster. In a move reminiscent of Fiorello La Guardia's banning of pinball, New York State in 2011 proposed legislation to add government oversight to whiffle ball. They claimed it was an unsafe game that posed significant risk of injury to children. Are you kidding me? Whiffle ball unsafe? Now playing on a city street, well maybe.

    Our preferred North Henry whiffle ball court was at the Norman Avenue end of the street, near the three-story brick apartment buildings. Since we were playing on pavement, we didn't have a ballpark, or ball field, it was a court. These buildings had two advantages for our court. First, above the third floor there was a higher than normal facade that significantly reduced the number of lost whiffle balls hit on the roofs. And second, there never seemed to be an owner that chased us from playing there. Other homeowners along the block were not as tolerant of us hoodlums hitting plastic whiffle balls off their screens and newly installed vinyl siding. Some of the older crabby ladies would sit by their windows and yell if a ball hit their house. If a ball were to drop into their aria they would yell out in broken English. "Hey ya kid, getta outta my aria! I calla the cops!" Like we were muggers or something!

This only enhanced our skills. We improved at directing our hits and outfielders improved at catching line drives. Mostly, we were quicker retrieving a ball from inside an aria, or our games coincided with the afternoon game shows the grandmas had to watch. The men, on the other hand, were more concerned if the ball hit their cars. Whiffle ball or not, they would be out on the street so fast yelling and screaming if a ball so much as grazed their car, we'd all have to scatter.

Some of the men, since I never saw any of the women drive, would run out as soon as they saw us coming with our white ball and yellow bat. "Waita minute. I mov-a my car!" It was no different than if they saw a meter maid coming on alternate side of the street parking days. Off they would speed, pulling their cars to the next block. I never understood this because there were whiffle ball games being held on just about every block north, south, east, and west, about every hour on the hour, in the neighborhood on a summer Saturday. So, these men never realized that they were getting spots because the men on that block, probably moved for a whiffle ball game whose teams were up at the candy store on their 7th inning stretch. I guess, if they couldn't see ball after ball being hit off their hoods and windshields, they figured they were safe.

For our court, we marked home plate at one end of a fire hydrant space. First base was a chalk mark near the rear bumper of the car at the opposite end of the hydrant space, or the bumper itself, depending on the car owner and if we had no chalk. To get to second base, we ran across the street, quickly checking for an oncoming car, and then ran between the two parked cars on the other side and up on the sidewalk to a marked outline of second base. If there wasn't a chalked outline of a base, that wasn't a problem, we just agreed the base was a certain crack in the cement.

Third base was down the sidewalk along the iron fenced arias. To get to home, we ran between the parked cars, checking again for oncoming traffic, and ran back across the street to step on home plate to the cheers of our team.

City whiffle ball was serious business. Entire games and amazing plays would be relived over sodas, as if we had just played the World Series. Pizza breaks were full of stories that started with, "Remember that game on July 28th, in the sixth inning, with one out and two strikes? I was on second, eating a Snickers, when Four Fingers..." The details were inconsequential but every bit could be recalled in living color.

The most memorable play I ever saw was when Ritchie was playing the outfield, which was essentially the entire street, both sidewalks, and all the arias past second base. Billy hit a high pop-up and Ritchie had a choice of letting the ball drop on the top of a car and gamble on the bounce, allowing Billy a single, or maybe a home run if the ball rolled under a car. Without hesitating, Ritchie decided to stand on the bumper to catch the pop-up. My team was cheering - until we saw the front door of Mr. Raviolo's house fly open.

"Hey! Get offa my car!"

Ritchie turned pale. I think he was just caught up in the game and had not thought about whose car bumper he was standing on. Mr. Raviolo flew down his stoop. Ritchie dropped the ball, jumped off the bumper, took off down the block, and rounded the corner to Norman Avenue. Mr. Raviolo was yelling up and down while inspecting his car. "It's scratched!" He picked up the ball and ran toward home plate. He grabbed the bat off the ground and beat the heck out of the fire hydrant. The yellow thin plastic bat crumbled and cracked in two. He then proceeded to stomp the remaining pieces and crushed the ball under his loafer.

We all stood in horror. "There! No more whiffle ball here!" he shouted and headed back inside, to probably watch the Yankee game.

The bat, being Tracy's, he yelled out, "Who do you think you are? Billy Martin!"

As we all had whiffle bats there was never a shortage of equipment to start a new game. The candy store on the corner sold official 'Wiffle' balls for thirty cents. They came packaged in a little cube box with instructions on how to throw curves and sliders. If someone hit a ball on a roof or it took a bad bounce down a sewer, it was never hard for everyone to throw in a nickel to get a new ball, especially Nickels. Even when we were short on cash, we always found ways to get more balls. About every week or so we would sneak up on a roof and collect the homerun balls by jumping from roof top to roof top.

The record number of balls collected was twenty-five. Since that was more than we figured we needed, we started dreaming of things to do with them.

"Let's hold a home run derby," said Billy.

"Nah. We'd just have to go back up on the roof and get them again," answered Nickels.

"Let's hit them over the pavilion in the park," suggested Jimmy.

"That's stupid. If they get stuck up on that roof, we can't ever get them back," sniped Tracy.

I said, "I bet I could hit one over Newtown Creek."

They all just looked at me with their mouths open. Now that was a different idea. We had never tried that before. So we had to try it. We filled a paper A&P bag with the balls and marched up to the lots at Greenpoint Avenue and then down to the edge of Newtown Creek. We found our way to a wharf, with rotted out boards, near some abandoned buildings.

We hit five balls each. Not one of us made it over the creek. We all blamed the wind. Before we knew it, we were back to no balls. We marched solemnly up on the bridge and watched until the last ball floated under on its way out to the East River.

To let Mr. Raviolo cool down, we moved the court down to the Nassau end of the block for a few weeks. The danger here was not Mr. Raviolo, but the fact that cars would turn off the avenue and give us no time to get out of the way. Kids catching pop-ups in the middle of the street were in the most danger. They always had to choose between standing their ground to make the catch, hoping the driver would stop, or jumping out of the way letting the ball drop, only to be crushed by the oncoming car. The other issue at this end of the block was the short six-foot-high fence that lined up with the outfield between second and third base. A grandmotherly lady, who we named Buster, short for Ball Buster, would sit in her yard behind the fence. She'd collect our stray balls and make us buy them back for a quarter. As this was a five-cent discount off a new ball, she had us, you could say, by the balls. If we tried to sneak in and steal them back, she'd let her dog out on us. She had a heck of a scam to support her bingo addiction. I always had my suspicions that she was Nickels' grandmother, explaining to me at least, why he always had a pocket of change. Between Mr. Raviolo, Buster, the dog, and the traffic, maybe whiffle ball was a dangerous sport!

We would hold the Greenpoint World Series toward the end of the summer. Teams came together for the best of seven games. The best players were drafted, while others were left flat to sit on the curb during these high intensity playoffs. In 1979 our street series was tied at three games apiece. Game seven was tied in the bottom of the ninth. I was on third base. We were down to our last ball. Buster was sitting in her yard, with her dog, and hoarding the balls that went over the fence earlier. It was all up to Billy, who hit a slow grounder. I had a split second to make the decision to bolt for home. There was no time to check for oncoming traffic.

Billy took off down the first base line. The play had to come home or the game would go into extra innings. Phin was pitching and headed to cover home plate. I took off from third and as soon as I came out from between the two parked cars, I was leveled flat against the asphalt. I blacked out. When I came around everyone was staring down at me. A tall girl with black hair was standing directly over my face.

She yelled, "Why don't you watch what yur doin! Look at my bike!" Her new ten speed was lying on the ground next to me. Her front rim all bent out of shape. I laid my head back on the pavement.

A few of the grandmas, who had been sitting in the arias gossiping, came "running" over. One yelled at Billy to go get my mother. I didn't want my mom coming out and banning me from playing in the street, so I struggled to my feet feeling very dizzy. Billy walked me to my house and left me at the aria gate. I went inside and laid down on my bed, probably just a mild concussion.

The end of the series was a point of controversy for days. I had never made it to home plate and I was never tagged out. Phin said that my leaving the court meant I was officially out of the baseline and thus by default was out. Billy argued there were no baselines, since we already had to swerve between parked cars to get to the bases anyway.

It was decided we had to replay the bottom of the ninth inning. During the replay game, I know I was way more careful in watching for cars and bikes when going out across the street. Jimmy was not as lucky during a game of slap.

Slap was the cheapest street ball game of all. All we needed was a pink spaldeen rubber ball and our palm. The real brand name of the ball was Spalding. I suspect our pronunciation of the name may have been due to our city accent. We had a problem, I think, with the ending 'ing' that no teacher, in the history of New York City has been able to correct in Brooklyn kids, even to the present day.

We pronounced parking, parkin as if it ended with "in." Dad would complain, "I had to go around the block eight times, there was no <u>freakin</u> <u>parkin</u> spot." Or when we were invited out to The Island for a weekend BBQ, Dad's first response would be, "Whata ya crazy? I ain't <u>drivin</u> out there. The traffic will be nuts and I'll lose my parkin spot," or during the blizzard, I remember him saying, "It's still freakin snowin!"

And so spaldeen must have been some Brooklyn adaptation to the shortening of the 'ing' ending on Spalding. Instead of it ending up as "spaldin," it became "spaldeen."

The pink spaldeen, and its blue cousin, were both staples of our handball games in Greenpoint. And slap was our all-time favorite. We spent hours playing this game since we only needed the ball and a few kids. There were no bats for the adults to destroy and the ball pretty much stayed on the court, not going into arias, hitting windows, and rarely going over fences.

As the name implies you slapped the ball to hit it. There were serious rules to this game and they differed by who was playing, what garage door we were using, and what block we played on. Closing your palm and punching the ball was an immediate out. Some kids thought they could be quick enough to pull it off and not get caught. But, if there was no painful stinging slap of the rubber ball hitting the palm, the cheater was called on it.

The pitcher would toss the ball such that it would bounce once at just the right spot in front of the hitter. Skilled pitchers could put some good old-fashioned English on the ball so that when it hit the ground it would spin away from the hitter causing him to swing at nothing but air.

At the Nassau end of our block the corner building had a three-bay garage with wooden doors we used as the outfield wall. We called it the "Brown Monster," our version of the Green Monster at Fenway Park in Boston. The object in slap was not to hit the ball over the wall, but to hit it past the pitcher and pray for a weird bounce off the doors that could turn a play from a single to extra bases.

The pitcher would stand at the curb in front of the garage. The 'batter' was across the street near the other curb. For the bases, we used chalk marks, a ball cap, or a piece of found cardboard. At the beginning of summer, we might get a hold of some old paint and at night we'd draw square boxes on the street and sidewalks for bases. The old men would complain and then spend hours scrubbing the boxes off the pavement, as if we had destroyed the neighborhood with graffiti.

The Brown Monster garage's owner had a garden patio on the roof. If the batter made a really bad swing and somehow hit the ball up into the roof garden, it was the end of the inning, or the game if we had no more balls. The owner's wife was nice, and if she was out watering her plants, she'd throw the ball back down.

However, the husband, hated us playing against his garage. If he was home, he would come out and open all the roll-up doors so we couldn't play. We had to time our games with his work schedule. If he came home and caught us playing, he'd chase us away. Usually, trying to run us down with his Impala.

Ritchie would yell over his shoulder at chubby Billy, "Run, Billy. Run. You're gonna getta Impa-lad."

It was on one of those Saturdays when the owner kept all the garage doors open so we couldn't play that Jimmy, Billy, Nickels, and I headed to the donut shop to drown our sorrows in sugar. When we hit Newell and Norman, a crew of kids were standing around. Nickels knew them from the public school and they challenged us to a game of slap. They had the best court in the neighborhood. A hydrant space was directly in front of a smooth, windowless cement wall. Across the street was another windowless brick wall. This was slap heaven.

The game was tied in the top of the ninth when Nickels took his turn at bat. We had the bases loaded. Jimmy was on first, I was on second, and Billy was on third. I know Nickels was looking to make a big play and give us a good lead going into the bottom of the inning.

I yelled at him, "C'mon, Nickels, get us some runs and I'll buy you a cruller!"

He hit a great line drive between the outfielders. The ball bounced off the brick wall and banked into a little corner. Billy and I scored easily. We were all yelling and screaming and watching Jimmy round third. He came screaming into the street headed for home. It was slap pandemonium if there ever was any. Nobody saw it coming. When Jimmy ran dead on into the passenger door of that moving Ford Mustang, he bounced backwards and fell to the ground.

The driver slammed on the brakes and ran around the side of the car. He was actually checking his door panel, as our friend was on the ground screaming and holding his leg. Billy and I ran over to check Jimmy. Nickels got right in the driver's face.

"You just ran into my friend. We're gonna sue your pants off!"

The guy was maybe thirty years old and was very calm. He said, "Technically, your friend ran into me. Look at the dent in my door, man."

By now there was a crowd gathering. The man looked down at Jimmy and said, "You want me to take you home or the hospital?"

All sorts of red flags should have went up at that suggestion, but none of us saw any. Jimmy was in agony and we all just wanted to get him some help.

"I think my leg is broken," Jimmy wailed.

Some lady yelled out, "You'd better get him to a hospital."

Why someone didn't call 911, I have no idea.

We loaded Jimmy into the backseat of a stranger's car and waved goodbye. Billy, Nickels, and I headed back to North Henry. We never did make it to the donut shop that day. We ended up sitting around on the stoop wondering if we'd ever see Jimmy again. For all we knew the guy could have dumped him in the East River. When Jimmy's dad pulled up and double parked that night in front of their house, we ran over to the car. Jimmy was in a cast and needed crutches to get around, which we all thought was pretty cool.

The spaldeen was used for plenty of other games besides slap. Punch ball was played lengthwise down the length of the block, manhole cover to manhole cover. Punching the rubber ball instead of slapping at it had the significant advantage that it would go farther and it did not sting your palm. The neurotic car owners didn't seem to mind us playing punch as much. I suspect it had something to do with no bat and the court was only the center of the street. This meant we probably hit their cars less often.

In punch there was no pitcher. The puncher would drop the ball and punch it on a bounce. For a more challenging game, the puncher had to throw the ball up in the air and punch it as it came back down before a bounce. A ball hitting a car or going on a sidewalk was out of bounds and a strike, so we were good at punching a ball straight down the block. The defensive team had an infielder and one or two outfielders. Since the field was not much wider than two car widths, the way to get around the bases was to hit the ball over the infielder as far as you could, before the outfielder could throw the ball back. The strategy to punch a ball between these fast guys in a field that was sixteen feet wide had to be planned out and took considerable skill.

Stickball was another of our street games where we needed to use the spaldeen, but we rarely played stickball on our street. Not that we didn't enjoy it. Stickball was a fun, fast-paced game. But, there were two problems. First, we had to have a stickball bat that would cost us a couple of bucks, and second, stickball was a dangerous game. If we weren't careful, friends could get injured from a flying bat, and also the angry car owners.

If someone had extra money, or we put our poker winnings together, we'd buy a bat at the Jiffy candy store. They always had a box of bats just inside their front door; some looked used.

Maybe angry men were confiscating our bats and then selling them to the candy store. It was a vicious cycle. The problem with buying a stickball bat was it was a short-term investment. These thin bats would split if we threw them to the ground after getting a hit. The only way to make them last was to gently place them down before running the bases. We never did that. After connecting with the ball we'd fling the bat and it would go sliding under a car. That was the best-case scenario. In the worst case, it would hit a player standing behind home plate or fly into the door of someone's Chevy. The owner would come flying out, grab the bat, chase us around the cars, and then either break the bat in two over the spears of an aria fence, or confiscate it.

If we had no official bat, or money to buy one, we made our own. Pop-Pop gave me a serious lecture when he found only the broom bristles, the end of a shovel, and the tines of his rake left after I sawed off the handles. He said, "Tommy, how am I supposed to sweep the sidewalk, shovel snow, or rake the garden to plant the tomato seeds?"

I replied, "Pop-Pop, it's September there's no snow and you can't grow tomatoes now," not taking into account his longer view of time.

"And what about the sidewalk?"

"Use the hose," I said, being a smart alec.

I had to work off buying a new set of garden tools. He made me paint the aria fence with a smelly oil-based black paint. It took weeks to paint all that intricate iron fencing as he inspected for drips and sections I skipped. I never sawed the tools up again.

Stoopball was another very popular spaldeen game that could be played by yourself or with one or two others. As our stoops had cement steps, we could play directly in front of our own houses. Dad would yell if I threw the ball against the front door, but for the most part he put up with stoopball. He even played now and then.

Not every stoop was the same. Stoops where the steps had an overhang were more challenging. Stoops with more steps provided more variation. It was always better to play this game at a house that had no aria, giving a much wider field. Luckily, for us anyway, the same man that owned the Brown Monster garage down the block had no aria in front of his stoop. The owner hated us throwing a spaldeen at his stoop just as much as he hated us playing slap against his garage. He had two darling daughters and must not have had any appreciation for boys playing ball.

Once again Ritchie figured something out. He "dated" one of the daughters and that gave us rights by association to play in front of their house. The girl would just look at her dad and say, "Aw, Dad, it's just a spaldeen." Then he'd let us play for a little while. Once we were older, he made sure the next generation of kids couldn't play in front of his house. He installed an aria gate and changed the wooden garage doors to roll-down metal ones that everyone knows are useless for slap games.

To play stoopball, I would wind up for the pitch and direct it at the cement stoop with as much might and force as I could. In the single player game, the objective was to have the ball come directly back at me. Missing it meant chasing it out into the street, looking for it under parked cars, or in the worst situation, watching it roll along the gutter and into the sewer before I could grab it.

In the multiplayer game, we had to get the ball past the outfielders. The strategy in stoopball was to fake out the outfielders by varying what step the ball was thrown at. The outfielders had to keep one eye on the ball and at the same time look out for natural disasters. There might be a small kid riding a Big Wheel directly into their defensive running path. These were easy to hear, the large black plastic tires vibrating over the pebbly cement sidewalk. The quick outfielder could jump over the annoying kid to make the play and catch the ball. I only recall one unfortunate time when a tike took a Puma sneaker to the side of the head when Paulie couldn't get enough height to clear the little urchin.

My sister, Jeanette, in the aria, standing in front of our stoop, ~1973. We had a great stoop for stoopball. It was smooth and there were no overhangs on the steps.

Typical Stoopball Plays:
- At the intersection of the rise and run.
- Off the front edge. Best chance for long fly ball.
- Directly off the back of a rise, sidearm style

*

The stealthy grandmas pushing their fold-up grocery carts were another natural interference to deal with. They were quiet and slow. On a brisk October Saturday afternoon, a not so nice lady, named Mrs. Flaherty, once took a direct hit. I threw the ball, and I turned as the ball ricocheted off the steps to see if it was going to get by Billy. I was surprised to see Mrs. Flaherty walking along the sidewalk. In slow motion, the ball bounced off her large bosom that was protected by her heavy fake fur coat. The fluffy fur stopped the ball dead, causing it to drop into her cart.

"That's a my ball now!" she yelled and continued on her way. What was the obsessive fetish with the ladies in this neighborhood confiscating balls?

We chipped in thirty cents, bought a new spaldeen up at the candy store, and played for another six hours before it went down the sewer. Every kid should be so lucky to have a stoopball court.

We'd spend hours throwing a pink spaldeen at a stoop, slapping it with our palm, or punching it with our fist. No other fancy equipment needed. A simple ball entertained a generation of Greenpoint youth.

Me in 1982.

Kid in a candy store, ~1969.
Dad trying to get me to eat some fruit. I don't think a candy apple qualifies.

Me on the sidewalk outside the aria during a city flurry.

I bet there are Wonder Bread bags on my feet inside those boots.

My brother Chris, my sister Jeanette, me, and our dalmatian Lady in the yard on North Henry Street.

Notice the whiffle ball bat. If a ball landed in Mr. Raviolo's yard, he never threw it back to us.

Uncle Ray, 1982.

My Great Aunt Dot in McGolrick Park near the pavilion. Around 1950.

I'm pretty sure there were no muggers around the park then.

Dad behind the counter at his candy store, about 1969.
He sold anything he could hang, stack, or tack up.

Dad and his sisters, Barbara, and Lucy.

The Pope is Coming!

I think Mickey came to work to eat more than to work. He would scrounge the water intake screens at the power plant for crabs, and volunteered for every overtime shift he could get for the free steak dinners. When we worked overtime together, he'd always page me to give him a hand with the food run. I didn't mind, since he usually had some funny joke or a story to tell. Sometimes, it was fun to see how he caused trouble.

There was a particular warm August evening, when we walked up to the lot where all the blue pickup trucks were parked. Mickey and I jumped in the same old blue truck we always used to get the takeout. Usually the keys were left in the ignition, or in the center console, or under the mat. Mickey looked in each of the normal spots, his grumbling getting a bit louder each time he came up empty.

"Check the glove compartment, will ya, Tommy?"

Did I just hear him right? He didn't call me kid!

"Nothin here, Mickey."

"Darn it." (Not exactly his words)

We tried the next truck in the line. The doors were locked. Same went for the next one after that. All of the trucks parked down the line were locked.

Now Mickey was getting sore. This meant we were going to have to walk back down to the plant entrance and sign out a truck.

"Heaven help the person who locked all these trucks up if my steak is cold," he grumped.

"I'll run down and get a set of keys, Mickey," I said.

"No. I wanna speak with the guard myself."

I walked down the hill next to Mickey with his perpetual limp slowing us down. Inside the guard shack Mickey turned from Mr. Hyde to Dr. Jekyll.

"Evening, Bill."

"Howdy, Mickey."

"Do you know why our shift truck has no keys in it and why all the rest of the trucks are locked up?"

"Yeah, the new night manager wants them locked unless signed out."

"Ya gotta be kiddin me? We're on a secure site here."

"I don't ask questions. I'm just a security guard. I do as I'm told."

Mickey shook his head. I thought I saw some steam escape from his ears.

"Well, let me have the keys to truck 11. Tommy and I gotta go pick up the food."

My head snapped quickly to look at Mickey. What was he doing?

"Do you have approval for that, Mickey?" Bill asked with some suspicion.

"Would I be askin ya if I didn't now?"

"I don't know, you usually take the old, shift truck for the food run."

"Bill, the steaks are gettin cold. I gotta get goin. Didn't you order a ribeye with steak fries tonight?"

Bill gave Mickey the once over, knowing who he was dealing with. Then he looked at me. I just nodded my head up and down, maybe to corroborate Mickey's statement, maybe just to say, "Nice night, Bill, huh?"

Not one to miss a meal on time, Bill turned and took down the key off the hook. Truck 11 was no ordinary company pickup. That truck was for management. They used it to drive down to meetings in White Plains. The white truck was always spotless. Why they had to have a truck we never knew; they never had any tools, parts, or gear in the bed of the truck. Compared to the blue working trucks that were dented and rusted on the outside, and greasy and smelly in the cabs, the supervisor's truck was a limousine. I heard they had air conditioning and an FM radio. I couldn't believe Mickey was thinking about driving their truck.

Back outside, I said in a low voice not wanting to arouse suspicion, "Mickey, we can't take number 11, that's management's truck."

"What time is it, kid?" I was demoted back to kid.

I looked at my watch. "It's 6:30."

"You ever seen management 'round here at this time a day?"

"Well no. But the supervisor might use it."

"Really, kid? That guy is gonna sit at his desk until we're back with his food. He ain't goin anywhere."

We walked back up to the top lot, Mickey whistling some tune I could tell was an Irish lullaby. He unlocked his door and hit the power lock button to let me in. Power locks? Who did these guys think they were?

The tan seats were immaculate. Not a coffee or ketchup stain on them. There wasn't a spot of dirt on any of the floor mats. There were no empty Styrofoam coffee cups rolling around. The two-year-old truck still had that new truck smell.

Pulling out of the lot, Mickey kicking up gravel with the big 350 engine, he slowed but didn't stop, as he drove by the guard at the gate. He gave the watchman a wave of his hand. I slid down low in my seat.

Mickey, noticing I was trying to hide, grumped, "What were ya an altar boy or sometin?" He laughed as if there was no possible way that could be true. Well, I was at one time, but I wasn't going to answer his question.

GREENPOINT AVE.

The altar boy program at St. Stan's Catholic school was close to a fraternity. It was an all-boys club. We all went to the same school, were about the same age, we hung out together, went bowling together, ate pizza together, and caused trouble together.

Fr. Ted was our altar boy advisor. His number one commandment was that we had to be at the church thirty minutes before Mass started. Once we checked in with the priest, we'd head down to the altar boy gowning room to get ready. St. Stan's had a huge dressing area for the altar boys. I've been in high schools with smaller locker rooms. We had closets full of different size robes and waist ropes in all sorts of feast day and holiday colors. Back in the heyday, there might be four or six of us serving with each priest. With that many boys with time on their hands, there's bound to be trouble, altar boys or not.

There wasn't much to getting ready as far as being an altar boy was concerned. We basically pulled a robe over our head and tied a long rope around our waist to go from resembling a Halloween ghost, to something respectable to be on the altar. The most difficulty I ever had was adjusting a waist-rope that was too long. Once we were ready, we'd sit on the bench and talk. It was mostly a social time. We didn't go up to the sacristy early since the priest was getting ready and we had to be silent. It was better to stay in the basement and horse around. If we were too loud, Fr. Ted would come down and tell us to be quiet. He never was mean, just stern and we all respected him. He wasn't one for letting anyone be out of line, and he had a way with words. His words weren't just for the altar boys either.

On Sundays, Mom required our family sit in the front row in the 'basement' church. We always went to the English Mass held in the downstairs of St. Stan's, because none of us could speak a lick of Polish, and the upstairs Mass was celebrated in Polish. Sitting us in the front pew was Mom's way of making my sister, brother, and I behave for forty-five minutes. Before I was old enough to be an altar boy, or when I wasn't serving, we always sat in the first pew on the right side.

The other reason we went to the 10 a.m. Mass was because Fr. Ted usually had that time slot. Nobody was allowed to get out of line at <u>his Mass</u>. If one of us kids so much as whispered, all Mom did was point a finger in Fr. Ted's direction (hidden behind the front of the pew, so Fr. Ted couldn't see her). That simple motion was enough to remind us to behave.

Fr. Ted never had to have a talk with our family about

behavior, which is a good thing, because Mom would have been so embarrassed we would have had to move to Jersey. You see, Fr. Ted didn't wait until after the service to lecture a misbehaving parishioner. No, Fr. Ted preferred to take care of things in real time.

The Talksalotski family also sat in the front row, directly across the center aisle. We sat on the right side of the church, they sat on the left, every Sunday. If we arrived late and some other family was in 'our' pew, Mom would just march us right out and we'd have to come back early to the noon Mass so that we'd have the front row. Being late, really put a kink in having fun on Sunday afternoons.

While Mom was smart to make our family sit in the front pew to have well-behaved children at Mass, she was also pretty shrewd. By taking the right side of the church that meant Mrs. Talksalotski had to seat her kids on the left side, right in front of the pulpit where Fr. Ted read the Gospel and gave his homily. The Talksalotski's were in the direct line of sight of Fr. Ted the entire time he stood there.

It was during one of Fr. Ted's homilies when little Bobby Talksalotski (I really have no idea what their names were, but it's a true story), was fidgeting and getting restless. He was pestering his mom for something. I kept peering around Mom's pregnant belly to see what all the racket was. She kept giving me the eye to ignore it and not bring any attention our way. I was trying to concentrate on what Fr. Ted was saying but Bobby was being very distracting; but not as distracting, or as loud, as the lady in the second pew who kept "shushing" little Bobby. At her last forceful "shhh," Fr. Ted couldn't continue, something had to be done.

In those days, priests didn't wear wireless mics under their robes and if they walked away from the pulpit microphone, people in the back couldn't hear them. On this day it didn't matter, I think people in the upper church may have been able to hear Fr. Ted. He didn't scold Bobby; he was just a child. He didn't scold Mrs. Talksalotski, as she was doing a fine job bringing six children to church each Sunday. No, Fr. Ted stopped his homily, which that morning was about patience, and walked off the altar and spoke to the "shusher" lady. Even Bobby paid attention to his message about the importance of being quiet in church. As he lectured, he used his index finger, not in a direct line scolding but more of a hook, as if he was pointing off to the side. Mom never had to tell us to be quiet and still again in church, and that's why all she had to do was hook her index finger in Fr. Ted's signature motion.

In the afternoon over rye bread and butter, Mom told Grandma about Fr. Ted's tirade. I remember Grandma saying, almost singing, "Patience is a virtue, virtue is a grace, and those that don't have it, have a bulldog's face." Did she mean Bobby or the shusher lady had a bulldog's face? She couldn't have meant Fr. Ted – could she? Not Grandma!

Grandma also had other sayings she'd spout to teach us a lesson. Her favorites were, "Can't means won't," and "Your face is gonna freeze like that." And when I was older and a bad 's' word slipped out when I hit my thumb with a hammer, she'd say, "You kiss your mother with that mouth!" I'd reply with, "And my grandma." She thought her daughter was raising really sassy kids.

When I was older and I became an altar boy, I always respected Fr. Ted. He was always nice to us altar boys and usually was very patient. It's not that the nuns weren't nice, but they were the disciplinarians, and carried rulers to prove it. Fr. Ted had a different style to maintain discipline. So when Paulie came down into the altar boy dressing room all excited over his latest discovery, I immediately wondered what Fr. Ted would do if he found out.

"Hey, guys, look what the candy store is selling!"

In one hand Paulie held an over-sized straw. I figured he had ideas for monster-size spitballs. In class, each morning after our milk snack, we would use the straws to shoot spitballs at one another while Sr. Elizabeth was writing fractions on the blackboard. The girls would tell on us because they didn't want to use recess time to clean up the salivary wads of paper.

Then I noticed in the other hand Paulie held a bag of beans. The candy store was now selling beans?

Seeing the look on my face, he explained, "It's a pea shooter!"

I had never used a pea shooter before because Mom was overprotective with these sorts of toys. She'd say, *"You'll shoot your eye out. N.O."*

Paulie put a pea in his mouth, lined up the straw, and blew a pea at high speed right at Peter. Luckily, Peter was wearing his robe already and he never felt it. But then Paulie just became a human machine gun. He was shooting peas all over the place and laughing hysterically. Then he began shooting at the metal lockers. Ping. Ping. Ping.

I screamed in a whisper, "Quit it! Fr. Ted is gonna hear!"

Paulie stopped for a second. Considering what I said, he aimed for a duller sounding target. Our heads. Within minutes, the floor was covered in peas. Peter had had enough and threw off his robe and disappeared up the stairs. I thought maybe he went to get Fr. Ted. I should have known better, even altar boys wouldn't rat on one another. Meanwhile, I tried to plead with Paulie.

"Fr. Ted is going to hear and come down here any second. We need to clean this up!"

It was no use. Paulie had a bag of a thousand peas and he was going to shoot them all. Jimmy covered his head with another robe to keep from getting beaned. I grabbed one and did the same. The attack went on for five minutes with Paulie shooting at us under the robes. Then Paulie yelled in pain.

"Ouch! What didya do that for?"

"How'd you like it!" said Peter.

"You shot me right in the ear," whined Paulie.

I lifted my robe to see Peter loading more peas into his mouth and now shooting at Paulie. He had run around the corner to the candy store and bought his own weapon. How in the heck candy stores thought it was a fine idea to sell these, so called toys, to boys I'll never know. But some of these stores also sold twelve-year-old kids cigarettes, so I suspect the owners didn't have a lot of concern for health and safety.

Now that Peter was in on the fun, Jimmy and I were the odd men out. Pretty soon, Peter and Paulie realized they could attack the unarmed and not get shot back. I bolted up the steps and out the side door getting blasted in the back with peas. Jimmy followed.

"Where ya goin?" asked Jimmy.

"To get a pea shooter!"

I had never left the church wearing one of my altar server robes before, but here we were, Jimmy and I, rounding the corner of Humbolt onto Driggs Avenue, in an all-out sprint, headed for the candy store. Preparing for a crusade, I grabbed a bag of peas. I twirled back around to the shelf and grabbed a second bag - to have extra ammo. It was a good thing I had cash - I had the change envelope for the Patron sales under my robe. Don't worry, I was going to pay it back with my tip money. The Patron, our church bulletin back then, cost ten cents. The altar boys would stand outside every exit of the church extorting a dime from leaving parishioners. Anybody that was anybody, gave us a quarter. Although, come to think of it now, that extra fifteen cents may have been a church donation and not an altar boy tip.

Ya'd think the lady behind the counter at the candy store, who could see the church from her cash register, might have asked, "What are you two altar boys going to be doing with these pea shooters?" She didn't say a word. She just took our money and went back to her crossword puzzle and puffing her Virginia Slim.

When we reached the alley along the side of the church, I stopped Jimmy.

"We need to sneak down there and get the jump on them. We need to partner up. Okay?"

"Okay, Tommy," he said.

The plan never had a chance. Peter and Paulie had already decided to partner up and they jumped out from behind the rose bushes next to the church rectory, pea shooters a blazin. We were under attack and bad. We hadn't even opened our bags of peas yet. I jumped behind a statue of the Holy Mother, hoping she was already praying for us sinners, and tried to open my bag. Poor Jimmy was standing in the courtyard taking full fire. My first bag of peas tore open and spilled all over the base of the statue and onto the ground. Good thing I bought the extra bag.

When I pulled my second bag open, I let Paulie have it. By now we were getting pretty carried away; we were laughing and yelling as if we were in a park. We had forgotten we were outside the church while a Sunday Mass was going on inside. Out of the corner of my eye, I saw the side door from the church open and someone stepped out. I turned, thinking it was just another enemy to fire upon, but it was too late to stop the pea that left my shooter and hit Fr. Ted square in the belly section of his black shirt. Peter and Paulie tried to conceal their shooters and bag of peas, pretending to be totally innocent bystanders. Jimmy was just standing there with the shooter still in his mouth and a bag of peas in his hands. When he saw Fr. Ted, he took a breath and swallowed a pea. He coughed it back up onto the sidewalk. It rolled to a stop at Fr. Ted's feet.

Fr. Ted said, "Peter, Paul, James, and Thomas!" (It was in the same tone as, "Holy Mary, Mother of God). He raised his right hand and with a curved index finger pointed us back inside and down into the altar boy dressing room. When he saw the floor covered in more peas, he gave us a lecture on safety, respect, and wasting food. After Mass we had to clean up every single pea inside and out and then we had to wash them. Later he asked where we had bought the peas and shooters. I suspect the candy store lady may have been given a view of Fr. Ted's index finger. But then again, where would he buy his cigarettes if he lectured her?

It was around the time of the pea shooter incident that the parishioners clogged the corner of Humboldt and Driggs Avenue. Without the blessing of the NYPD and no blue police barricades, the faithful had shut down the streets. All of Greenpoint had a special holiday that October of 1979. Throngs of parishioners stood on the front steps of St. Stanislaus Kostka Catholic Church gazing south towards the Brooklyn Queens Expressway (BQE), which no one could see from where we stood, but it was out that way somewhere. There had been rumors that the Pope might make a stop at St. Stan's on his way to Shea Stadium to say Mass.

When Karol Józef Wojtyła was elected Pope, it was rumored he wanted to take the name, Pope Stanislaus I. As the first non-Italian Pope in 455 years, his advisors convinced him that the name Stanislaus was not a "Roman" name – go figure. He instead took the name John Paul II.

Based on the rumors the Polish Pope might stop at his almost namesake church, Mom dragged me up to Driggs Avenue with hopes of seeing the Pontiff. The altar boy fraternity pushed closer to talk.

"Did you get in trouble from your mom because of the peas?" asked Paulie.

"Ya know, I don't think Fr. Ted said anything to her," said Peter.

"Mine either," I said.

"He's pretty cool," said Jimmy.

I stood on the base of a light pole, which only put me at the shoulder height of the men. There was nothing I could see, and nothing to see anyway. Fr. Ted was standing on the front steps of the church and when he caught my eye he gave me a crooked index finger that I took to mean, "Good to see you. I am sure you will behave, and no peas," all in one shake.

Standing on the light pole, I was caught up in the excitement of the crowd. The parishioners were jubilant because ten years earlier, when he was a Cardinal, the man who was now Pope had visited the parish. Grandma, who was standing beside us, told us how she remembered attending the Mass said by Cardinal Karol. This naming confused me. He was Karol, wanted to be Stanislaus, settled for John Paul II? Was this something like I was Thomas, wanted to be Superman, but answered to Tommy? I didn't realize, at the time, that Popes started taking more common names back in 533AD.

The original names of the Popes are quite uncommon. For example, Pope Leo XII was originally **Count Annibale Francesco Clemente Melchiore Girolamo Nicola Sermattei della Genga**. That's one long name! No wonder he chose Leo. Even modern-day Popes have unique names. Take Pope Francis, whose given name is Jorge Mario Bergoglio. What a great name! Why change it? We could have called him J.B.

Why is it there has never been a Pope whose given name was Paulie (Paul), Tommy (Thomas), or Jimmy (James)? Are these names destined to rise only to altar boy or apostle status and no further? Even Saint Peter, was originally Simon, or Simeon.

The papal itinerary noted that the Pope would travel through Brooklyn on his way to Shea. The Greenpoint faithful of 1979 were hopeful that Pope John Paul II would make a second visit to their parish as Pope, even if with just a wave from the limo.

Men lined Humboldt Street, within shouting distance of one another, all the way up to McGuinness Boulevard watching the BQE for the motorcade traveling from the city. If the Pope's caravan exited the highway, their plan was to relay a signal down to the church, somehow faster than a police-escort with sirens blasting. How did they figure this was going to work?

A pair of walkie talkies might have been more useful for such a mission, rather than trying to shout over a siren coming from an NYPD motorcycle, especially since CBs were all the rage in 1979. That's about when men started installing CBs as must have equipment in their cars. In the evenings, after dinner, the men of North Henry would sit in the front seats of their parked automobiles, smoke, and talk on their CBs. This, it appears to me, was the start of the downfall of the evening aria conversations, with each CB station the precursor to the first chat rooms.

Channel 9 was usually the police. If people started talking on it, they were quick to remind everyone to clear off. Maybe the other channels were reserved for discussions about sports, politics, or gossiping about women. I have no idea. My CB was a cheap base station, with a pullout antenna that had limited ability to pick up anything more than twenty feet away. I'd sit for hours near the front window waiting to catch a piece of a conversation over the airways. The best I could do was if Billy was down on the street in front of our aria with a walkie talkie and we could talk with the window closed. That wasn't very useful, since I could have just opened the window to talk to him.

"Whatcha doin?"

"Standin down here in the street talkin to you! What's it look like I'm doin?"

This pretty much lost its appeal after a few exchanges. I'd shutdown and put the batteries back in the freezer.

Four Finger Frankie's older brother Robbie had a van with a more elaborate CB setup. His antenna was massive and could probably intercept Russian intelligence. Robbie was always "working" on his van. He had installed door-to-door shag carpet and fake leather trim that we'd sniff as he glued it on. Robbie's mom had a base station in the house and she'd use it to call him in for dinner. Working in his van, he'd keep the sliding door open and we'd hear her calling, "Mom to Robbie, Mom to Robbie, time for dinner. Come back."

One afternoon when he was "working" on his van and Mary Angelica was "helping" him, they had the door closed, and his CB malfunctioned. Mrs. Budinski was getting no response so she schlepped herself out to the van wearing her housecoat and slippers to tell him the pierogi were ready. She was obviously not aware of the common Greenpoint courtesy we gave van owners, "If the van's a rockin, don't come a knockin."

Not only did the CB malfunction, but Robbie and Mary Angelica, in the heat of the moment, or maybe from the incense they were using, had forgotten to lock the sliding van door.

Sitting on the stoop near the candy store, I saw Mrs. Budinski headed to the van. I poked Jimmy, "Isn't Robbie in the van with Mary Angelica? This is gonna be good."

The scream from Mrs. Budinski was so loud, it could have been heard above the roar of the Pope's motorcade.

Given the reliability of CB technology, the men of St. Stan's were probably right to form a human relay team for the message. It didn't matter; the Pope stood up St. Stanislaus and kept right on going to Queens. Maybe the church should have renamed itself Church Johnny Paulie, or something more Roman to get his attention.

Twenty-six years later, and 4,000 miles from Greenpoint, I found myself closer to this Pope than on that day in Greenpoint. Unfortunately, it was a sadder time.

St. Stanislaus Kostka Church, Brooklyn, New York. The corner where I stood on the light pole base waiting for the pope to arrive.

We Lost Mom - in Rome

If Pope John Paul II wouldn't come visit us at St. Stan's, we'd go to him. It would just be decades after we had waited for him at the corner of Driggs and Humboldt.

Our trip was planned months in advance. I arranged to meet my mother and youngest brother, Nick, for a week in Rome. My flight was to arrive from Germany, a side excursion to Italy on the way home from a business trip. Mom and Nick were flying in from New York. To say Mom was excited would be an understatement. She reminded me of a six-year-old going to Disney World. Mom had even ordered tickets to be part of the weekly Papal audience.

In Frankfurt, the morning of my flight, I awoke to the news that Pope John Paul II had passed away. By the time I landed in Rome's Leonardo da Vinci airport Sunday morning, the third of April 2005, it was an outright fiasco. Italians were hugging and crying in their espressos. Every traveler was glued to the television monitors that were tuned to different Italian TV stations covering the Pope's passing. Images of John Paul II flashed on the screens. His many pilgrimages around the world were being hailed by reporters who recounted his remarkable life, including the last twenty-seven years as pontiff.

While waiting for Mom's flight to land, I survived without a French cruller and enjoyed a perfect cappuccino with a warm chocolate brioche at the airport bar. (Why is it, that in Italy, even food at the airports and highway rest stops is amazing?)

"People will come from all over the world to Rome. They are already pouring in," claimed a broadcaster from somewhere in the airport. He reported that airlines were running out of seats and hotels were selling out as far as Florence. We were already here, but I hoped we'd still have a room waiting for us. I had no idea what the protocol might be for a papal funeral in this eternal city full of interesting history and annoying quirks. Would we be sharing our flat with a contingent of arriving priests or be quartered with guards from Switzerland?

In the taxi on the way to our rental, the driver was speaking faster Italian than I could understand, especially, since Mom was poking me in the ribs telling me to tell the driver to slow down. The digital readout of his C class was showing 110.

I asked him in English, since there was no way I could piece together the question in Italian while trying to explain to Mom that 110 km/h was 68 m/h, "Do you know when the funeral will be?"

"Si potrà visitare martedì, mercoledì e giovedì, e il funerale sarà venerdì." (Visitation would be Tuesday, Wednesday, and Thursday. The funeral would be Friday).

He zipped us from the airport to our rental apartment in record time, all the while complaining about the traffic. "Ora il traffico sarà ancora peggio!" (Now the traffic will be even worse). He may have been worried about the traffic, but I was worried about our holiday, what terrible timing. Was this bad form on my part? I couldn't express that to Mom, for she was now in Rome for the Pope's funeral, a place where millions and millions of faithful would want to be right now.

After we checked in at our B&B, close to Piazza Navona, the first thing my mom wanted to see was St. Peter's. As we walked, the passing of the Pope was already overshadowing everything in Rome. The bars along the streets had their TVs tuned to the news. Soccer could wait. People were crying into their cell phones. We crossed over Ponte Sant'Angelo to people sobbing under the shadows of angels.

I was walking at a brisk pace to get close to the portico and getting impatient with Mom for taking her time. A lifelong devout Catholic, Mom was on her first pilgrimage to Rome and she deserved the time to take in the space and to process the immensity of it all. She was admiring the architecture and observing the Italians. I had forgotten how I felt on my first trip here and how every little detail was something to absorb. Right then I heard Grandma whisper, "Patience is a virtue; virtue is a grace."

Mom wanted to stop in all the little stores that sold Christian relics, books, and statues of popes and saints. I knew that every one of these stores were selling slight variations of the same stuff. It's the same as Times Square, every store sells t-shirts with "I Love New York," and "NYPD" on them; just pick one and move on. Here the shops sell postcards of the Vatican with scenes from St. Peter's, imitation marble statues, religious books in multiple languages, and challises in gold and silver displayed behind locked glass cases. Evidently, even visiting priests are not immune to buying souvenirs from the land of the Holy See.

Knowing we would be back the next day to visit the Vatican Museum, I wanted to do a quick walking tour through the area and then find a place for a thin crust pizza that served a good table wine. Mom instead dragged us into a small corner store to examine rosary beads. I think I mumbled a choice word.

At that moment, I heard Grandma whisper a second time, "Patience is a virtue, virtue is a grace…" This made me slow down. I began to notice that the people sitting on the sidewalks crying were not the homeless, but the popeless. I noticed those wandering the streets were not tourists, but Roman mothers pushing baby carriages towards the square. I noticed the tears in Mom's eyes. It was joy and sadness all at the same time.

We walked along Via della Conciliazione, the wide obelisk lined street leading to St. Peter's. I feared everything was going to be locked up tight. At Piazza San Pietro, the mourners were already gathering. Some were holding candles and others were on their knees praying. The Pope was not yet lying in repose, so those going into the Basilica were there to see the church. Knowing this might be the one and only time Mom would have to see St. Peter's Basilica, we decided to get in line.

The line to enter the largest Catholic church on the planet was longer than I had experienced on any prior visits. Security was extra tight. Our bags were inspected and we had to pass through metal detectors. I suspect these measures were post 9/11 additions, maybe with some added diligence for the passing of the Pope. I began to get agitated again. Why couldn't people have their bags open and ready for inspection? Grandma's voice came a third time finishing her rhyme, "And those that don't have it, …."

Once inside, we stopped at The Pieta, my favorite Michelangelo sculpture. I lingered admiring the sculpture longer than Mom even had patience for, and she started to walk down the aisle. (Hey, Grandma, how about a whisper to Mom?)

Nick and I followed to keep her in sight. The distance from the entry doors to the altar is a long walk, but as the staff were already preparing for a Vatican State funeral, the center aisle was only open at the rear of the church. We stood there for a moment in silence. Knowing St. Stan's would fit in a small section of St. Peter's is humbling. I was in awe considering the generations of men who worked more than one-hundred years building the great basilica by hand. It is miraculous.

On this day there was no walking at will and wandering into the side alcoves to admire the statues was not permitted. Along with all of the pilgrims in the church, we were directed through barriers along the right side, in one direction only. Mom didn't seem to notice, because she was living in the moment. The interior of St. Peter's has always felt cool to me, no matter how hot the day. Maybe it was the mood, or the overcast damp April afternoon, but it felt cooler than ever. Barely any lights were on and the somber darkness started to hit home. Suddenly, I wanted to move through the space as quickly as possible. I needed a brighter location.

After what seemed to be an hour, filing slowly through the barricades, we reached the main altar where Mom knelt and prayed. She lingered a long time. That was understandable; she was realizing a lifelong dream. She should have been able to kneel and pray the rest of the day if she wanted. Nick and I decided to walk behind the Papal Altar to explore. By the time we circled around, there was an older man with a long gray beard, dressed in all black, kneeling where we had left Mom.

Nick and I looked at one another and started through the crowd. We snaked through the barricades being pushed along in the current of visitors.

Nick said, worry in his voice, "Where's Mom?" We had misplaced an almost senior citizen inside a very large crowded church, in a city she was unfamiliar with.

Nick and I were not in control of where we were going. There was no allowance to go backwards to retrace our steps. Security and Swiss Guards enforced the one-way traffic. We were dumped out on the far side of the square in a torrent of tourists, mourners, and pickpockets. Turning to go back inside, two Swiss Guards in their colorful Michelangelo-designed uniforms, didn't have to say a word to us. We knew we were not getting back in that way. Nick and I looked at each other, and did the only thing we could do, we went to get an espresso.

We paid "extra" for our three ounces of coffee so we could sit at a table. We were hoping Mom might just wander by. I was a little worried and not sure what to do next. But why should I be? She was a New Yorker. If she could navigate the city subway system, she should be able to find her way back to the rental apartment. Then I thought about it a bit more. She didn't have a cell phone. Had I even given her the address? Finishing our second espressos, a side of Disaronno with mine, Nick and I decided we had better head back to the apartment and wait.

As the hours passed, Nick fell asleep and I watched an Italian TV game show with curvy Mediterranean women in bikinis. I love Italian TV. I eventually fell asleep and had a dream about the time I was not so lost in New York.

GREENPOINT AVE.

My family didn't do a lot of outdoor things growing up. We never hiked up a mountain, or went camping, or did a backwater canoe ride. Our outdoor times were spent in the aria, the yard, the park, and at my grandparent's country house.

To learn about how to survive in the wild, I joined the boy scouts. We had den meetings and worked on our merit badges all in the safety of our Brooklyn apartments. When our scout troop voted to go on an overnight camping trip, I was ecstatic. Finally, I'd have a night in the wild sleeping under the stars. Mind you, I was in maybe sixth grade at the time so this was a big deal for a city kid.

Our small troop, of five boys, was combined with other troops from Greenpoint and Williamsburg. I had visions of the Flintstone Boy Scout Jamboree. There would be scouts camping in a huge open field, bigger than Central Park, surrounded by mountains, with white scout tents as far as my eyes could see. We'd have huge bonfires and scouts from all over Brooklyn, maybe New York, no, the world, would be there singing Old MacDonald in their own languages. (Why did Fred and Barney choose *that* song?)

I didn't realize my unit would be shipping out by boat until Dad and Mom dropped me off at a terminal on the Hudson. The scout troops filed on the huge craft in military marching order, two by two, knapsacks and sleeping bags over our shoulders. We stood on the deck and waved our red bandanas to our crying mothers as our vessel headed out to sea. When the boat docked, it felt as if we had been at sea for hours. After being given instructions, we disembarked in orderly fashion and marched into the woods. My troop was on the lookout for Russians. We had to stay on a path that was lined with a wooden boardwalk. To the left and right of the boards was quick sinking mud that a scout could fall into and end up in China (or so we teased one another).

We arrived at the camping site after hours (six minutes) of hiking through the mosquito infested woods (a State Park). I took a look around. Where were the scouts of the world? Where was the field? Where were all the tents? None of it was there. Instead, we had three log cabins arranged in a semicircle, each with a screened-in porch. In the center of it all was a small fire pit. (I thought it was very cool).

To choose cots we played rock, paper, scissors. Then we looked around the cabin. Not much to see. Then we said, "So now what?" We had three hours before what the scout master called, "chow time," and I was bored. I wandered off following the wood planks deeper into the woods.

After an hour's walk (5 minutes), and a few turns on the boardwalk, I knew I was lost. Now what? I kept following the planks hoping to find civilization. This was no way to die. At least I'd be buried in my scout uniform.

Walking for another hour (3 minutes, I was just about running by that point), I happened upon a trader's cabin (a camp candy store). I bought a candy bar, a soda, and a pack of baseball cards and sat on a log (a park bench) next to the lake (a frog pond the size of a pool).

I evaluated the cards in the pack. I cracked the stale piece of hard pink gum in two and slid it into my mouth. Then I heard the noise. It sounded as if the entire Soviet Army was on the march, headed my way. I looked around for a place to hide. But wait, were they singing? Yes, they were. They were marching and clapping while singing Queen's *We Will Rock You*. It was a far cry from Fred and Barney leading a sing along of *Old MacDonald*, but it was music to my ears, I'd been found!

The rest of the troop came marching around the bend. I was lectured for going to the camp store ahead of the rest of the gang. We had hot dogs for dinner and s'mores by the fire. The next morning, we marched to the boat and went home to have lunch and take a shower.

During that camping trip, I thought we were way out in the woods, somewhere far from the city. Within the cover of the trees, I couldn't see any buildings or skyscrapers. Being 'lost' on that plank trail, even if I wasn't really lost, was a bit unnerving. There were no sounds I was used to. No squealing buses. No cars honking. No grandmas yelling from a second-floor window for kids to come in for dinner. It was a different experience to be in a strange land. I found out years later, we had simply taken the Staten Island Ferry. The cabins in the woods were no more than five-hundred yards from the road.

GREENPOINT AVE.

When the bell rang, I jumped up. I answered the intercom, "Chi e?" (Who is it?).

"It's your Mother!" She didn't sound too happy. I buzzed her up.

I waited by the 3rd floor door. I could hear her coming up

the marble steps. She paused at the first landing. This was at a time when she was still smoking half a pack a day. Then her steps continued. She paused at the second landing. When I heard Mom starting up the third flight, I placed a book in the door and went back inside. She was probably in no mood and I didn't want to find out about her patience, virtue, or grace.

I woke Nick and we were standing by the sink when she came in.

"Very nice. You just leave your own Mother in a strange city. Very nice."

She was wet. To make matters worse it had started to rain on her way back.

Nick spoke first. "We looked for you, where'd you go?"

"I knelt down for a few minutes to pray. When I turned around, expecting you to be waiting, you were gone. You couldn't wait two minutes? Now I know how Jesus felt at Gethsemane."

I guess it's a good thing she didn't walk in and catch us both napping.

I said, "I'm just glad you found the apartment. I wasn't sure you had the address."

"Lucky for me I had a scrap of paper with the name of the place written down. No address. A nice Italian policeman was kind enough to call it in and gave me the address and directions. He could not believe my two American sons had left me stranded. Especially when he found out our name was Carbone!"

She threw her wet coat over a chair and continued, "The two of you have no patience. You should both say a prayer. You know your grandmother had a saying, *Patience is a virtue, virtue is a grace, and those that don't have it, have a bulldog's face.*" And with that she stormed into the bathroom to re-do her hair. That's when I noticed that she couldn't have been too distraught wandering around Rome. By the doorway she had put down three bags filled with rosary beads, medallions, and books. In the bags I also noticed a scontrino (receipt) for two cappuccinos and a brioche. She had evidently made good use of her walking tour of the city center.

Mom eventually softened up again. Waiting in line that night to get into a pizza place, she told us how she enjoyed her time in St. Peter's. She recounted the inner details of the church, the shops, and the streets she walked.

On Monday morning, we again walked across Ponte Sant'Angelo. As we turned along Piazza Pia, I thought we were in New York. The American news media had platforms setup along the wide street with their cameras trained on the basilica. All the major networks and cable stations were there. We watched as our typical TV hosts from NBC, CBS, and ABC delivered broadcasts on how many people were paying a visit to St. Peter's in honor of the Pope. What happened to our Italian Holiday? The paper reported that Pope John Paul II's funeral would be the single largest gathering of heads of state outside the United Nations. The Pope was moved from the private Apostolic Palace to St. Peter's, where over three days millions would file by his coffin paying their respects.

On Friday we took a train to Florence since pretty much every shop, restaurant, and attraction in Rome closed for the funeral. We spent the day walking haphazardly through the

Duomo where there were no barricades, security, or Swiss Guards. After a pizza lunch we visited the Accademia Gallery where Mom stared a little too long at David. As we walked around, it seemed to me that the city had fewer tourists than normal. It also occurred to me that everyone was speaking Italian. When I asked a group of people where they were from, they said, "Roma!" Enough said.

Watching the late-night news coverage of the funeral, I thought about Pope John Paul II. He was Pope for so much of my lifetime. Even in 1979, the people of St. Stanislaus that stood waiting for him knew, well before much of the world, what a great leader he would become. It may not seem like much, but to me this coincidence in timing, twenty-six years apart, of a Polish Pope, with a connection to St. Stanislaus, was something I always remembered.

GREENPOINT AVE.

Back in 1979, the men of Greenpoint never had a chance to shout out, "The Pope is Coming. The Pope is Coming." Everyone was just thrilled that the motorcade passed by the church on the highway. Maybe Pope John Paul II made the sign of the cross with his outstretched hand if he saw the steeple of St. Stan's from the BQE.

For the next two days, during that October of 1979, many in the parish were glued to their television sets watching the visit unfold. At school, the nuns wheeled TV carts into the classroom so we could watch significant portions of the visit. The St. Stanislaus faithful had something else to cheer about when the parish choir performed at the Shea Stadium Mass for the Pope.

GREENPOINT AVE.

Mickey made the restaurant place the to-go orders in large cardboard boxes and he placed them in the bed of truck 11. Evidently, he didn't trust the kid to hold the food in the front seat of the ridiculously clean truck. That was probably a wise decision, given the way Mickey drove. I didn't want to have a vision of Fr. Ted's finger pointing at me as I cleaned French fries off the floor.

Pulling back into the parking space at the plant, Mickey said, "See that, kid. Back safe and sound. Not a scratch on the truck and management will n'ver know. I bet you'd never guess, kid, but I was an altar boy."

I just smiled, and thought, "Weren't we all back then."

Mom tossing a coin into the *Fontana* di *Trevi*.
Probably making a wish that Nick and I didn't give her the slip again.

Nick at St. Peter's Basilica.

Where's Mom?

Pickles for Nickels

Our fast food in 1970s Greenpoint was totally different from today's fast food. Sure, McDonald's and Burger King were up on the avenue, but I could count on one hand the amount of times I ate at either of them combined. We had plenty of other options we discovered around the neighborhood to fulfill our cravings.

The bottom of the fifth inning of whiffle ball was snack time and with only a few minutes to spare from our street game competitions, we needed something fast. Sometimes the teams would split up. Some would head to Baldo's Pizza for a slice and Italian ice, others to the candy store, and a few kids would run inside to a cooked meal of pierogi or kielbasa prepared by a grandmother who kept track of the innings from her front window. Peter's grandma would always watch our games, as long as the Yankees weren't on TV. I swear she kept a scorecard and a little black book of our summer-league stats.

During a summer playoff double header, when the fifth inning ended, Peter made a beeline for his house. The rest of us were arguing about what we wanted to eat – pizza or knishes – when Peter called us over from his stoop, "Guys, come on over here."

We reached the aria gate as a basket was being lowered from the second-floor window. His grandma had made us all lunch. In the basket were hotdogs, pickles, and warm homemade chips. Once we unloaded the food she pulled the basket back up and down it came again, this time with a pitcher of lemonade. We sat on the stoop, eating hotdogs and chips, feeling as if we were in the center field bleachers at Yankee Stadium.

Playing whiffle ball in the morning always presented a dilemma for our fifth inning break. Since the pizza places weren't open yet, we'd settle for a ring ding and a soda from the candy store. That was all fine, until we found a place that was open in the mornings for a cheap snack.

After five innings, in the summer morning sun, dodging cars and grumpy ball-busters, we were sitting on the curb drinking our sodas. Peter poked me in the side and pointed. I looked over to see Nickels walking down the street eating a big pickle like it was a Snickers bar. We didn't think it was odd that he was eating a pickle at 9:30 in the morning, we just all wanted pickles all of a sudden.

"Where'd you get the pickle?" Peter asked in a demanding tone.

"Right over there," said Nickels, pointing towards an open garage. I had passed that place a thousand times to and from school or on the way to the candy store. There were always barrels inside the garage bay, I just never cared what was in them. It's strange how nonobservant kids can be and yet sometimes never miss a beat.

"Hey, how much?" I chimed in.

"Five nickels." Nickels jingled as he walked with the pocket full of nickels he carried around. There was a rumor that his brother made his coin being able to open pay phones. I still think Buster was his grandma, but he denies it.

"I've got a quarter. I want to try one of those," I said.

"I'll get a quarter from my grandma. Hold up guys! Grandma!!" yelled Peter, turning and running toward his house.

The teams cleared the stoop and our whiffle ball gang paraded down to the pickle garage. Once we were close to the open garage door, the smell I never associated with pickles before, became instantly obvious. We stepped into the dark shade of the garage. Covered barrels were arranged in haphazard rows. It smelled briney and skunky. Sawdust covered the floor and Peter started kicking it around.

A guy in a thick black rubber apron appeared from a dark corner in the back.

"Whatta yu kids want?"

"You sell pickles here?"

"What kind does ya need?"

We looked at one another.

"The regular kind," I said. I knew there were different kinds of pickles, I just didn't know what they were called. The man with the wild hair and stubbly face stared me down. I tried to think of the name of the pickles my grandma made in the summer. By the time the Jersey pickling cucumbers could be bought at the farmstand and pickled, it was late July. She would put the special cucumbers in jars on the windowsill at the bungalow to let them pickle. By the end of August, not nearly enough time for the pickling process, she would give in to my begging and open a jar. This meant the pickles were not yet pickled but were cucumbers with weak salad dressing. So, having little patience to wait, I preferred Vlasic. I was hoping the pickles in the barrels were not cucumber tasting pickles, but regular - you know - like from a jar.

The fat guy smirked and shook his head, knowing we had no idea what the difference was between a dill, sour, half-sour, German-style, or any of the thirty pickles he had fermenting in his garage turned into a pickle distributor. He walked over to a large barrel, lifted the wooden top by a dirty rope handle and pulled out an immense fat pickle.

"This kind?"

"Yeah," said five salivating boys, what did we know. I personally had no idea what type of pickle he was holding in his hand.

"How many? It's Twenty-five cents EACH," he said, stressing the word each, apparently assuming we had no idea how to add or the going price of a pickle. Considering he was talking to the Diamond Street poker club, he was seriously mistaken about the first point. As to the value of a pickle, we had no idea, he could have charged a buck at that moment, we were so caught up in the pickle frenzy.

He handed us each a pickle wrapped in a square of butcher paper he tore off a roll hanging on the wall. He wiped his hands on a dirty towel, took our silver, and returned to doing whatever pickle people do.

We walked out of the dingy garage and back into the bright summer sun, proud of our pickle purchase. Yet, I don't think any of us really were sure how we just got suckered into buying pickles for our second breakfast.

I pulled back the wet, soggy, brown paper. A strong pickle smell wafted through the air. I took a bite. Juice squirted out both sides of my mouth, some hitting Peter in the face as he was gently peeling back the paper to get at his own pickle.

"Hey, watch what you're doin!"

It was the tartest, coldest pickle I ever tasted. I can still remember the garlic and pepper flavor. It was delicious. Some of the guys, anticipating sweet gherkins, hated the taste and dumped theirs in the nearest trash can.

After our trip to what we christened The Diamond Pickle Factory, I noticed grandma after grandma stopping at that garage and emerging with bags of pickles. Throughout that entire summer, I sampled all the different types of pickles that the pickle guy sold. Thinking back, how a pickling operation, in an unassuming garage, could operate in the middle of a residential block is just part of Greenpoint magic.

With the discovery of the pickles, we had added a new fast-food summer snack, direct from the barrels. There was no store, just an open garage door. The pickle guy, as we referred to him, would take our quarters and put them in a cigar box that rested on a wooden plank over two barrels. He always closed the garage in the early afternoon when he would load his truck and leave to make deliveries. If I needed a pickle fix in the afternoon, I was forced to go over to the Park Deli. They had a large jar of dills on the counter. It was the next best thing to one direct from a moldy barrel in a dirty garage. The guy behind the counter at the deli was always a bit annoyed when I stopped in to buy just a pickle.

Knishes were a favorite to have with a pickle. We'd pick up a pickle and then go over to the candy store for a hot knish. Nick would yell that we were dripping pickle juice on what were already sticky floors. With the knishes heating up, he'd be yelling, "If I wanted pickle juice dripped around, I'd sell pickles. Next time come and get your knishes first, then go to the pickle place." He found something to complain about every day. If we bought our knishes somewhere else he'd complain we didn't stop in.

Double headers of ball games played into the afternoon meant finding different nourishment to tide us over to dinner. It was about then that we discovered another garage door up on Norman Avenue. It turned out this was a pretzel distributor that was open later in the afternoon to sell the stock left over from the morning deliveries. We caught Nick there several times buying the day's leftovers to sell at his candy store; that explained why they were always a little stale. The lady would sell us two pretzels for a quarter. We never shared, because how could you go halfsies on something that cost twenty-five cents? So, we each ate two huge pretzels. There were a lot of things I remember buying for a quarter back then. A pickle, a candy bar, two stale pretzels, and a flat fountain soda - that was our 1979 dollar menu.

Tired of the same old pizza, pretzels, Italian ices, knishes, and pickles, we branched out for our between inning breaks. As our crew was made up of mostly Italian, Polish, and Irish kids, we found places based on where our grandmothers dragged us shopping to carry home the grocery bags. Those were still the years when grandmas went to the butcher for meat, the bakery for bread, the fish place for fish, and the garage for pickles. It must have made for a long day of shopping for them. We discovered another treat the day Jacek pulled us towards a butcher up on Driggs Avenue for our snack break.

"Why are we going here, Jack?" We always called him Jack even if the nuns, priests and his babcia used the Polish pronunciation, Jacek.

"This is where I go with my babcia. They have good stuff in here, it's more better than pizza. Trust me." We teased him on his saying 'more better.' He didn't get why. We liked the sound of it, so everything we did became 'more better' for the rest of the summer. I suspect Jack's choice of words had something to do with his being a second generation American, where only Polish was spoken in his home. I don't know about Polish, but in Italian, the word for good is meglio. Italians could say più meglio to mean better. Più being the word for more. In Italian, this is not exactly saying, 'more better,' but rather, better. And meglio alone would do just fine. It could have been language confusion on comparative phrases, or maybe just a simple slip of Jack's tongue that day. I just remember that 'more better' phrase he used and sometimes I find myself wanting to use it to make a point.

When eight kids entered the butcher shop, all the Polish ladies waiting turned and looked at the gang of eleven-year-olds, who might mug them for their sausages. The butcher eyed our dirty hands from behind the counter. Jacek led us to the display case.

"Jack, why are we in here? We have no way to cook any of this!" moaned Peter.

"Yeah, Jack. Let's go get a slice, man," I said.

"No, no. These you don't have to cook, it's already cooked, like ham."

I stared at the meat case. The names of the sausages and

kielbasa in the case were all in Polish, but it may as well been written in Russian since none of it made any sense to me.

"No way, man. We have kielbasa at my grandma's and she always cooks it. We can't eat this raw," said Peter to Jack.

We were talking loudly and I could tell the butcher was listening but he was dealing with a lady who was complaining about too much fat on her lamb chops. When he finished ringing her up, he held open the door so she could push her grocery cart out of his shop.

He turned toward us and asked, "Jacek, how's your Babcia?"

"She's good," Jack answered.

Then he asked, "You needa sometin, boys?" looking us over one at a time, his glasses perched on the end of his nose.

Peter asked, "Mister, Jack here says we can eat these sausages raw, is that true?"

"Not all of them. But these here in this case are smoked. They ar'not raw, but already cooked. And ah yes, you can eat them just like-a this."

I was a little apprehensive of trusting an answer from a guy who wore a white paper hat and had bloodstains all over his apron and pants. The butcher took out a link, the size of a large middle finger, and cut it into pieces. He placed the pieces on a slice of butcher paper and walked out around the counter. He gave each of us a sample.

"Wow! That's really good," I said.

"Yeah. I never had these before," added Peter.

Jacek was all smiles, having just introduced us to a new exotic food from his Polish mother's homeland – Greenpoint.

We all paid for one small finger link each. They were expensive, maybe forty cents each, way more than we typically spent. We were still hungry and stopped for a slice on the way back to the game. The smoked sausages were a mild departure from our norm, until the day we crossed under the BQE to play ball.

A few weeks later, we were playing whiffle ball up near St. Cecilia's. As usual, around the middle of the game we were getting hungry. Although we were just four blocks from our own part of the neighborhood, we may as well have been in a foreign country, and we realized we had no idea where to buy our snacks. One of the local guys on the other team, Patty, a Polish-Irish fellow, said he knew a place and led us down a side street.

He took us into a warehouse type building that was full of smelly fish. Fish hung from their tails on clotheslines that were strung from end to end of the red brick room. It looked like some kind of fish Chinese laundry. More fish were stacked in wooden bins along the wall. Other fish were on ice behind the counter. I'd never seen so many darn fish. Not even in Pop-Pop's bathtub!

"Patty, are you crazy? You want us to eat raw fish?" asked Jack.

"Nah, that's disgusting. Nobody eats fish raw stupid. Haven't you ever had smoked fish?" replied Patty. *(I wouldn't be introduced to sushi until my first trip to South Korea, decades later).*

"C'mon, man. Where's the pizza place around here?" Peter said.

I, on the other hand, actually liked smoked fish. My grandparents often put some out during the holidays and this place seemed strangely familiar. I think, I might have even been to that same shop a time or two with my grandmother, when I was little. It was hard to tell. The factory streets in that section of Greenpoint were usually red brick unassuming buildings, usually with no signage. You just had to know where to go to get what you wanted. It all looked the same from the outside. Not knowing where you were going, you had about an equal chance of stumbling into a pickle factory, a pretzel bakery, a smoked fish house, or a numbers joint.

"You kids got money?" barked a guy from a small office, an unlit cigar hanging from his mouth.

"Yeah, we got money," snapped Patty.

All the other guys, except me and Patty, hightailed it back out to the street. Patty and I bought one small fish each. The guy unclipped the clothespin they were hanging from and wrapped them in pages of the Daily News. I think it was probably a smoked mackerel or just what my grandmother always referred to as "white fish."

Outside, we were teased by the others, but I thought it was pretty good. As we had no utensils, we had to skin the fish and pull pieces off the bone using our fingers and the newspaper. My hands smelled of fish the rest of the day and were coated in black newspaper print. The other guys had found a candy store and bought Hershey bars.

This was our type of street food – pickles from barrels, slices from hole in the wall pizza joints, knishes from candy stores, leftover pretzels, sausages from butchers, and smoked fish off a clothesline. It was rarely a full meal, but more something to tide us over. I'd leave the house early in the morning, spring, summer, and fall and might not come back until dinner time. Depending on what corner of Greenpoint we were hanging out, and who we were with, we had great adventures trying different foods. Street games, friends, and cheap snacks - the way life was growing up in Greenpoint.

Fortune Cookies

Working a double shift at the power plant always meant big meals paid for by the company. The first choice, or should I say demand, was take out from a surf and turf house just up the road. The dinners were mostly turf. The place would pack Styrofoam to-go boxes with large steaks and thick cut homemade fries; the surf being a single jumbo butterfly shrimp on the side. And that was just fine with all of us, the more meat the better.

Mickey paged me at 6:30 to head out for what I thought would be the dinner steak run. I met him at the front door and we grabbed the keys to a truck. He complained and grumbled on the walk up to the lot. Mickey's patience was worn thin because a temporary manager from corporate was covering and the guy wanted Chinese food. Nobody wanted to say anything to get on the wrong side of the boss, so they ordered Chinese.

"You like Chinese food, kid?"

"It all depends. I haven't had really good Chinese food since living in Greenpoint."

"Don't get your hopes up then. Around here it's terrible."

We pulled into a strip mall where the red neon sign in the window flashed, "Chinese Food." Very imaginative. The woman handed us five shopping bags full of little white boxes with metal handles. Mickey made her give us extra fortune cookies, even though she kept saying, "Max is two per meal!"

She gave in when he replied, "Big tip or little tip?"

He was right; the food was terrible. The rice was wet and sticky and the sweet and sour pork was swimming in a bland orange sauce that may have constituted nuclear waste the way it was glowing. The on-loan boss made no complaints. He ate as if it tasted the same as all other Chinese food he ever ate.

Making sure the boss didn't see, I chucked the barely touched food into the nuclear waste spent fuel pool (if the Nuclear Regulatory Commission is reading this, I'm just kidding). Mickey and I grabbed a handful of fortune cookies and walked out to the grated walkway to get some air.

"That stuff was just terrible," Mickey started in.

I agreed, saying, "I picked out some of what was supposed to be pork, but that was about it."

Mickey told me about how he and his wife enjoyed eating in Chinatown every year for their anniversary. I don't know why, but this hit me as a surprise. Not so much that he enjoyed good Chinese food, but that the old curmudgeon was a bit of a romantic.

Leaning up against the railing, I told Mickey about the Greenpoint Chinese restaurant I remembered from when I was a kid. Since then I have been to different parts of China and the food there was nothing compared to the Greenpoint restaurant. The food in China is mostly regional, so you can't really generalize it as simply, *Chinese food.* Some of it I loved, some of it not so much. But the fancy Chinese dinners my family ate at the restaurant in Greenpoint were some of the best dishes I ever had. Maybe it was eating with the family, maybe it was the food, or maybe it's just a memory.

GREENPOINT AVE.

We didn't eat out much when I was a kid. When we did it was because my grandfather, or my Uncle Tony, would take us out for some special family occasion. These celebrations were usually held in the backroom of a neighborhood bar called Clancy's or Bruno's, or something of that nature. The menus were simple. Combinations of steak, chicken, or shrimp. Unless it was near St. Patty's day, then obviously Clancy's served corned beef all week long.

Drilled into my memory, the fanciest dinners I had growing up were at the Chinese restaurant on a corner of Manhattan Avenue. The restaurant was a throwback even then to some long-gone era. The dining room was on the second floor and, in my memory, it was the size of an airplane hangar. All the dishes were shiny white porcelain. My grandmother would say, "Real China from China!" I think maybe she was kidding, maybe not. At her house we ate off of blue chipped Melmac, unless it was Thanksgiving, Christmas, or Easter. And even on those special occasions, at the kids-table we still had Melmac. So, to use real plates at a non-holiday meal was a big deal.

The wait staff at this restaurant looked ancient. They were perpetually hunched over, most likely from carrying huge trays of rice for forty years. Their damaged posture aside, they were attentive and quick. They spoke very little English and would speak to each other in their native language. All the wait staff at the restaurant were in a constant state of hurriedness and yet they spoke in a calm sing-song rhythm, never any yelling. It was so different than the yelled Italian phrases common at Nana's house over dinner. At least there, I partially understood Pop-Pop and my uncles when English words were injected in a sentence if the Italian word was unknown, or when they were over excited.

The waiters, there were no waitresses, were dressed in black pants, crisp white shirts, and red silk vests. Walking up the stairs to the restaurant, they would spot our large party and jump into action. A small food army, stationed at the ready.

The headwaiter would sing, "How many?"

Dzia Dzie would give a quick response of, "Eight."

Grandma would inject, "No. Tell him fourteen." The waiter's eyes popped open and a confused look came over his face.

"The kids are small, Kitty," Dzia Dzie would say.

"They still need seats, Anthony," she'd counter.

The headwaiter would sing to the underling waiters, "Table for furteeen." They would look at him with questioning faces. Then he would repeat in Chinese. At that command they would go about scrambling to set chairs around the table. I don't ever recall there being a problem fitting everyone, the round tables being the size of Jupiter's moons.

Following the headwaiter to the table, I was impressed with all the pristine white tablecloths and the carved wood armed chairs that were upholstered in dark red cushions. Each table was set to perfection with matching plates, no chips, and real glasses. Very fancy indeed.

The ordering process was slightly less complicated than fixing the city electric grid after the '77 blackout. It started with the votes at the table for what dishes to order. These arguments went on for some time, requiring Dzia Dzie to send the waiter away several times until we were ready. As the adults debated, I'd start to cause trouble.

Each table had a doorbell button stationed on the side of the table. Usually, Dzia Dzie, being the patriarch, and the paying person, sat near the bell. The button, when pushed, would sound a soft "ding," barely audible out in the dining room, and light up a table number over at the headwaiter's station, which looked to me to be about a quarter of a mile away from the table. I don't remember exactly how far away it was, but it was pretty far.

The adults would be arguing over getting the Emperor's Delight with brown rice or white and I'd stand next to Dzia Dzie and ring the bell. The waiter would come running over.

"You ready now?"

"No, No. Come back," Dzia Dzie would say. The waiter would look puzzled and go back to his station.

The adults would negotiate an order maximization process. They needed enough of the dishes that each wanted for dinner and just the right amount for Grandma to take home in a doggy bag, for the dog she didn't have. When my mother was young, Grandma did have a monkey named Poncho, a gift from Uncle Ray. Let's just say having a monkey in a Greenpoint flat didn't end well.

I'd ring the bell. Over to our table the headwaiter would run.

"You ready now?"

"No, No. Come back," Dzia Dzie would say again.

"Why you ring bell?"

"I didn't," said Dzia Dzie, feeling he'd been accused of launching a missile by Brezhnev. Mom, at that point, would grab me and sit me down. The waiter would go back to his station.

On the occasion burned into my memory, I don't think there were any other people in the restaurant. Of the twenty tables, we may have been the only group.

"We have it now, right? I'm going to ring the bell," Dzia Dzie would declare and he'd press the buzzer. The headwaiter looked over but made no run for our table. Dzia Dzie pressed again. The light behind the waiter's station flashed on and off. Dzia Dzie waved at the waiter and remarked, "What's the matter with this guy? First, he comes when we don't call him, now he's not coming?"

The waiter walked over, all enthusiasm lost.

"You ready now?"

"Yes, we're ready," replied Dzia Dzie with a big smile.

Then the hysterics started with the actual ordering. This would make the most politically incorrect episode of Seinfeld seem mild. Polish, Irish, and Italians, with Brooklyn accents, attempted to order Chinese food to authentic Chinese immigrants who barely spoke English. Each dish on the menu, I suspect to take care of the translation problem, was numbered, but that did not matter. Within a minute, everyone was lost.

"We need three number fives, two number fours, one number one, and two number two poo poo platters." Dzia Dzie rattled off way too fast for the waiter to understand and get the numbers straight. The waiter repeated to be sure he had heard correctly.

"Two poo poo platters, one number one?"

"Yes, Yes," confirmed Dzia Dzie.

I whispered to Mom, "I don't want any of that!"

Then there was the question that stumped everyone, "Brown rice or white rice?"

Such a simple question. The same question was asked every time. Why it even deserved a conversation, I do not know. After arguing over who wanted what type of rice, Grandma would declare, "Bring some of both – white and brown." To this the headwaiter always made a concerned look as to how he was to handle such a request.

The waiter disappeared through the double doors to the kitchen and another waiter would bring the tea. The tea was addicting. Never since my childhood at this Greenpoint Chinese restaurant have I had such good tea. Of course, this is just a childhood memory and cannot be true from a tea perspective. I've had amazing tea in South Korea, Singapore, China, Taiwan, Malaysia, and the Philippines, and my Asian friends take their tea very seriously. They always watch and await my reaction from my first sip of a particular four-ounce cup of tea they've served me. They do have good taste in tea, and I do have to admit, a visit to a tea house on a cold dark winter evening in Seoul is a warm and welcoming event after a twenty plus hour air journey.

But none of the teas have approached the taste of my memory from that Manhattan Avenue Chinese restaurant. They served it in little stainless tea pots that held only enough for five tiny cups at a time. That was bad because the tea never lasted.

It was good because I was allowed to ring the bell for more tea, especially when the adults had added a spicy dish to the order. And as far as I can tell, the tea must have been included with the price of the meal, or Dzia Dzie would have put a stop to the deliveries.

The cups were tiny porcelain, almost doll house size. I was constantly bugging Mom and Grandma to pour me a refill. Maybe that was the allure of it all. Maybe the tea was Lipton. Maybe they never washed the tea kettles. Maybe I was just a thirsty kid. Who knows.

When the food came, it was delivered by General Tso's entire army. The headwaiter, waiters, kitchen staff, family members, and the cooks, delivered our meal. The brigade marched from the kitchen in a single file procession to the table. The headwaiter would place the first dish on the Lazy Susan. He would then rotate the platter for each subsequent dish to be set down. Once everything was placed, he would rotate the platter announcing what we had ordered.

"Here are your three-number fives, two number twos, one number twenty-one, and one number twelve." By now, the numbers made no sense to us, he may as well have been talking in Chinese, because with the menus long gone we had no idea what each number represented anyway.

"All set?" he would ask in a tone that stated he was looking forward to sitting down for a few minutes.

"Yes, yes. All set," Dzia Dzie said, anxious to dig into his Peking duck.

Just as we all were spinning the Lazy Susan to dish out some food, Dzia Dzie put out his large hand to stop the platter from spinning. Holding the wheel and everyone's appetite hostage, he exclaimed, "Where on here is the duck sauce?" Nobody could locate the duck sauce. He rang the bell.

The waiter looked over. Seeing I was in my seat on the opposite side of the table, he sprinted over.

"Yes?"

"Duck sauce?" The waiter beckoned a junior waiter and spoke in a foreign tongue with a command so long it sounded as if he was reciting Sun Tzu's "Art of War."

The young man never spoke a word back. He disappeared with a slight bow and returned with two platters of orangey sauce. He gave them to the headwaiter, who was still waiting at attention beside my grandfather's chair. The waiter placed the first on the Lazy Susan platter and gave the wheel a spin. The platter came to a stop on the exact opposite side.

Grandma said, "He'd be a ringer on Wheel of Fortune." She had a crush on Chuck Woolery.

"All set?" asked the headwaiter, stressing the ending, not catching at all what Grandma meant.

"Yes, yes. All set," Dzia Dzie said. Of course, we were not.

"I need chopsticks," stated my older cousin a minute later.

"Why? You don't know how to use them," replied my uncle.

"Well, how can I learn without trying them?" She made a good point.

It was an argument Dzia Dzie wasn't willing to have as his Moo Goo Gai Pan was getting cold. He rang the bell. The waiter was speaking to another waiter. He looked over at our table, glaring at me in my seat and then hurried over.

"Yes?"

"Chopsticks?"

There was never a need for full sentences, it only tended to confuse. The waiter surveyed our family, doubting any of us had a clue how to use them.

"How many?"

My grandfather looked at him strange and said in a tone, completely serious, as if the Chinese man had no idea how to use the utensils, "We need two sticks. One would not work." The waiter frowned and walked away.

He returned with two pairs of stainless chopsticks and handed them to Dzia Dzie who passed one set to my cousin. And gave the second set back to the waiter.

"ALL set?" he asked, stressing the collective ALL this time.

"Yes, yes. All set."

Of course, we were not. Everyone was busy eating, spinning the Lazy Susan, and drinking tea, which by now had run out, and Dzia Dzie wanted more.

Dzia Dzie rang the bell. I think he liked ringing the bell as much as any of the kids. "Kitty, we should get a bell like this next to my armchair."

"You can try, Anthony, and we'll see where it goes."

The waiter appeared.

"Yes?"

"Tea?"

The headwaiter beckoned the younger tea waiter who took the empty tea pots and bought two new ones.

"How come you are not using the chopsticks?" my aunt

asked my cousin.

"They gave me the metal ones and those are too slippery."

"Do you want the wood ones?"

"That would have been good. I can't learn using these." She was obviously upset.

My aunt looked at Dzia Dzie. He rang the bell.

The waiter appeared at our table.

"Yes?"

"Wood chopsticks?"

The waiter looked at my fourteen-year-old cousin. He should have known.

He came back with a pair of wooden chopsticks wrapped in paper and handed them to her.

"All set now?" he asked. The waiter had just added a new word.

"Yes, yes. All set."

I'm pretty sure the waiter knew we were not. On the other hand, given the terrific level of service, the 'all set,' may have been meant in a different way. It may have meant, "Have I provided what you asked for?" Or, "Did I get it right?" Either way, they had the best service in the neighborhood.

After the food was packed in the to-go containers, Grandma always ordered everyone ice cream. Always vanilla. Scoops of white in little white porcelain bowls. After we finished our dessert, the waiter scooped fortune cookies by the handful from a decorative basket, onto the suzy platter. As soon as the waiter turned his back, Grandma was giving everyone <u>one</u> cookie and the rest were scooped into her purse.

Everyone then cracked their cookie and we read our

fortunes out loud. There was always a good amount of laughter at the sayings. Sometimes for the funniness of what was written, sometimes for the typos that were found on the little strips of paper.

When we stood to leave, the waiters lined the way to the door, bowing and all saying repeatedly, "Thank you, come again," as we marched down the two-story staircase.

GREENPOINT AVE.

An hour after we had finished up the Chinese takeout, Mickey paged me. He was skipping out for a burger and fries. I jumped at the chance for something else to eat. He made some excuse to his supervisor that he needed to check something at the substation. The supervisor was pretty slick and told Mickey to bring him back a cheeseburger.

"First, we have to stop at the convenience store," Mickey told me.

"How come?" I asked.

"I want to play the numbers from the fortune cookie I had. Look at these!" He handed me the slip to read.

It read, "Do Not Take Unnecessary Gambles." Typed under that was a list of six so called, "Lucky Numbers." I don't have a clue what the numbers were, but Mickey thought they were special; the irony of the fortune surely lost. If the numbers were so lucky, why then were some Chinese people stuck in a hot kitchen someplace making those cookies?

I handed him back his slip. By this time, New York State had long legalized the lottery and Mickey was going to be playing in the official game.

Mickey said, "Wait til you taste the fries from this burger place. You've never had fries this good anywhere. I can tell you that."

I wasn't so sure; I remembered a place in Greenpoint that had the best fries I ever had.

Greenpoint Fries

Growing up, Burger King and McDonald's were on the far end of the avenue. When they first opened, Billy, Jimmy, and I'd head up just to buy fries. When we were feeling lazy, walking ten blocks was a far hike. Lucky for us, we discovered the 'fry man' much closer to home.

In the 1970s, many Greenpoint stores modeled their businesses as it was in 'the old country.' Grandma would tell me how in Poland there were particular stores for fruit and vegetables, other stores for cheeses and dairy, a butcher for meats, a fish market for seafood, a bakery for breads, and the pastry shop for cakes. While the A&P and Busy Bee sold pretty much all foods, it seemed to me that Greenpoint was organized similar to the old country she was describing. Probably because the shop owners were only one, two, or maybe three generations removed from their home country.

I remember our family was pretty picky when it came to gathering our food. Deli meats for a sandwich came from Busy Bee along with a sliced Rye. For milk, Dad would drive miles to the dairy distributor in Maspeth. He'd say, "The milk was fresher from the dairy." I never saw any cows in the back parking lot. I knew he drove over there because the milk was five cents cheaper. I always jumped at the chance to go with him on these dairy trips.

I didn't go because it was exciting to get milk, I went

because he let me drive the VW bus on the deserted industrial road. I'd stand in front of him, steering, while he worked the gas, the brake, and the stick. This was a lot of fun, until our van started to rust out.

Driving along, I was in front of the wheel one second, and the next second, my leg went through the floor. In a panic I jerked the wheel while trying to pull my leg back up into the van. My sneaker got caught on the jagged rusted floorboard and fell off. Visions of Fred Flintstone flashed through my mind; my toes inches from the cobblestones.

Dad grabbed the wheel before we hit a parked tractor trailer. A single Puma was left somewhere on 56th Road. Dad covered the hole in the floorboard with a piece of cardboard. After that, I had to be careful where I stood when driving. The worst of it was driving during a rainstorm. Dad wore Wonder Bread bags over his shoes to keep dry.

While our milk came from the dairy distributor, much of our fruit and vegetables came from the corner fruit stands. Mom could get off the subway and grab a few carrots, some tomatoes, and a half dozen apples. A block later she'd stop at Straub's butcher to buy the dinner's main course. There were no cuts of meat under cellophane with a date on it. No, here you ordered and the butcher would prepare the cut you wanted as you watched. He'd wrap it in brown paper and say, "See you tomorrow." Our butcher was right across from Grandma's. She'd send me down with a note written on a ripped off piece of paper bag. She'd write specific instructions for Mr. Straub, basically saying, "Don't make me come down there, and I will, if you send Tommy up with a poor cut of pork!"

Uncle John picking out some fruit on Fresh Pond Rd., ~1984.

When it was Friday, we bought our fish from the fish store. The fish place was busiest on Fridays all through the year, but it was a zoo on first Fridays and all Fridays during Lent. Maybe the details behind abstinence and no meat on Friday was originally petitioned by the early Roman fishermen to the Pope himself, a way to drum up their end-of-week business. Saint Peter was perhaps a member of Matthew's Chapter of the International Brotherhood of Fisherman – Local 4:19.

The line on Fridays at the fish store would stretch out the door onto Nassau Avenue, and sometimes it could go around the corner, since the interior of the store only held three to four customers at a time. An old-fashioned wooden screen door, the blue paint faded and peeling, would creak and then slam with each patron, releasing a few flies back to the street while letting in ten new ones.

The storefront had a huge plate-glass window, behind which were displays of fish in wooden crates on ice over beds of straw. The fish that were permitted to lie with their heads still on would stare at me as we waited in line. Growing up, we ate mostly flounder. Passing by the store with my mom on a Wednesday, which was not Ash Wednesday, and hoping to avoid the Friday line, I asked, "Can we have flounder for dinner?"

"No, Tommy. It's only fresh on Friday."

Was she serious? The guy only had fresh fish once a week? I doubted that. But that was the conventional wisdom. Whatever the case, on all other days of the week when I went to the fish store, I bought a snack that wasn't fish. It was better.

I discovered my latest Greenpoint culinary snack standing in the long slow-moving line at the fish store on a Friday. Waiting with my Mom to place our order, the lady ahead of us was getting a full meal cooked to go. The fishmonger cracked an egg, breaded the fish, and stuck it in the frying oil while we all waited. As the fish fried, he dipped another metal basket of fries in a second vat of hot oil. The little store went from raw fish smell to fried greatness in a minute.

"When I was little we'd come here just for fries," Mom said as we waited.

I made a mental note. The next week I was walking up Nassau Avenue with Alison. I asked her, "Do you want some fries?"

"I don't want to walk all the way up to McDonald's for

fries," she said.

"No, we can get some right here." I pointed to the fish store.

"Really?" She made a face looking at the crates of headless fish in the window.

We went in and I ordered. In hindsight, this wasn't the best way to impress a girl. The place smelled like, well dead fish. Alison turned and decided to wait outside as the man fried the potatoes. The owner dumped the oily hot fries into a brown paper bag and placed it on the counter. Before I even paid him the thirty-five cents, the bag was soaked through with oil.

"You want ketchup for the fries?" he asked.

"Sure," I said.

He opened the bag and banged out half the bottle of Heinz, shook the bag, and handed it back to me.

I must have looked at him with a, "What the heck did you just do?" look.

He pulled two tiny white napkin squares from a dispenser and handed them to me.

"One for you, one for your girl," he winked, as if he was doing me a great favor.

Back outside on the street, the oily ketchup soaked bag wasn't going to hold together much longer. Unfolding the crease, steam poured out. The fries looked injured.

Being the gentleman, I held the bag of fries out to Alison, "You want some?"

She just gave me a look, shook her head, and laughed her eighth-grade midnight laugh, probably thinking, "You're gross!"

I stuck my fingers into the bag and pulled out a long crinkle cut fry. I bit into it. Once I was over the pain of burning my tongue, I realized it was a GOOD fry! Crunchy outside and perfect potato inside.

My hands got very messy eating the ketchup soaked fries. Alison, I think, was a bit disgusted. Trying to salvage her impression of me, we walked the half block to Grandma's apartment and I rang the bell. The door buzzed open. At the top of the first flight of stairs, Grandma yelled down, probably holding her big frying pan in case it was a burglar, "Who is it?"

"It's Tommy. Can I come up and wash my hands?"

Grandma was excited to have a visitor. Seeing I brought along a little Polish girl, she tried to feed Alison zimne nogi (pickled pigs feet), czarnina (duck blood soup), and smoked whitefish. I had the impression that Alison's Polish roots didn't run as deep as my family. She said she never had any of those dishes. Alison and I didn't hang out anymore after that. Maybe it was me. Maybe it was the fries. Maybe Grandma could have offered Alison a soda and a Chips Ahoy.

Even though I never took another girl for fries, the guys and I added the fish store to our favorite places to go for a snack. The man still poured the ketchup in the bag over the fries. He still shook it up. It was still an oil soaked mess. Over time, we developed a better strategy to eat them. First off, we stopped placing our entire hand and arm down into the bag. Instead, we'd sit on a stoop along Eckford Street and tear open the bag. This provided a much easier and neater way to eat the entire bag of fries. I remember those were the best fries ever.

We were eating our bags of fries during one of our inning breaks and Billy said, "I wish that fish place sold burgers to go with these fries." Now that would have been a great idea. As it was, there were a few times, we'd walk far out of our way to get the burgers we would get a craving for.

In the summertime we'd be sent out right after breakfast to "Go play." Mom always said she needed us out so she could 'clean.' Given we lived in a four-room apartment, how much cleaning did she need to do? If Nana was watching us, she wanted us out because she had hours of *The Price is Right* and the *Newlywed Game* to watch. Although, in reality, there was no 'sending' us outside to play by parents. We'd be outside playing in the street from right after breakfast until dinner time. We couldn't wait to get outside; that's where all the action was taking place.

After dinner, we'd be back out again until the nightly reminder would come on TV, "It's ten p.m., do YOU know where YOUR children are?" Then Mom would panic, realizing she didn't know, and run to the front window. Every other mother was doing the same. The yelling would begin, "Thomas! Billy! Paulie! Come Home!" What would they have done without broadcast TV reminding them they left the kids out?

On a lazy summer morning, Billy, Jimmy, Paulie and I started our day as we usually did, sitting on a stoop. There was no action on the street. Nobody wanted to play any ball games. It was too hot to move.

"Whaddaya wanna do?" asked Paulie.

"I dunno, what do you wanna do?" I replied.

"I don't know. How about you Billy" Paulie asked.

"Doesn't matter to me," Billy said with little doubt.

This went on for some time. The July day was heating up by the minute. The asphalt was hot enough to fry an egg. We had already tried that yesterday, and it had worked.

This morning, I knew Pop-Pop wasn't going to let us take any more eggs to fry. Nick had already kicked us out of the air-conditioned candy store. Going home to sit inside and watch TV or play Atari never entered our minds.

"You guys want to go up to the park?" I asked.

Now that would have been a sensible idea. Here we were, sitting on a cement stoop, the sun beating down on us, when we could have been sitting on a park bench in the shade of a hundred-year-old oak tree.

"I don't wanna walk up there," griped Jimmy. Because we were half way down North Henry and that would have meant walking about three hundred paces.

"I'm pretty hungry," Billy said.

"It's ten o'clock, didn't you just eat breakfast?" I asked.

"Like two hours ago. I could go for a box of burgers," Billy replied.

"Me too," added Paulie

We didn't have to say what place. Everyone knew what Billy meant when he mentioned he wanted a box of burgers.

"It's not even open yet," I said.

"It'll be open by the time we get there," Paulie corrected.

"I'm pretty sure it's open 24 hours," Billy said.

And so began the burger adventure of the summer of 1981.

We weren't totally sure how to walk to White Castle. Until that day, we'd only been driven there by our parents. It was in

Queens, almost another country, as far as we were concerned.

"We just take Greenpoint all the way," I said, pretty sure that's how Dad would drive us there. And that's how the hike to Queens began; we just stood up and starting walking. We were too lazy to walk up to the park, but walking to another borough, now that was a way to spend an 85-degree summer day. We didn't have trails to hike where at the end there'd be a cool pond to dive in. We had cement sidewalks and at the end of the hike there'd be a castle.

North Henry Street, north of Norman, was all industrial. It was pretty deserted the morning we walked up it. There were a lot of squat brick buildings with unmarked roll down doors covered in graffiti. Once we reached Greenpoint Avenue and headed for the bridge, it was noisy and the traffic was constant.

We walked block after block seeing nothing but garage doors and auto shops. Finally, we hit a neighborhood and passed a pizza place, tempting Billy to give up.

"Hey, guys, I'm pretty hungry. That pizza place back there looked pretty good. They had a Sicilian pie in the window."

"No, Billy, we're gonna make it to White Castle."

When we hit Calvary Cemetery, Billy started to get all freaked out. "Why are there so many graves? Why'd they put them so close to the sidewalk?" he asked.

We had to cross over to the other side of the street to calm him down. When we reached the overpass going over the LIE, we stopped and looked out at the skyline of New York City.

"Looks pretty close. Why don't we walk over there?" asked Paulie.

Standing on the overpass, I watched the traffic below.

"Let's keep moving. The LIE goes through the tunnel, we can't walk that way," I said. I was sweltering in the sun and I think Paulie was getting delirious.

~ ~ ✦ ~ ~

A few days after our hike to the castle, when we were bored again, we acted on Paulie's idea. We crossed the Williamsburg Bridge, explored Delancey Street for no particular reason, and then headed back to Greenpoint. Walking through Williamsburg back then was not a fun hike. We were chased and had to hide out in a candy store. Luckily, Greg K was with us (he always had money) and he asked the store owner to call us a cab. The cab dropped us off at Humboldt and Driggs. When we were climbing out of his cab, the driver, a large Irish guy in a stained white t-shirt, yelled to us, "You kids better stay closer to your own neighborhood from now on."

~ ~ ✦ ~ ~

None of us were sure of the cross street off Greenpoint Avenue to take to get to White Castle up on Queens Boulevard. And there was no way we were asking anyone, that would just highlight we didn't belong there. We just walked until we hit Queens Boulevard and then, on a total guess, went left.

After two short cross blocks, Billy spoke up, "Did you see that Jewish deli? They have knishes."

"We didn't come all this way for a knish, man!"

"How many more blocks?"

"We should go back, my mom's gonna kill me."

"Look, as long as we are headed towards the city skyline, we're fine."

Then, just as I was about to give up hope and thought we

had made the wrong choice in direction, the buildings gave way and there it was – the White Castle parking lot.

All at once we took off in a sprint to the door, not so much in anticipation of the burgers, but for the cool air conditioning. There was only enough room inside the small building to order at the register. Paulie, Jimmy, and I ordered a box of six burgers each, Billy ordered ten. We sat outside on the greasy blue tables under the white and blue awnings. A White Castle burger, with small square holes and tiny chopped onions, with a pickle slice, and a dot of ketchup, made the walk worth it.

"Ya know, I think this side street will take us right back to Greenpoint Avenue," said Billy. We debated whether to take the side street or go back the way we came up Queens Boulevard.

In the heat of the argument we didn't see the two guys come up to our table until they were standing over us. The skeevy looking one with long slimy red hair spoke first. "You guys not from around here, are ya?"

Billy, not yet street smart, opened his mouth full of cheeseburger, "No. We're from Greenpoint." The two guys looked at one another, as if they just stumbled upon kids from some rich neighborhood.

The other guy, sporting a face full of red pus-filled zits and smoking a Marlboro said, "You kids got any extra money? We're pretty hungry and those burgers look good." Billy swallowed hard, finally catching on. We looked at one another. I had a few bucks left for the walk home. It was getting hot and I was figuring on buying a soda at the deli near the cemetery. By the looks of these two, I was wondering if I might be getting to the cemetery another way.

"C'mon on, guys. Don't hold out and make it hard. Just hand over what you have and we'll leave you alone."

Just then a White Castle Samaritan came out the door and walked up to our table. "Wow. You boys ate fast! It took them forever to make my order." We had no idea who the man was. He sat down next to Billy. He grabbed a burger from his bag and took a bite, making half of it disappear. "Mmm. I love White Castle."

He then looked the long-haired guy in the eyes, "Who are you guys?"

The two of them just looked at him and walked off down Queens Boulevard.

The man finished up his first burger in one more bite and then said, "I've seen those two harassing people around here before. You looked like you needed some help."

"Thank you, sir. We appreciate that," I said.

None of us had any appetite to finish our burgers, so we just stood up to go.

"Do you know if this side street connects back to Greenpoint Avenue," I asked the man.

"Sure does. A few blocks down. Stay alert and good luck," he said as he picked himself up and walked away.

The three of us were a little spooked. The worst that happened on the way back was that a mangy dog started tagging along. Billy, being afraid of dogs, threw the rest of his burgers to get him to stop following us. A few minutes later, the dog came bolting down the street and followed us anyway, mostly barking at Billy for more burgers. Billy was all bummed out for not having his burgers and still having to deal with the dog. This turned out to be to our advantage because Paulie and I wanted to walk through the cemetery on the way back. We bribed Billy with a slice of pizza to get him over his fears of walking by the graves.

Aside from all of Billy's complaints, the cemetery was a pretty nice place to walk. We explored the paths and had fun reading the names on the gravestones. From the top of a hill, there was a nice view of the city. The dog was having a wonderful time peeing on the bushes. When he caught sight of a squirrel, he took off and we never saw him again.

Back on the street, we took a detour to cool off in the air conditioning of a pizza place and get Billy a slice. By the time we were back in Greenpoint, we were hungry again. We detoured to the fish store for bags of fries. When we finished, we walked back to North Henry and sat on the stoop, exactly where we started our day. It was four o'clock and the heat hadn't let up at all; the concrete, the asphalt, and the bricks trapped the heat, cooking the city.

"Whatcha wanna do now?"

"I dunno, what do you wanna do?"

"I don't know. How about you?"

"Why don't we go hang in the park?"

"I don't want to walk up there." (That would have been three hundred paces.)

"Why don't we go up to Russ's for an Italian ice?"

"That sounds good to me." Because we had no problem walking almost a mile to get an ice from someplace particular, even if it was almost one hundred degrees out.

Swims with the Fishes

Mickey and I were sitting on the metal stairs outside the power plant, looking out over the Hudson River. A boat went buzzing by pulling a skier.

"Ya know, they could be out there fishin, instead of driving around in circles, yelling and screaming," Mickey said. I didn't say anything. I knew his idea of water recreation was all about catching something to eat.

He went on. "Did you and your friends jump off the Greenpoint piers into the East River, kid?"

"Heck no. That water was disgusting. Besides, we stayed away from that area of Greenpoint in the seventies and early eighties."

"Good thing. People drowned doin' that."

Mickey was right about the drownings. I've heard that has happened there. Others have taken to swimming in the river to cool off on hot days as well. None as famous, I guess, as Cosmo. While, my Pop-Pop's given name was Cosmo, he wasn't the one swimming in the river. He'd more likely be down on the pier next to Mickey with his pole and tackle. I'm thinking of another Cosmo.

In the Seinfeld episode, *The Nap (Season 8, Episode 18)*, a kid is looking out over the East River with his dad and says, "Hey, there's a man swimming in the water." The dad replies, "Nah, that's probably just a dead body, son. You see, when the mob kills someone, they throw the body in the river." In the episode Kramer (a.k.a. Cosmo) takes to swimming in the river for exercise. As kids, we did some crazy things, but not once did we ever consider jumping in the river. I told Mickey how we found other ways to cool off.

GREENPOINT AVE.

During the second night of the blackout, when Mom wouldn't let me go in Billy's pool, and we were sweltering in the yard, Dad took our side.

"Ah, Mary Lou, he can go in for a little bit."

"Are you going to take him to the doctor when he gets sick?"

Dad let it go, knowing he couldn't argue with a mother's instinct. Instead he pulled out the box of water guns and we had a water fight in the backyard. Nothing like running around, working up a sweat, spraying each other with mists of water on a ninety-degree night to cool you off. At least, we had fun and forgot about the pool. Well, my sister, brother, and I did; Dad not so much.

Finding ways to cool off during a city heat wave was always a challenge. Our best possibility of getting cool was when Paulie's dad opened a fire hydrant. If we weren't lucky enough to be outside when the water started to flow, we pretty much missed it because Mr. Raviolo called the NYFD to shut down the fun. There was never enough time to run in and put on a swimsuit, we just ran under it with whatever we had on. It was better to take the punishment for getting our new sneakers wet, than miss the fun.

With no pool and a strict NYFD, we were desperate, and

desperate times called for desperate measures to beat the heat. A gang of us seventh and eighth graders hatched a plan to take the train out to Coney Island. It took a lot of negotiation with Mom and Dad for them to let me go with no adult supervision. Especially since the trains to the beach ran through some of the riskier neighborhoods.

This was also the summer I had my first steady girlfriend, as serious as a grade school relationship could be, with JC. She was a year older than me and I couldn't tell her, "My parents won't let me go." She'd have punted me like a football. Mom and Dad gave in to my whining, or maybe I just went. I can't really recall.

Twelve teens, dressed in sneakers, swimsuits, and carrying nothing but towels met up at various corners on the way to the station. I had five singles in my left shoe for lunch and two train tokens, one for the ride out and one for the way home, in my right shoe. The trip across Brooklyn was almost over before it began.

We were spread out in three groups across a city block as we made our way down the avenue to the Nassau Avenue GG station. The lead group heard the train as they reached the stairs. Paulie yelled over his shoulder to the second group, and Billy relayed it to JC and I who were leisurely walking holding hands in the last group.

"Hurry up, it's coming!" they shouted.

Missing a train that's pulling into a station is right up there with eating the crust off your pizza first – that's crazy talk! Given the next train wouldn't be along for another twenty minutes, an entire lifetime, we made a run for it. JC pulled me along. She had long legs and ran faster than me. We never thought to stop holding hands even as we ran. We jumped the turnstile. There was no time to take off a shoe and get a token.

The first group made it on the train easily. Running down the stairs, I saw Donna and Billy getting on. The doors started to close.

JC screamed, "C'mon, we can't lose the others."

We reached the train as the doors were halfway shut. I thought, "That's that. May as well head back home. We'll never find the rest of them out on Coney Island."

JC had other ideas in her head, or maybe not. Without thinking, she wouldn't have done it if she was, at least I hope not, she stuck her head right between the closing doors.

Now, I've seen men stick umbrellas in, women have been known to jam in their shopping bags, but I had never seen anyone stick a body part between the closing doors of a subway car before. I went into panic mode. Mom and Dad were always warning us to stay clear of subway car doors and elevator doors.

I yelled, "Back up!" It was too late. The doors closed on her ears.

Lucky for her, her head was big enough to activate the emergency switch and the doors opened up again. Or maybe the conductor saw her and hit the switch. Either way, he was not happy. With his head hanging out the window a few cars ahead, he started yelling. We jumped into the car with the others, the doors closed, and the train took off. JC wasn't going to live down her action. Right away everyone was making wisecracks.

"Way to use your head!"

"What's on your ears, JC? A subway car?"

"Now that wasn't thinking with your brain!"

JC's older brother, Kenneth, wasn't as amused. He read her the riot act for being so stupid and how she could have been dragged to her death. He always had a way of bringing down the crowd.

We made it to the beach at ten o'clock with all our heads still attached. I spent most of the next five hours of the overcast day lying on my stomach, my arm over JC's back as the two of us laid on a towel together. JC's sister rubbed suntan lotion on her back and the back of her legs for her. When we stood up to leave I noticed the first pain in that sensitive spot behind my knees.

Getting close to the station, we heard the train. When the group started to run, the skin on the back of my thighs felt as if it was being pulled off my dermis and my muscles in one pull. I had to stand the entire train ride because I couldn't bend my legs. No-girlfriend-Billy, thought it was funny to keep hitting me on the back of my red legs with his wet towel.

By the time we reached the Nassau Avenue stop, I could barely walk up the steps to the street. My skin was on fire from my calves to the back of my neck; so much for going to the beach to cool off. I spent the next three days also on my stomach and Mom applied aloe vera to my sun blisters. The jelly being patted on my cooked lobster-colored skin might as well have been ice cubes. Never since, has going to the beach with a girl in a bikini been so painful. I was never allowed to go to Coney Island again with just friends.

When we did go to the beach as a family, we went to Breezy

Point. Dad loved going to the ocean and jumping in the waves. I enjoyed that too, but I had more fun at the nightly bonfires, especially if Eileen was there. She was a blue-eyed Irish beauty and my first beach crush. A Ritchie Cunningham look-a-like would play guitar and we'd all sing *Bill Grogan's Goat* or *You Are My Sunshine*, and other corny, but fun songs. It was a far cry from the heavy metal being played back in Winthro.

If there was a weekend without an invite out to Breezy and Dad wanted to go to the ocean, that meant one thing, a road trip out to Jones Beach. He'd start off in a happy mood singing, "Under the Boardwalk" as we packed up the VW bus. A three-hour bumper to bumper *freakin* traffic packed drive later, with *parkin* two miles from the sand, we'd find a postage stamp size spot a half mile from the surf for the five of us. By then, it was two in the afternoon, everyone was hot and grumpy, and Dad was ready to head home.

When Dad had the entire weekend off, we'd head to the lake in Jersey to visit Grandma. I preferred the lake over the ocean because there was a dock that we'd jump off of - over and over again. For some reason having a lake to swim in wasn't good enough for some of my uncles, and they decided to put up a pool. I don't ever remember swimming in the pool, but what I do remember was the weekend it was full of fish. Some wise guy went fishing and brought back buckets of perch and sunfish and dumped them in the pool. To keep the fish alive, we couldn't treat the water. My uncle thought it would be fun to swim with the fishes. Only he went in. My aunt called him Luca Brasi. Dad reminded her, "Luca Brasi slept with the fishes. Luca was in no condition to swim with them."

Within a day the water turned an awful green color. The bottom of the pool was full of dead worms and balls of bread the size of golf balls that some little cousin thought the fish would eat. Another cousin decided to fish with his fishing pole and only succeeded in getting the hook caught on the liner, causing a hundred little leaks. I don't know who had the job of taking down and cleaning that mess, but the pool at the lake gave Dad an idea.

The summer after the blackout, Dad double parked and called us over. He slid open the sliding door on the VW van to show us stacks of boxes and metal tracks.

"What's all that?" I asked.

My sister, Jeanette, read the side of the box that said, "Pool Filter," and we all screamed at once.

Nana asked, "Did you hit the numbers?"

We were all gung-ho dragging boxes and pieces of the pool through the aria, down through the basement, and up into the yard. I had visions that within the hour I'd be floating on my back like the otters I saw on *Grizzly Adams*. My sister and I had no idea the effort it was going to take to get the pool up and how long we would have to wait before we could get in the water.

Just getting the pool assembled took up most of our summer. After two weekends picking out rocks and leveling bags of some kind of puffed up mixture on the ground, there was a Saturday designated to assemble the pool. A barbeque was announced in an effort to get other family members to show up and help. Since they were all cursing the assembly of their own pools, nobody did.

Putting up the pool was left to the five of us and Nana, who had no choice since she lived in the ground-floor apartment and we knew she was home. My brother Chris, being as young as he was, wasn't much help. My sister was designated to hold the cup of screws. Why the manufacturer thought it was smart to use sheet metal screws to attach a rim around the top of a pool liner, I'll never understand. Besides, Jeanette was constantly dropping the cup of screws into the fake sand piled up along the outside of the pool frame, losing half the screws each time. Likewise, Dad would drop a screw about one in three times trying to attach the rim. He lost so many he had to make do with replacement screws from his workbench in the basement. This meant that the rim was attached with ten percent of the correct size screws, forty percent with screws too small, and thirty percent with screws too big. Yes, your math is correct. The other twenty percent of the places where screws were supposed to go, were just left empty. What could go wrong?

Once the rim was in place, we realized we were supposed to first put the liner in. The rim would come off with a lot of yelling. The liner would have to go on with a plastic snap on gasket that was near impossible to bend in the shape of the pool. Finally, we'd be ready to try putting on the metal rim again.

By now, thirty percent of the screws were missing. I'm sure people up and down the block were sitting at their windows laughing hysterically at our pool assembly crew. What else did they have to do? Nobody had cable or computers back then.

This was not a kiddie pool. No, my dad had to buy the largest oval pool he could fit in our Greenpoint yard. It included a regulation size "wallyball" net across the middle. Of course, he was not going to have the pool place come and assemble it for the fifty bucks. We could do it on the weekend. No problem.

You have to picture this. My mom, my dad, my nana who weighed less than I did and was so short she could barely reach the top of the pool rim, and my sister who was mostly on the ground looking for screws, were stationed around this monstrosity of what was essentially a wall of killer sheet metal. Chris was mostly pulling tomatoes off the few surviving tomato plants. Mom had to keep chasing him to keep him from touching those horrible looking horned green worms that camouflage themselves on the stalks.

Our motley crew was trying to keep the bottom in the track, while Dad put on the plastic snap gasket, and attached the rim, with all the wrong size screws. He was about fifty percent done when a freak wind blew down between the row of houses. At the same time Chris was bit by a snapping turtle (we had a lot of those in Brooklyn), and Mom let go of the metal frame, causing it to knock Nana down, and the entire thing popped out of the track. The gasket flew in the air, scaring Jeanette, who dumped the rest of the screws on the ground.

Dad yelled, "Tommy, why the heck did you let go?"

I couldn't answer because I was screaming. The sheet metal was full of little sharp spurs that had ripped my fingers apart when the wind whipped the frame from my hands. After triage from the turtle bite, the torn fingers, and picking Nana up, we started all over.

Eventually, the frame was secured and the liner was in. The hose was turned on. Immediately the water started to leak out in all different directions. Mom had to brave the fifty degree water with a patch kit to try and seal all the holes that sprung up from the frame's metal spurs, the incorrect screw sizes puncturing the liner, the screws dropped on the ground before the liner went in, and all the rocks under the bottom that were never taken out, but were just covered over with only about half the recommended amount of fake rubbery sand stuff, because Dad knew the guy at the pool store was just trying to oversell him.

We'd wait another week for the water to warm up (at least a little), then weeks more waiting for the chemical balance to level out. A problem made worse by the filter that kept blowing a fuse. Mom was worried we were going to be the cause of another New York City blackout.

Dad spent each weekend dumping in chemicals in an attempt to turn the water from a cloudy milky color, to something resembling clear liquid. While he concocted different chemical mixtures, we sat in our bathing suits waiting and pleading to go in the pool. There was no way Mom was letting us swim in cloudy water or after he had just dumped in a fifty-five-gallon drum of industrial concentrated bleach flakes. (Investigation would later show that many of the holes in the liner were caused by this plastic eating crystal chemical mixture.)

Mom used a test tube contraption with an eye dropper containing some radioactive chemicals to measure pH, chlorine, and alkalinity. She would insist on taking water samples at multiple water depths just to be sure it was consistent, trying to match the results on the test strip to the color-coded key on the cover of the plastic test kit.

To add to the insanity of water chemistry, Dad would go into the chlorinated water and run in circles to create a whirlpool effect to uniformly stir up all the stuff he dumped in by the bucket. He once was running in a circle so fast, the sides of the pool started to bend inward; the pool almost sucked itself into a vortex and disappeared, Dad along with it.

The testing and adjusting of the chemical went on until Labor Day, when finally, the water was declared to be in balance and we were able to use the pool. About a week later the days were too short, the temperatures would drop, and that would be the end of our swimming. I think we had forty-five minutes of swim time that summer. Most weekends, we just gave up and sprayed one another with the hose, while Dad added chemicals and Mom tried to work the test kit.

Dad was determined to get the best of the pool gods and he decided to leave the pool assembled all winter. This meant he had to add different chemicals to the water and buy a winter cover. Dad knew the guy at the pool store was trying to oversell him on chemicals, so he never did buy the right amount. He also found a deal on two smaller covers instead of the one to fit the exact model pool. I was at the store the day he bought it.

"Sir, you really should purchase the proper size cover for your pool. If it snows and you have these smaller covers on, they're not going to hold the weight. It will just sink in. You will then have a mess to deal with."

"I'm not worried about that. We live in Greenpoint. Have you ever seen more than a couple of inches of snow? And it melts in a day." This, of course, was the summer of 1978 and we had just had one of the snowiest winters ever. The man at the store pointed this out to Dad.

"Exactly! That won't happen again for another thirty years," was Dad's reply. On February 19th of 1979, the city received almost thirteen inches of snow. Certainly not a record, but enough to weigh down an improperly sized pool cover.

The following spring, when the pool was opened, we all just stood around it and stared at the gross green water. The covers never did stay on. They ended up slipping into the water, letting in all sorts of debris. Interestingly, the pollution you might not see in the city air accumulates in a thick black layer at the bottom of a pool. During the cleanup process, Dad was grossed out when he came across a creature that was - sleeping with the fishes, Luca Brasi style. Mom was forced to make a command decision.

Maybe Dad hadn't followed the exact directions for the winter chemicals or something else had happened because Mom took one look at the green-colored water, the creature lying on the bottom, and declared the pool had to be destroyed. No kids of hers were going to be allowed into water that had gone through some type of metamorphosis. Dad tried to convince her it was normal after the winter and that with the right amount of chlorine and cleaning it would be perfect. I think she knew it would take her until at least Thanksgiving to get the chemical balance correct again.

Facing another hot city summer, Mom packed us up and we spent most of July and August at the lake with Grandma and Dzia Dzie. It wasn't so bad, thanks to Uncle Ray and his ever-expanding Playboy magazine collection. Grandma also cooked up a lot of her specialties for us all summer long, along with five-inch perch and sunnies I caught in the lake and begged her to fry up for me. Being the wonderful Grandma that she was, she labored cleaning and deboning these tiny fish to make me a snack. I do remember, those fish from that shallow, man-made lake weren't very tasty – not in a good sense anyway. I went back to catch and release fishing after that. Thankfully, Grandma was talented in the kitchen and she cooked up some of her specialties all summer long.

North Henry Street backyard pool.
Me, Jeanette, Chris (on the ladder), Dad, and Nana.
Nana enjoyed the pool most of all.

Pasta and Sauerkraut

Mickey and I would bail out of the plant every couple of weeks to go grab pizza for lunch. We both enjoyed our slices of pie.

"You must miss city pizza, kid, heh?"

"A few places. Some were good. You had to know where to go. I like a thin crust," I said.

"Yeah, I know what you mean. The sauce makes a big difference too."

"Cheese, dough, and sauce. Doesn't seem all that complicated, but there's a wide variation in the taste," I added, as he turned into the parking lot of the pizza joint on Route 9A.

After placing our order, Mickey told me his mom was Italian and he ate a mix of Irish and Italian food growing up.

"It's funny, my mom was Italian, but my dad made the pasta sauce. Go figure. Does your dad make the pasta sauce?" Mickey asked.

"Not so much. My nana and Pop-Pop would make it when we lived in Greenpoint. We'd have Sunday dinner with them a lot growing up. Mom made it after that."

"What does your mom put in the sauce for seasoning?" he pressed.

"The usual. Garlic, onions, thyme, oregano, basil, parsley, always fresh herbs," I said.

"I don't like too much oregano in mine. It makes it bitter. So I only add a little," Mickey told me. I never had considered that. Now when I make the sauce, I cut back on the oregano. He was right, it is better.

We sat down in a booth to eat our slices. We both ate them the same way – folded with the grease dripping from the crease onto the white paper plate. When I looked up, I saw him shaking his head.

"What's the problem, Mick?"

"Look at that," he said with a jerk of his head. I looked over to see a guy in a tie eating his slice with a fork and knife.

"Eh, what are you gonna do," I said.

Mickey wanting to dig more into my family history asked, "Did you have big family dinners growing up?"

"We sure did." I sat back and told Mickey a bit more about growing up in my large extended Greenpoint family.

GREENPOINT AVE.

My parents may have had a Romeo and Juliet love story growing up. Dad was an Italian guy with Brylcreem hair, always wearing a white t-shirt with a pack of cigarettes folded in the shoulder, courting a Polish girl whose father envisioned she'd become a nun. Dad must have had an uphill battle. Somehow, he won Mom (and her parents) over and they had four children. I think it was only because he enjoyed kielbasa with sauerkraut and she learned to make a good marinara sauce, although, he always said Nana's was the best, just never in front of Mom.

Dad had eleven siblings who moved from one Brooklyn flat to another growing up. How they all fit, I have no idea. If Nana and Pop-Pop's Manhattan Avenue apartment was crowded on a normal day, Sunday dinners were small conventions. By the time my parents were married, some of Dad's brothers and sisters already had their second child. You can do the math, eleven siblings, spouses, kids of various ages - coming and going to Nana and Pop-Pop's small Greenpoint flat for pasta and sauce; close barely describes it. In the dead of winter, with all the windows open, we'd all be sweating. My Uncle Mike recently said, "720 on Sundays was a zoo." Our home movies show that he loved every minute of it.

Nana would do all the cooking in her tiny galley kitchen. Being somewhat height challenged, she could barely reach to stir the sauce in the ridiculously tall pots on the stove. One pot was never enough to feed this crew. She had two five-gallon monster pots with red sauce bubbling over and down the sides. The pasta was cooked in a pot that was as round as the stove was square.

Nana had loaves of bread piled high on the table. Starving, my cousins and I would grab pieces and dip them into the sauce pot, asking, "Can we eat yet?"

When the meal began, it was mayhem. Plates of ziti and meatballs were passed around. People ate sitting anywhere they could find a seat – at the table, on the couch, on the floor, on the stairs in the hall. And the talking – Mamma Mia - it never stopped during the entire meal. A dozen conversations would be going on at once. I don't know how anyone kept up with it all.

On more intimate gatherings, of twenty or so, we'd eat lasagna. Pop-Pop would make the ragù. He'd start early Sunday morning browning the meats and preparing the sauce. Pictures from my Aunt Lucy show Pop-Pop rolling dough while wearing his pajamas. While the sauce was cooking and the dough was rising, he'd fry peppers in olive oil. He'd hand me a big hunk of crusty day-old bread, he'd soaked in the warm oil, and cover it with one of those sweet peppers. It was delicious.

Nana and Pop-Pop, 1988.   Dad's youngest brother, Michael, 1963.

When the mozzarella was melted on the lasagna, Pop-Pop would yell for everyone to sit down to eat, "Mangiamo!" (Let's eat). Twenty people for a dinner around a small table, in a tiny flat, was still very crowded and loud. Silent home movies show the laughter and the covered faces yelling at my Dad, "Tommy, don't take my picture!"

When the meal was done, the conversation volume rose

even louder. My cousins and I talked, tossing a spaldeen back and forth to one another sitting on the floor in the living room. We talked chewing on our Lucky Lights candy cigarettes. We talked because we couldn't go out and play; Manhattan Avenue was no place for kids to play stickball. When my Uncle Mike was home, he'd play his 45's and Zeppelin albums. He gave me his Wild Cherry 45 of *Play that Funky Music* because I made him play it so much – he wasn't going to part with a Grateful Dead album.

When the plates were cleared, the desserts came out. No family ever arrived at Nana's without bringing a sweet or a basket of fruit. Desserts came by the box. Pastry, cakes, cookies, and cannoli would fill the table. At Sunday dinner, we all felt rich.

Dad with seven of his eleven brothers and sisters, around 1950.

Barbara, John, Betty, Terry, Lucy, Tom, Pat, and Gus.

My mom also grew up in a Greenpoint flat on the other avenue – Nassau. Mom was the only daughter amongst four brothers. Supposedly, the hot water for the bathtub was at a premium in those days, the days of her childhood being the 1950s and 60s. Once the tub was filled, all five of them took turns getting cleaned up – in the same water. At least in her case, being the girl in the family, she used the bath water first.

Food was a big part of gatherings on Mom's side of the family as well. At Grandma's, it was important that everyone had a chair, everyone was seated in the same room, and everyone ate together. She would borrow tables, chairs, and dishes from her neighbor Margie. The small kitchen would become an eat-in restaurant. The food would go directly from the stove to the table. It was orchestrated order. I have no memories of there being pots all over the counters and stove. We would all be seated to food in serving dishes that were passed around. Maybe Grandma had it all prepared ahead of time and she made it look smooth.

Lunches were kielbasa and sauerkraut with coleslaw and potato salad. Easter, Thanksgiving, or Christmas there would be ham or turkey. For special dinners, she made czarnina a traditional Polish duck blood soup. In this case, we always had one extra guest of honor arrive for the dinner – the duck.

The duck would be bought from the poultry distributor alive. There was a year I recall when someone thought it would be good for us kids to arrive before the duck was sacrificed. For this soup, as the name implies, the blood is the essential ingredient. How this occurs is probably not something a ten-year-old should witness, but Grandma thought it was important to pass on all traditions.

I'm sure you've heard the expression, "To run around like a chicken with its head cut off." I'll tell you there's no problem substituting the word "duck" in place of "chicken" in that statement. When Grandma cut the neck to drain the blood, (Dzia Dzie wouldn't do it), the duck ran around her kitchen. I thought I was in a live Daffy Duck cartoon. That was until I realized what was really happening and I ran screaming to the other end of the flat, traumatized by the dinner preparation. It must not have scarred me too much, because until this day, duck is one of my favorite meals. Since Grandma passed, we've never had czarnina again. It's a tradition we let go, since nobody in the family knows how to prepare it anymore. Besides, the duck distributor, a brick warehouse that was somewhere near the BQE, is long gone.

Grandma also made gołąbki, we called it gawoompki, an adaptation of golumpki, a Polish word for stuffed cabbage. My all-time favorite were Grandma's sweet pierogi. These were filled with a soft cheese she called, "Farmer's Cheese." Since all cheese starts on a farm, it always confused me as to why the farmer had decided to make this sweet cottage type cheese his namesake. Grandma would also make pierogi with fruit filling. Once I was hooked on Grandma's, I never enjoyed the pierogi we'd find at the Greenpoint Polish festivals filled with meat or potato.

For dessert, Grandma would make cheesecakes and pies. She'd also make chrusciki, a pastry covered in powdered sugar. It was so crispy, when I bit into it, the sugar would fly off and coat my face, shirt, and pants.

Mom, with Dzia Dzie and Grandma, and three of her four brothers – Anthony, Eddie, and Thomas.

When the meal was done, the family would break out the cards. That went for both the adults and the kids. The kids would play crazy eights at the little card table, while the adults played rummy or some game with an odd name like scat or spit. As my cousins and I got older, we played rummy or poker, and by then, we were playing for money.

We started off playing with pennies or nickels, and by the time we were teens we were 'playing' for quarters and dollars. The losing kids would always borrow money from the adults. The oldest cousins could go home with winnings of five dollars or more by beating the pants off the little kids. This was great training and I used my knowledge to run poker games on the corner near the candy store. I'd cleanup. It was better than having a job.

Dzia Dzie and Grandma

Sunday dinner at Grandma's was rarely the same, and that was the point. Sunday dinner at Nana's was always the same, pasta and sauce, and that was the point. Romeo and Juliet just had to adjust if their marriage was going to work.

While Nana and Grandma were different from one another, their differences were nothing compared to the differences between Pop-Pop and Dzia Dzie.

Pop-Pop loved to fish. Dzia Dzie liked to watch baseball.

Pop-Pop loved to cook. He'd make noodle pie and

mountains of struffoli at Christmas time.

Dzia Dzie liked to help Grandma cook, but his jobs were done sitting down, while watching the ball game on the kitchen TV. He'd sit and grate beets so Grandma could make the barszcz czysty czerwony, a polish red beet soup, a borscht that I loved with a dollop of sour cream on top. He'd also cut noodles from the dough Grandma would roll. By the time I was six, I'd be sitting next to him helping cut the dough into strips. "Not too wide. Like this, Tommy," and he'd take my hand in his with the knife and show me how.

For my love of wine, I thank Pop-Pop. For my hate of whiskey, I thank Dzia Dzie.

When it was time to eat at Grandma's, I'd sometimes have to go and find Dzia Dzie. I'd run down the flight of stairs, out into the street, and down the block to Stash's bar. Slowly I'd open the large door with the stained-glass window. Inside it was always dark. The only light came from the neon lights of some alcohol sign behind the bar. The ball game was usually playing on the TV, no sound though, it was a quiet hangout. Dzia Dzie would be wearing his signature outfit, a plaid shirt, green work pants, and black dress shoes.

Stash's place would smell of whiskey and hard liquor. I knew I wasn't allowed in there, but the owner knew I was there to collect Dzia (jaj) for dinner. He was always proud to introduce me to the one or two other regulars who'd be in the place. We'd talk on the way back to the apartment and he'd ask me how I was doing in school. He'd give me a dollar if I could solve a math problem. After dinner, he'd have a shot of whiskey. He once gave in to my asking and let me have a sip from his shot glass. The burning sensation kept me from ever wanting another taste.

Towards the late 70s, when Pop-Pop and Nana lived on the first floor of our apartment building, I'd sometimes bring Pop-Pop down a bowl of pasta. Many times, I'd find him sitting in his chair, eating olives and oranges. During the winter, his dining room would smell of citrus since he'd place the peels on the hot radiator. A habit that would drive my dad crazy, but I thought it smelled nice - better than the fish in the tub, that's for sure.

Pop-Pop wasn't much of a talker. I suspect after raising eleven kids he'd had enough. But if he was cooking something, he'd always pull me over to watch.

"Tommy, this is how you roll the struffoli. Never too big."

"Tommy, this is how you brown the meat for the ragù. Don't let it burn."

Dzia Dzie, Pop-Pop, Grandma, and Nana all passed on wonderful cooking traditions from two family cultures, a little at a time, year after year.

Many of the old Greenpoint traditions of my youth are almost lost now. We hold on to some at our house. Sunday is still pasta and sauce night, just not every Sunday. For Easter we try to have Polish kielbasa, but it's not as easy to find as it was in Greenpoint. We've never had anywhere close to fifty aunts, uncles, and first cousins for dinner; that would be a statistical improbability with the shrinkage of the family size and the distances between all of our families now. We still play cards -

sometimes. I try to teach my girls how to make the sauce, hopefully they will remember.

New traditions have probably taken the place of the old. I'm not sure what they are, my daughters might be better able to describe them to their children. For me it's just how we are living in the moment. I suspect it's not much different from the way it was in that regard.

Nana and Pop-Pop's Sauce – My Way

I watched Nana making sauce a lot. I should say Nana **and Pop-Pop**. Pop-Pop would start the sauce and then Nana would have to stir it for hours to finish it. I don't know if this is exactly how they made it, but it's pretty much how I do it.

To start, Pop-Pop would dump in olive oil that came in gallon cans covered in pictures of Tuscany, tomatoes, and Italian words. I use the best extra virgin olive oil we can find and coat the bottom of the pot. To this I throw in chopped onion and garlic to sauté for several minutes, but NOT to brown. Then I add a little chopped carrot, plenty of diced red and green peppers, and salt. The pot is then covered so the vegetables will soften. Sometimes, I put in a very small amount of celery to this base.

After ten to fifteen minutes, Pop-Pop would throw in the meat – sausage, pork, and veal. He was cooking for a small army so he added platters of meat. I add enough for my small family. After the meats brown, I dump in cans of sauce, puree, paste, and chopped tomatoes. I never witnessed Pop-Pop measuring, and that was never a problem, so neither do I.

Pop-Pop would add a little water. He'd say, "It needs some water to boil off, but too much makes a watery sauce." He'd add a little more water as the sauce slowly cooked for hours.

For the seasonings, I use handfuls of fresh basil, thyme, oregano, pepper, and parsley. I follow Mickey's Irish wisdom and put less oregano nowadays. I remember watching Nana prepare the herbs that had to be just the right sizes, or Pop-Pop would hand them back to her to chop some more. I do the same to my wife Meredith. My daughter, Gina, will not chop the parsley because I am too particular.

Once all the ingredients were in, Pop-Pop would sit and drink a glass of wine, always red, always from huge gallon jugs. Nana would stir the sauce.

Nana and Pop-Pop feeding me. When I was older, Pop-Pop used to give me sips of his wine when he was cooking the pasta sauce.

I cook the sauce on a low heat. The sauce needs stirring or it will burn and stick to the bottom of the pot. This is not a gentle stirring around in the middle of the sauce. This is a stirring that scrapes the bottom. There is to be NO, and I repeat "N.O.," build up that sticks to the bottom.

After an hour of simmering this hybrid ragù / sauce / gravy, Pop-Pop would get up and he'd add red wine. He'd taste the sauce and add a little sugar to remove any acidity. More seasonings would be added according to the taste test. I do the same – both with the wine and the sugar.

I remember, Pop-Pop used to call to me, "Tomas, vieni! Assaggia." (Tomas, come! Taste.) Pop-Pop would hold the spoon for me to taste the sauce. After that, he'd give me a little bit of wine in a juice cup.

Meatballs were made from a freshly ground pork, beef, and veal mixture. To the meat, I add a little of the sauce (the amount depends on the amount of meat), breadcrumbs (don't be stingy), and eggs that are lightly fork beat with a little water. Sometimes I add a little more seasoning directly to this mixture. The meatballs would be rolled (by Nana) and she'd quickly fry them to brown the outside and then put them in the sauce to finish cooking.

Over the years I've experimented with this recipe. The best sauces are those with the proper amount of time taken during the initial vegetable and meat braising. Rushing this step will make a poor base and a lousy tasting sauce. The wine is not necessary, but I find it goes well with the cooking. I open the bottle when I begin the sauce preparations and provide a little to the pot when called for, but mostly I drink it as I cook, just as Pop-Pop did. I call my girls away from their video games to taste the sauce and a meatball with a crusty piece of bread – this builds the anticipation to the meal.

The other VERY important ingredient is music. Not just

any music. When I make the sauce, I listen to Jerry Vale, Dean Martin, and Lou Monte, mixed in with modern day Italian artists - Zucchero, Laura Pausini, Biagio Antonacci, and Andrea Bocelli. This makes the sauce making an experience to savor.

Eat. Talk. Sing. That's amore.

Buon appetito.

Pop-Pop – Our Big Ragù

Goodbye to Greenpoint

I'm told I was angry when my parents sat my siblings and I down to inform us we were moving. I don't remember the feelings exactly, but I can imagine. Not only were we moving out of Greenpoint, we were leaving the city. Sure, it was still New York, but it was the other New York, not even The Island. Mom tells me I didn't speak with them for months after getting this news.

I did everything I could to get back as often as I could to the old neighborhood. I stayed with Grandma or my cousins, so I could visit with friends. As soon as I bought my first car, I'd take every opportunity to get to the city, even though the car I was driving was more likely to break down in the Lincoln Tunnel, than make it to Greenpoint.

When my new upstate friends wanted to see where I grew up, I jumped at the chance to drive into the city and show them. Melanie, Bobby, Kelly, and I skipped school and piled in my sardine size ten-year-old car. I figured on following the same route Dad always drove. I'd cross from upstate New York into Jersey, go through the Lincoln Tunnel, and head straight across midtown, through the Midtown Tunnel and into Long Island City. A quick right over Newtown Creek and we'd be at North Henry Street. I had it memorized. As long as there were no detours, we'd be fine. (There was no such thing as GPS back then.)

I breathed a sigh of relief when my car emerged from the Lincoln Tunnel into midtown. So far, so good. It was a straight shot from there. The one kink was I hadn't anticipated that driving a stick shift in city traffic would be so stressful.

Then the pretty girl in the short skirt next to me asked me to drive through Times Square. She'd never been and wanted to see the sights. That route wasn't in my memory bank, but for her, anything. I snaked through traffic trying not to get in an accident as Bobby and Kelly in the back seat snapped pictures on their disposable cameras. They reminded me of Japanese tourists and not technically "New Yorkers!"

I was distracted by Melanie's bright blue eyes admiring New York, or maybe it was her legs on the dash; somehow, I must have made a wrong turn. From the back Bobby said, "What happened to all the traffic?"

I was thinking the same thing. It was strange that I was the only car on a New York City street. The calm lasted for less than a second.

I don't recall what I saw first, Melanie's panicked hand squeezing my right thigh, the silver grill of that huge truck, or the line of yellow cabs coming directly at me blaring their horns. Didn't these people have any PATIENCE? A cab driver, whose irate face I locked onto for a split second, actually resembled a bulldog, so I guess not. Pulling a stunt only seen in movies, I swung my tiny 1976 Oldsmobile Starfire around in a U-turn that The Bandit would have been proud of.

I made a right and landed back on a street with a sign pointing to the Lincoln Tunnel. When we passed the "Welcome to Jersey" sign, Melanie asked, "Did we go through

Greenpoint?" (She was sexy, okay!)

That night over dinner, Dad asked his usual question, "How was your day?"

Dad's office was in midtown, high above Broadway, in a building that now houses the Hard Rock Café and the Bubba Gump Shrimp Company. He would take the bus from our sleepy little town to the Port Authority and walk each day to his building in Times Square. I went to work with him a couple of times when I was in grade school. He'd set me up in an empty office and within twenty minutes I'd be calling his phone extension asking, "Dad, can we go get a French cruller?" That was an offer he couldn't refuse (he went for coffee six times a day), so back down to Broadway we'd go for a donut.

It did cross my mind that Dad would be getting a coffee and he'd see me driving around near Broadway during the middle of a school day, but then I considered the odds and realized that would be ridiculous.

"It was fine. Same old. Classes and then track practice," I replied.

"You know, it was interesting. I was out for coffee today and a car that looked just like yours came down 43rd going the wrong way."

I swallowed hard.

"That's the only time I've ever seen another one of those cars. The girl in the passenger seat almost looked like Melanie a little too," he continued.

"Isn't that funny, what a coincidence," Mom chimed in, giving me enough time to think.

"Not really. It was a very popular car in the day. In a city as populated as New York you're bound to see a few of them. It's just basic statistics," I said. I don't think he considered that this mathematical jargon was coming from me, who almost failed algebra. Dad didn't push it. The way I figure it, he knew it was me and figured if that's the worst thing I'd be doing, he was pretty lucky.

With each visit I made back to the city, it was never the same. Friends had moved on. The city had moved on. I had moved on. Eventually, the city became a place to visit, but not someplace I needed to be.

Some years after we moved upstate, Dad opened up a store. Not a candy store, but a place to sell work clothes, similar to the products Pop-Pop used to sell from the back of his station wagon. It was going to be Dad's ticket out of the commute and something to do in semi-retirement. Soon after, Dad was diagnosed with terminal cancer. I don't know what went through his mind when he knew he was dying. My last memories of him are seeing him through a slightly open door, lying on the bed in his dark bedroom, weak from the chemo treatments.

Mom and Dad, 1985.

There's a saying you've probably heard, "You can take the boy out of Brooklyn, but you can't take Brooklyn out of the boy." I think that is the best of both worlds. I'm grateful for having grown up in Greenpoint and the experiences I had there, but looking back I'm glad Dad and Mom decided to move.

After going to college, I found that even our 'upstate' suburban town had too much concrete, too many cars, not enough trees, dirty streams, and crowded hiking trails. I needed more space, cleaner air, a different kind of wildlife. I didn't know at the time that this wildlife, meant I'd get chased by a moose, more than once, and one bull would tip me out of a canoe into an icy-cold lake.

When I resigned from the power plant, and told Mickey I was moving to Maine, he said, "Ya know, kid, you're gonna miss the good pastry, Chinese food, and real Italian Hero's around here."

Mickey was right. I still can't find knishes and it was ten years before another New York transplant opened a store nearby that sold imported Italian prosciutto. And real Italian ices? Fuhgeddaboudit!

The October I was twenty-five, I sat next to Dad on his bed and told him I had accepted a job, five hours away. He held my hand and said, "Don't go, Tom."

Mom said, "He has to. He has to pursue his dreams, as you did yours."

The Lord called Dad home that December. He was forty-eight.

I never got to tell Dad how great a decision it was to move the family. He sacrificed and commuted so we might know something different. Being a city boy, he loved the country and he left me with that gift.

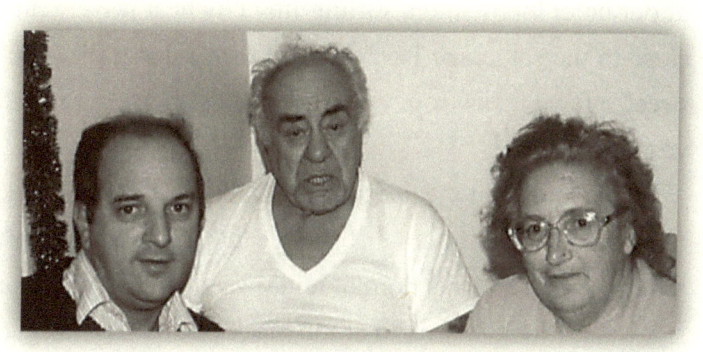

The last photo of Dad, Pop-Pop, and Nana together.
Christmas 1992.
Pop-Pop would pass away in March.
Dad the following December.

I moved to a place where through my land there is a clear running stream that reaches the Atlantic. Deer gather in small herds, turkeys roam by the dozen, and birds come by the flock in the spring. We don't have an aria. We have acres of trails that are carpeted in thick coats of pine needles, no raking needed. We lose power for days at a time and just deal with it. We don't call these times blackouts, we call them quiet times. Snowstorms of thirty-five inches and blizzards that last for days are not that uncommon, although the shoveling is still no fun.

Miles of sand beaches are just minutes from our house, no subway token needed. I smell the salt air through my bedroom window when the wind blows from the east. I own pine trees that are six stories tall that scent the air with evergreen after a spring rain.

I was reminded just how different this is from where I grew up on a recent visit to the city. My daughter and I walked out of our hotel lobby into a stifling July city heat wave. Gina was close to the same age I was when I drove down that one-way street, a few blocks from where we were standing, almost thirty years earlier.

Gina looked at me and asked, "Dad, what's that smell?"

I tried to figure out what she meant. It smelled as I always remembered it. It was normal midtown smell. Standing on the sidewalk, I looked around at the black plastic bags of garbage lining the edge of the curb. Commuters, residents, tourists, and delivery people navigated around the piles as if it were an obstacle course. At the same moment a train was pulling through the station below, pushing up a gust of hot, foul-smelling air from deep below the city. A dried urine stain ran from an entry way along the sidewalk, person or canine? A pretzel was burning on a street cart near the corner.

"That's just the city."

"That is **not** a good smell," she said. I laughed.

"Did you live right near here, Dad?"

"No, honey. We lived across the river – in Brooklyn. Come on, I'll show you."

We rode a cab downtown and took the elevator to the observation deck of the Freedom Tower. I pointed out the Statue of Liberty ("It looks so small," she said), Jersey, Ellis Island, where her Great Great Grandfather entered the country from Napoli, the Brooklyn Bridge, and to the northeast Greenpoint.

"It's so flat over there," she said.

I think she envisioned that the entire city would be skyscrapers. I remembered standing very close to that same location, height included, at the top of the South Tower of Two World Trade Center, with Dad so many decades ago. I thought about what she said. To me, it appeared Greenpoint hadn't changed at all since 1977. But then again, I knew it had changed a lot.

"Welcome Back."

My daughter, Gina, at the Freedom Tower with the view of the bridge leading "home."

Dad and I were the last to leave the house on North Henry Street. Mom, my sister, and my brother were already at the new house waiting for the moving van that was on its way. I walked with Dad through the house one last time to make sure we hadn't forgotten anything. The basement was completely cleared out. We locked the heavy metal aria door that went up to the street, went up the stairs to the hall, and turned out the light. The ground floor apartment where Nana and Pop-Pop had lived was empty. They had moved to Queens.

We did a final walk through of what had been our second-floor apartment for ten years. How strange it looked with all our faded furniture missing. It smelt dry. Dusty. Old.

Dad swept up the dog hair that had accumulated behind where the fridge used to be. I noticed the rug rake in my closet.

"Dad, we forgot to pack the rake!" My voice echoed through the bare rooms.

"That can stay, Tommy, we don't have any shag carpet at the new house." I wondered if the new owners knew they had to rake the carpet every Saturday morning.

I picked up the milk crate I had stolen from behind the dairy. Inside it, Sparky, the Greenpoint kitten a neighbor had asked we take to have a country life, purred and looked up with his big black eyes.

Dad and I stood in the hallway looking at the empty living room where we used to laugh on the couch, and the dining room where we ate so many family dinners.

He put his arm on my shoulder and said, "Why don't you turn off the lights."

The apartment went black. We walked out.

City Terms

Aria – the small front yard in front of the house. So says my Mom.
BQE – Brooklyn Queens Expressway.
Egg cream – drink from a candy store that contains no eggs and no cream.
English – to put spin on a throw.
Halfsies – splitting something in half with someone. Just be sure it's something that can be split equally in two.
- *"I'll go halfsies with you on a candy bar." "Okay."*
- *"I'll go halfsies with you on a slice." "What? Are you freakin crazy!"*

Hero – a sandwich on a torpedo or Italian bread.
LIE – Long Island Expressway
Malted – a shake, sometimes with malted mix added.
Play my number – playing a string of three or four numbers in the lottery with the guy that came to the corner store. In the 70s, this was NOT the legal lottery that people play today.
Punch – a game played with the spaldeen, lengthwise down the center of the street.
Skelsy – a game with the top of a glass soda or beer bottle. The top was removed by rubbing a glass soda bottle over the grate of a manhole cover.
Sleeps with the fishes – A reference from the Godfather movie. If you don't know it, that's a shame.
Slice – one piece of pizza, always eaten by folding it in half.

Slap – a game played with a spaldeen against a garage or wall.

Spaldeen – what we called the pink ball made by the Spalding Company.

Stoop – the set of three or four steps outside an apartment building.

Straight and box – the way Nana played her address in the daily numbers.

Stoopball – a spaldeen game played against the steps of a stoop.

The lots – any place there weren't apartment buildings where weeds grew. Sometimes used for games.

Whiffle Ball – our term for wiffle ball; probably because when someone missed the ball with the plastic bat, they 'whiff'd,' as the sound would indicate. Term based on the brand name, Wiffle, of the most popular version of the plastic ball.

Winthro – Our short name for Winthrop Park now named Monsignor McGolrick Park.

Dad, my brother Nick, and Mom. ~ 1990.

Thank you for reading. I hope you enjoyed these memories I have of Greenpoint and my childhood. Maybe they brought back some memories of your own childhood.

Please visit my website

www.tommycarbone.com

where you will find updates and links to my social media sites where we can stay in touch.

Discussion Questions for Book Groups

1. How do you think Tommy's personality was shaped growing up in Greenpoint?
2. Why was a childhood in Greenpoint so memorable for Tommy?
3. What is different now in how teens and pre-teens interact in urban centers, such as Greenpoint?
4. How are sports organized differently for children today as compared to the 1970s?
5. Would you have allowed your children to roam the city streets in the 70s from morning until night? How about now?
6. What words for foods or games are unique to where you grew up? Did you ever find yourself explaining them to others?
7. Do you remember recipes or foods your family ate when you were a child that are no longer commonplace? What were they? Do you still eat these foods?
8. What traditions did your family have when you were young that you have passed down to your children? What traditions have you stopped and not passed down? Why?
9. What relatives do you think had a positive influence on Tommy growing up?
10. How would you describe the relationship between Tommy and Mickey?

Acknowledgements

This memoir would not have been possible without the support of my family and friends. I want to thank my Mom. She not only read the book to provide encouragement, but she gave me valuable constructive feedback – all bad words have been eliminated.

I want to thank my Uncle Mike for giving me his 45 of *Play That Funky Music* back in 1977 and introducing me to all music other than oldies and country that played in our house. There was no way he was parting with a *Grateful Dead* album! Thanks also for being the family archivist with all the photos you share of the family.

I am forever grateful to Katherine Wilson. Katherine not only took time to review my writing and use of Italian, she has also been an inspiration to me during this project. I came across Katherine's wonderful book, "The Mother-in-Law Cure," while researching memoir writing. Of the more than one-hundred memoir books I've read, Katherine's is one of my favorites. Katherine also has a wonderful TEDx talk with an inspiring message. Grazie mille, Katherine.

To my wonderful daughter Marisa, a scholar, an athlete, a musician, and now a book editor. Thank you for your assistance – even if I left some of my Brooklyn-English the way I wrote it, your input was extremely helpful.

My wife, Meredith, was instrumental with this project. Meredith provided the day-to-day support and read and re-read the pages so many times, she remembered more of the book than I did. If Meredith laughed, I kept the story in the book. Ti Amo.

About Tommy Carbone

Tommy Carbone grew up in the Greenpoint section of Brooklyn. It wasn't until he was ten that he realized Greenpoint wasn't the center of Brooklyn, much less the center of the universe, not everyone was good at pinball, and not all families ate pasta on Sunday nights.

After nearly failing algebra at St. Stan's, he became an electrical engineer, thanks to his interest in electricity being sparked by the great New York City blackout of 1977. Leaving Greenpoint and New York to memories, he now writes from a one room cabin on the shores of a lake that is frozen for more than six months out of the year and moose outnumber people three to one.

www.tommycarbone.com

Novels by Tommy Carbone

The Lobster Lake Bandits
Mystery at Moosehead

A Maine Novel
The first novel in the *Moosehead Mystery* series.

Poachers, game wardens, and unknown characters roaming the Maine woods make for a suspenseful assignment for New York writer Sarah Molloy.

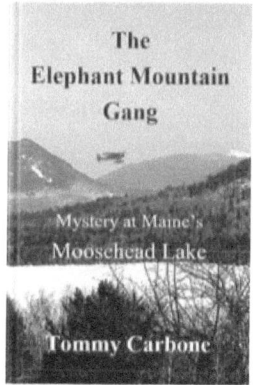

The Elephant Mountain Gang
Mystery at Maine's Moosehead Lake

The second novel in the *Moosehead Mystery* series.

Game Warden Henry Ford, Joe Parker, and Sarah Molloy get mixed up in a crime that brings to the small town of Greenville a mystery man who may be up to no good.

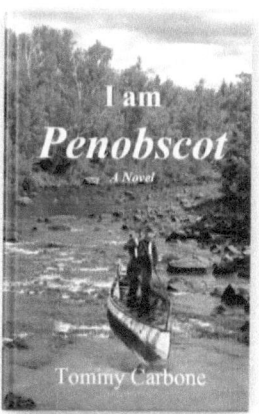

I am Penobscot
A Novel

A novel based on the life of river-driver, Civil War soldier, miner, and writer, **David Stone Libbey.**

Maine History and Legends

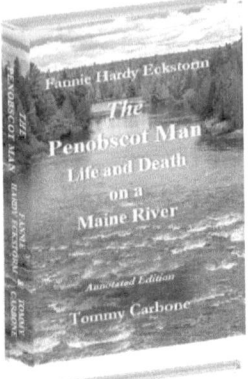

An annotated edition of Fannie Hardy Eckstorm's classic river driver stories.

Hubbard's Guide to exploring Northern Maine. 2020 Edition

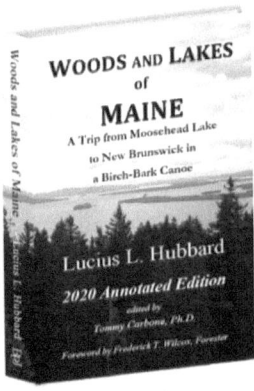

Hubbard's adventure through Maine to Canada.

www.ingramcontent.com/pod-product-compliance
Lightning Source LLC
Chambersburg PA
CBHW031057080526
44587CB00011B/721